BALANCE SHEET RECESSION

Japan's Struggle with Uncharted Economics and its Global Implications

BALANCE SHEET RECESSION

*Japan's Struggle with Uncharted Economics
and its Global Implications*

RICHARD C. KOO

John Wiley & Sons (Asia) Pte Ltd

Other Wiley Editorial Offices

John Wiley & Sons, Inc., 111 River Street, Hoboken, NJ 07030, USA
John Wiley & Sons Ltd, The Atrium, Southern Gate, Chichester P019 8SQ, England
John Wiley & Sons (Canada) Ltd, 22 Worcester Road, Rexdale, Ontario M9W 1L1, Canada
John Wiley & Sons Australia Ltd, 33 Park Road (PO Box 1226), Milton, Queensland 4064, Australia
Wiley-VCH, Pappelallee 3, 69469 Weinheim, Germany

Library of Congress Cataloging-in Publication Data:
ISBN: 0-470-82116-7 (cloth)

Typeset in 10.5/13 points, Times Roman by Linographic Services Pte Ltd
Printed in Singapore by Saik Wah Press Pte Ltd
10 9 8 7 6 5 4 3 2 1

To my mother
Amy Koo Ma

CONTENTS

ACKNOWLEDGEMENTS

This book would not have been possible without the help of many people. In particular, a number of institutional investors around the world and clients of Nomura Securities, who made me think deep and hard about the problem of the Japanese economy, were of immense help in shaping my ideas. The fact that they had their money in Japan meant that they never allowed me to go off on a tangent. I am also grateful to the Japanese from all walks of life, from top political leaders to the operator of a small hobby shop, who trusted me and shared with me their ideas and concerns.

I have also benefited from countless discussions with Mr. Shosaku Murayama, who headed the research department of the Bank of Japan until recently and is now the president of Teikoku Seiyaku Co., and Mr. Robert McCauley, a former colleague at the New York Fed who is now with the Bank for International Settlements. I must also thank Mr. Edward Frydl, my former employer at the New York Fed, who coined the expression "balance sheet recession." Any mistakes in the book are, of course, mine and mine alone.

In the actual preparation of the book, I benefited greatly from the initiative provided by Mr. Noriyasu Yoshizawa of Nomura Securities Hong Kong, as well as from the help and encouragement provided by Mr. Takashi Yakabe of Nomura Research Institute and Mr. Setsuya Tabuchi, a former chairman of Nomura Securities.

My secretary, Ms. Yuko Terado, helped me with the preparation of the text of the manuscript, while my assistant, Mr. Takaaki Shimizu, produced the graphs and provided the numerical data. They both worked very long hours in order to get the book out on schedule. I cannot thank them enough for their efforts. I am also grateful to Tokuma Shoten, the publisher of the initial Japanese version of this book.

Finally, I wish to thank my wife, Chyen-Mei, and our children, Jackie and Rickie, for enduring my absence on so many weekends and holidays. I am truly indebted to them.

Richard C. Koo
Tokyo
February 2003

Introduction

Contrary to popular belief, the root cause of Japan's economic weakness during the last decade has much more to do with balance sheet problems at the corporate level than with the lack of structural reform within the overall economy. Today, 70–80% of Japanese companies are paying down debt, even at 0% interest rates. As a result, the corporate sector in Japan is now a net supplier of funds to the banks and the capital market to the tune of ¥20 trillion, or equivalent to 4% of gross domestic product (GDP), a year. Furthermore, this move to pay down debt started years ago, when Japan still had inflation.

The situation is unlike any described in any economics or business textbook. After all, corporations exist because they are supposed to be able to make better use of the public's money than the average member of the public could do on their own. The fact that so many companies are paying down debt at a 0% interest rate goes completely against the conventional notion of the firm. Indeed, for most companies in Japan today, their implicit first priority is no longer profit maximization, as is assumed by most economists, but restoration of their balance sheet through debt minimization. With so many companies trying to repair their balance sheets at the same time, it is no wonder that Japan's economy remains so stagnant.

While most economists are well trained to analyze macroeconomic indicators such as industrial production, the inflation rate, money supply, and so forth, few are accustomed to looking at micro indications such as corporate balance sheets. Even fewer economists are familiar with a world where most companies are no longer maximizing profits, but instead are minimizing debt.

Furthermore, business executives from the corporate sector have no incentive to speak publicly about their balance sheet problems, especially when they are already in or near negative equity territory. The same holds true for bankers who lent money to those corporations.

As in the Zen proverb "Those who know it cannot say it, and those who say it, cannot know it," the recession brought about by balance sheet problems is typically invisible and inaudible. Indeed, a prominent Japanese business executive called the current balance sheet recession a "managers' and bankers' recession," meaning that only those two groups are aware of the seriousness of the corporate balance sheet problems, the real driver of the recession, but they are not well disposed to share that information with the general public.

As a result, the general public, including economists and journalists both at home and abroad, conclude that since the traditional macroeconomic remedies such as fiscal and monetary policies seemed to have failed to revive the economy, the problem must be structural. Although that is a possible conjecture, and there is certainly no dearth of structural problems in Japan, balance sheet problems can produce the same results as structural problems, but with far better consistency with actual market and economic indicators such as super-low interest rates and large trade surpluses.

More importantly, once the possibility is recognized that, from time to time, a large number of companies could be minimizing debt instead of maximizing profit, established economic theories and their policy implications will have to be altered to account for such occasions. Indeed, once this possibility is included in the picture, what constitutes the correct policy to remedy the recession changes completely. Moreover, if the government is hell-bent on correcting structural problems when the real problem lies in corporate balance sheets, this could throw the entire economy into a horrendous depression.

The key theme of this book is that companies do shift their focus from profit maximization to debt minimization when they are faced with daunting balance sheet challenges. The book then goes on to explain what policies will work, and what ones won't work, in a balance sheet recession. It is argued that when companies are maximizing profits, the smaller the role of the government, the better it is for the economy. In this normal world, monetary policy is sufficient to tame the economy. But when companies are minimizing debt, proactive government is essential in not only keeping the economy going, but also in maintaining money supply and the effectiveness of monetary policy.

In terms of economic theory, the possibility that a large number of firms may be minimizing debt instead of maximizing profits fills the logical gap that was always present in the Keynesian theories. At the same time, this possibility also indicates the clear limitations of monetarism. It is shown that the balance sheet argument makes far more sense than the conventional "speculative demand for money" argument used to explain the liquidity trap.

Regarding fiscal stimulus, a number of new ideas are presented on whether budget deficits really cause the transfer of income from one generation to the next. In particular, it is emphasized that each generation has an obligation to leave a healthy economy, as well as sound government finances and social infrastructure, to the next generation. It is argued that the excessive emphasis on the last two, to the detriment of the obligation to leave a healthy economy, has resulted in a somewhat biased conclusion toward fiscal deficit in the conventional literature.

The banking crisis that often accompanies a balance sheet recession is also discussed in detail. This discussion is very much influenced by the author's first-hand involvement with the most devastating of U.S. banking crises during the last 20 years – the Latin American debt crisis, which erupted in 1982. As an economist in charge of syndicated loans to Latin America at the Federal Reserve Bank of New York, I was at the very center of the crisis where virtually all the major U.S. banks were under water. Based on this experience, it is argued that the way the U.S. authorities under the then Federal Reserve chairman Paul Volcker handled this crisis is much more relevant to the Japanese situation today than the much smaller Savings and Loan crisis, which blew up in 1989.

The banking crisis is then divided into four categories and it is shown that the rapid disposal of non-performing loans (NPLs) is advisable in only one of the four categories. This section also indicates how poor reporting by the Western press over the years has produced a huge misunderstanding surrounding Japan's handling of its banking crises. That misunderstanding is still with us today.

The theoretical implications of balance sheet problems are applicable far beyond Japan's borders. Indeed, the collapse of the Asian bubble in 1997 and of the information technology (IT) bubble in the United States in 2000 caused behavioral changes in the affected entities that were similar to those observed in Japan over the last 10 years. Chapter 8 explains how the Asian currency crisis appeared from the Japanese perspective. Chapter 9 is devoted to the similarities and differences between the Japanese and post-IT, post-Enron U.S. economies.

Lastly, the long-term structural problems faced by Japan are discussed. It is argued here that budget deficit or NPL problems should be viewed as "a clean-up job after the bubble." From the macro perspective, real structural challenges lie in whether it is possible to change the ethics and lifestyle of the Japanese people. In particular, it is argued that the way the Japanese view savings and leisure must be changed in order to match the country's level of economic development. One of the largest structural problems in Japan, if not one of the largest economic distortions in the world, Japan's land problem, is also discussed here.

From the balance sheet perspective, it is the view of the author that Japan has been conducting, albeit unknowingly, one of the biggest economic experiments in the history of mankind. The experiment conducted here is to see whether it is possible to keep the economy going and allow companies to repair their balance sheets in the face of the tremendous loss of wealth that resulted from the collapse in asset prices.

So far, over ¥1,200 trillion in wealth has been lost due to the massive fall in asset prices over the last 10 years. This figure is 2.7 times Japan's GDP in 1989, the last year of the bubble economy. As a proportion of GDP, it is also 2.7 times larger than the wealth lost in the United States during the Great Depression of the 1930s. Historically speaking, an economy that has fallen into this plight has invariably plunged into a depression, the recovery from which has taken massive amounts of time and fiscal expenditure.

Japan's GDP, however, has remained more or less static during the past decade despite the above-mentioned loss of wealth. This amazing feat was made possible because the country lost no time in mobilizing aggressive fiscal policies and has maintained them year after year in order to prevent the onset of a vicious cycle that would plunge the country into a depression. This is the first time in the history of mankind that a nation has taken such an action from the very beginning of an asset price collapse.

Nevertheless, as the decline in asset prices has been so large, as will be examined later, the treatment will have to be continued for a few more years to ensure that the patient is sufficiently recovered to be discharged from the hospital. Corporations' efforts to compress their debts have been paying off, but it will take a little more effort in that direction before businessmen will stop worrying about their balance sheets.

Unfortunately, because the balance sheet explanation was never offered by Japan's political leaders, people both within and outside Japan are losing patience, and some, such as the current Koizumi government, are on the verge of abandoning the experiment in favor of a leap in the dark. They are now willing to try anything that is different from the past, not realizing that they have been extraordinarily fortunate to have avoided a depression so far.

The primary objective of this book is to sound an alarm about the recent arguments for abandoning the big experiment that has proven to be effective. Moreover, this book is not alone in sounding the alarm. Plunging share prices and super-low interest rates are sounding the same alarm.

The fact that so many countries are encountering a similar balance sheet recession today means that Japan has the responsibility to learn from its own painful experiences and inform the world of what to do and what *not* to do in such a recession. Failure to do so will mean that other countries will end up taking the wrong medicine and repeating the same mistakes made elsewhere. It is hoped, therefore, that Japan will press the buttons for structural reform and macroeconomic policies in the right order, and explain to the world why it has chosen that course over any other.

1

THE JAPANESE ECONOMY IN BALANCE SHEET RECESSION

ALL INDICATORS ARE THE OPPOSITE OF THOSE IN THE U.S. AND U.K. 20 YEARS AGO

The Japanese economy has deep-rooted structural problems. The problems of the inefficient use of land (which is said to be the worst in the world), insufficient competition policies, and still-prevalent trade barriers, resulting in a high-cost economy, should all be rectified quickly. However, these problems did not come to the surface abruptly in the 1990s to torpedo the Japanese economy, which had been so robust over the preceding 40 years. Many of these problems had been in existence for 20 or 30 years, if not longer.

When talking about structural reform in Japan today, many people, including the Koizumi administration, do not mean rectifying the grossly inefficient use of land, which will be mentioned in Chapter 11. Instead, they mean the need to implement supply-side reforms that have been pushed ahead in the United States and the United Kingdom since the 1980s.

But, having worked as an economist with the Federal Reserve Bank of New York in those years, I can safely say that the situations in present-day Japan, and in the United States and the United Kingdom then, are completely opposite in every sense.

During those days in the United States, short-term interest rates had climbed to 22% and the yields on 30-year U.S. treasury bonds rose as high as 14%. There was double-digit inflation, and labor strikes were everywhere so that finally even air traffic controllers went on strike. When I bought a house in New Jersey, which is across the river from Manhattan, the interest rate on the 30-year fixed-rate mortgage was 17%. The U.S. trade balance was deeply in the red and the dollar was near collapse.

These indicators all pointed to a serious supply constraint in an economy with a strong domestic demand. In view of this fact, I was very much in favor of President Ronald Reagan's supply-side economics, which was, at that time, not at all popular with mainstream economists.

In contrast, the interest rate in Japan is now close to zero, which is literally unprecedented in the history of mankind. Deflation, rather than inflation, is spreading and there is not even a hint of labor strikes. Workers are grateful just to have a job, even if there is no increase in their pay. Japan's trade surplus is still one of the largest in the world, and the yen is still one of the strongest currencies.

No matter how one looks at it, this is a world in which there is plenty of supply but no demand, and it is a situation that is the complete opposite of the one seen in the United States and the United Kingdom 20 years ago. The huge trade surplus alone is sufficient to suggest that supply and competitive problems are not the key constraint on the Japanese economy.

It is terrifying to think that even though economic and market indicators are all screaming that the disease which Japan contracted during the last decade is not the same disease the United States and the United Kingdom suffered from 20 years ago, the authorities and the media are ignoring all such indications and are hell-bent on using the same cure that those countries used all that time ago.

BANKING PROBLEM NOT A CONSTRAINT ON GROWTH?

The same holds true with the problem of non-performing loans (NPLs). The present government and many commentators claim that banks' money has been frozen in unpromising traditional industries and that the souring of these loans has worsened the capital ratio of banks, making it impossible for them to extend credit to promising new businesses with interesting projects. Therefore, they claim, if the problem of NPLs is solved promptly to allow banks to function as intermediating financial institutions, money will begin to flow again and the economy will head toward recovery.

However, if this argument that NPLs are preventing the banks from extending credit despite the existence of a large number of creditworthy borrowers with interesting projects is correct, the lending rates of Japanese banks should be rising sharply. That is, if there are a large number of creditworthy businesses with projects that promise high returns, there must be fierce competition for funds among these would-be borrowers for the limited amount of funds available from the banks. Such competition should necessarily push lending rates higher, as would-be borrowers vie with one another for the limited funds available.

In fact, when U.S. banks were unable to lend due to their capital problems between 1991 and 1993, bank lending rates stayed well above 6%

even though the Federal Reserve had lowered banks' funding cost to as low as 3%. This is because it was the availability of bank capital, not liquidity, which constrained bank lending at that time, and there were still many people and companies in the U.S. who were willing to borrow even at such high rates.

In contrast, Japan's interest rates have been going nowhere but down, and yields on government bonds and bank lending rates are both at their lowest levels in human history. Furthermore, the *Tankan* survey, the Bank of Japan's quarterly survey of more than 5,000 companies, both large and small, on the question of bankers' willingness to lend, has revealed that, except for two occasions, banks have been willing and accommodative lenders for most of the last 10 years (see Chapter 3 for details).[1]

The exceptionally low interest rate, which is fully consistent with the Bank of Japan's survey of borrowing companies, is telling us that there is a serious flaw in the above interpretation of the problem of NPLs. If the NPL problem is really the constraint on Japan's economic growth, then the lending rate of those banks should be much higher, not lower, and bankers should be unwilling, instead of willing, lenders.

If the structural argument, including the NPL problem of Japanese banks, is not consistent with the voice of the market, such as low interest rates and strong trade performance, what could possibly explain the sudden loss of forward momentum in the Japanese economy over a decade ago and its sub-par performance ever since?

LOSS OF ONE OF THE TWO KEY WHEELS OF THE JAPANESE ECONOMY

The answer to this question lies in the collapse of asset prices starting from the first business day of the 1990s, which forced Japanese companies into a balance sheet repair mode the likes of which no one had seen since the Great Depression of the 1930s. This collective sea-change in corporate behavior threw the Japanese economy into a balance sheet recession, a very rare type of recession that occurs perhaps once in half a century.

An examination of the remarkable growth of the Japanese economy prior to the 1990s shows that the economy actually had two big wheels, which revolved with exquisite timing. One wheel was the high savings rate of the household sector. The fact that households did not spend all of their income and saved a considerable portion of it means that they were offering those saved funds to businesses via financial institutions or the capital market.

The other wheel was the equally high investment rate of the Japanese corporate sector. Until the end of the 1980s, the investment ratios and degrees of debt dependence of Japanese companies were very high by world standards. In other words, Japanese businesses were aggressively borrowing funds saved by the household sector in order to develop new products and expand capacity to an unparalleled degree. Indeed, in the early 1980s, the leverage ratio of the average Japanese company was five times the average in the United States.

This exceptionally high investment rate, combined with the high savings ratio of the household sector, enabled Japan to become the world's second-largest economy. Fifty years ago, no one in the world could have predicted that a war-torn Japan would soon become the second-largest economy in the world, but its actual growth was beyond anyone's expectations.

In the meantime, corporate debts grew to an enormous scale, especially in relation to their capital. But the value of their assets rose even more sharply. Thus, the world's credit-rating agencies, including Moody's Investors' Services, Inc. and Standard & Poor's Corporation, routinely gave Japanese businesses and financial institutions their highest ratings. Prices of assets grew particularly rapidly in the late 1980s, allowing Japanese companies to procure funds with ease and expand their business even faster.

The asset-price bubble, however, collapsed from the first business day of 1990, triggering a crash of asset prices. The prices of many shares fell to a fraction of their peak levels. The price of land, which had been believed to be absolutely safe, plummeted, with the price of commercial land in the six major cities tumbling 85%. That is to say, it is now worth only 15% of its peak price. Golf club memberships, which are important in the scheme of things in Japan, are now worth less than one-tenth of what they were. Exhibit 1.1 shows how far asset prices in Japan have declined.

During the 1970s and 1980s, Japanese companies took out massive loans with which to expand their business. These debts are still there, but the value of the assets, which should be at least as large as the size of their debts, has collapsed. As a result, the balance sheet, or the financial health of the companies, has deteriorated drastically. The sheer magnitude of the decline in asset prices suggests that perhaps there are hundreds of thousands of businesses in Japan whose liabilities exceed their assets, or whose financial condition is close to it. For these companies, the excess liabilities mean that they are actually bankrupt.

The concept of bankruptcy, however, really has two levels. First, there are companies that are hopelessly bankrupt in the sense that both their main line of business and their balance sheets have no future. Then there are companies whose main line of business is still sound, but whose balance sheets are completely out of whack.

When one looks at Japan today, many, if not most, companies are in the second category in that their core businesses are still doing fairly well. The fact that Japan still chalks up the largest trade surplus in the world means

(1990 = 100)

Exhibit 1.1 Asset prices collapsed in Japan

Sources: Tokyo Stock Exchange; Japan Real Estate Institute; Nikkei Sangyo Shinbun.

that consumers around the world still want to buy Japanese products. Even so, an enormous number of these companies have disastrous balance sheets brought about by the collapse of asset prices within Japan.

THE JAPANESE ECONOMY IN A "FALLACY OF COMPOSITION"

Any (responsible) business executives who find themselves in the situation of running a company with reasonable cash flow but disastrous balance sheets will do one thing: they will repay their debts with the earnings from their core businesses. Even for businesses whose debts are enormous vis-à-vis their assets, given sufficient time, they should be able to repair their balance sheets by paying down debts, because asset prices will not move into negative territory.

Once the balance sheets are restored and the businesses move out of their negative equity territory, executives would feel free to start looking forward again for new money-making projects, instead of looking backward and trying to restore their balance sheets. But in the meantime, the first priority of these executives must be to put their companies on a sound financial footing by paying down debts as quickly and quietly as possible. In addition, businesses in this predicament are likely to cut costs anywhere they can and use the funds so saved to repay their debts. As the behavior of individual businesses, this is a very proper and responsible action to take.

The problem is what will happen to the economy as a whole when a large number of businesses, all at the same time, begin to behave this way. It goes without saying that with so many businesses paying down debts and not investing, the demand in the overall economy will shrink compared with the case in which such funds are used for expansionary projects such as capital investment or new product development. The contraction in aggregate demand weakens the economy. The weakness of the economy further depresses asset prices, which further worsens corporate balance sheets. That, in turn, drives businesses further to cut costs and pay down its debts. The more such efforts are made, therefore, the greater the shrinkage of demand, and the economy deteriorates at an accelerating rate.

The point is that, even when businesses individually take proper and responsible actions, it is possible for the economy to deteriorate further and further in a vicious cycle when everyone takes the debt-minimizing action at the same time. Such a situation is called a "fallacy of composition" in economics, and this is exactly what is happening in Japan today.

NO CHANGE IN PERSONAL CONSUMPTION OVER THE PAST DECADE

Exhibit 1.2 shows how disastrous the situation is. The exhibit shows flow of funds in the four major sectors of the Japanese economy (that is, the household, corporate, government, and overseas sectors). The sectors above the horizontal line at zero are those sectors that are saving funds, while those below the line represent those that are borrowing and investing funds. Although the flow of funds statistics, from which this chart was compiled, are designed so that the sum of all sectors will be zero, Exhibit 1.2 entries do not add up to zero because it has omitted the financial sector in the interests of clarity. However, since the financial sector would be neutral in the long run, this omission should not present a problem.

The exhibit shows that the household sector is at the top of the chart, indicating that high savings, one of the two wheels mentioned above, are still intact. Moreover, savings behavior of the household sector hardly changed during the 1990s. The sector saved an equivalent of around 7% of GDP at the peak of Japan's asset-price bubble in 1990 and continued to do so until 1999.

This means that the savings behavior of consumers has hardly changed between the bubble period, when the Japanese economy was booming and the nation was billed "Japan as Number One," and the present, when the Japanese economy is the whipping boy of the world due to its poor performance. The combination of unchanged savings and zero growth and zero inflation means that there has been almost no change in personal consumption either.

In fact, Exhibit 1.3 shows that consumption has remained flat during the past decade. If the Japanese people were really worried about the future

Exhibit 1.2 Falling asset prices forced companies to move away from profit maximization to debt minimization

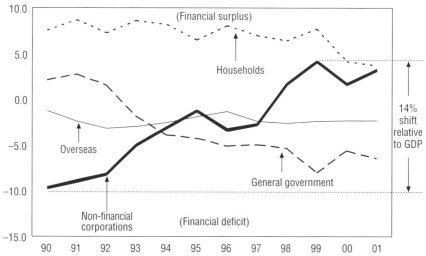

Financial surplus or deficit by sector

(as a ratio to nominal GDP, %)

Source: Flow of funds data, Bank of Japan.

budget deficit or the collapse of their pension programs, as some people claim, then consumption would have shrunk rapidly and savings would have increased. However, neither has changed significantly during the past decade. This means the frequently heard argument that the economy is faltering because consumers' worries about the future are driving savings and depressing consumption is not supported by the data. (The fall in household savings in recent years is due to the fall in income and employment. That is bad news for those who are experiencing the fall in income, but from a macroeconomic perspective it means that deflationary leakage has narrowed for the economy.)

DISAPPEARANCE OF CORPORATE DEMAND FOR FUNDS

If the household sector is not responsible for the weakening of the Japanese economy, who is? Exhibit 1.2 shows that in 1990, the non-financial corporations (represented by the bold black line) borrowed an equivalent of 10% of GDP annually to invest in all sorts of projects. The existence of such a large demand for funds means that businesses were borrowing and spending that much money, thus supporting the economy.

Exhibit 1.3   Consumption has been flat since 1990

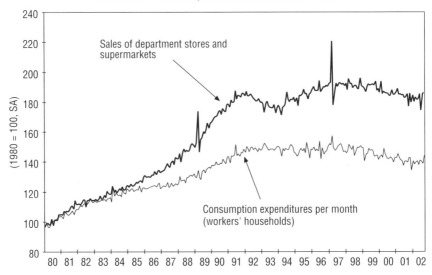

Sales of department stores and supermarkets

Consumption expenditures per month (workers' households)

Sources: Management and Coordination Agency, "Monthly Report on the Family Income and Expenditure Survey"; Ministry of International Trade and Industry, "Current Survey of Commerce."

Since 1998, however, the non-financial corporations line is in positive territory, which means that companies are now repaying their debts – that is, they are now net suppliers of funds to the capital market and the banking system. Between 1990 and 2001, for example, the shift in the behavior of business corporations was equivalent to 14% of GDP, as their position shifted from a net borrower of funds to the tune of 10% of GDP to a net repayer of debt to the tune of 4% of GDP. This means that Japanese companies have not only stopped borrowing money to invest, they are now redirecting ¥20 trillion in corporate earnings from reinvestment and other uses to repaying debts. This means a loss of nearly 14% of GDP from the income stream compared to 10 years ago. A loss in demand of this magnitude would certainly plunge any economy into recession.

Why, then, have businesses behaved this way? The answer lies in Exhibit 1.1. Faced with the devastating crash of asset prices that hit their companies hard, businessmen throughout Japan began placing their highest priorities on repairing their balance sheets by repaying debts so as to avoid being labeled insolvent. Indeed, it was around 1993 when businessmen all over the country started talking about "balance sheet scare syndrome." In other words, a large number of Japanese businesses shifted their management priorities from profit maximization to debt minimization in around 1993, thus causing a loss of demand equivalent to 14% of GDP.

BUSINESSES ATTEMPT TO REPAIR THEIR BALANCE SHEETS

A large number of commentators have been "bashing" Japanese businesses for bringing the economy to its present sorry state by procrastinating on corporate restructuring and other reform efforts. However, their view is fundamentally wrong. If corporations had really ignored the decline in asset prices and procrastinated on taking countermeasures in the belief that land and share prices would soon recover, there was no reason for the Japanese economy to plunge into a recession. This is because the corporate sector would then still be borrowing and spending the equivalent of 10% of GDP.

In fact, some companies in Japan did maintain their expansionary ways. For example, Sogo, a major department store chain operator, continued to increase its investments because it believed that the economy and asset prices would recover in due course. Other businesses, in the meantime, assumed that asset prices would not recover to their former levels and rushed to repay their debts in order to clean up their balance sheets. Because many more companies were doing the latter instead of the former, the economy sank deeper into recession. Under these circumstances, Sogo, which had remained on a solitary expansionary course, went bankrupt, as demand failed to increase as it had forecasted. It can be said, however, that Sogo was providing underpinnings to the economy, while other firms were collectively pushing the Japanese economy toward a contractionary equilibrium.

The economy is in recession precisely because business executives took the plunge in asset prices seriously, attempted to repair their balance sheets promptly, and are paying down debts as quickly as possible. Those analysts who complain about the lack of structural reform in Japanese companies are missing the most important reform, which is taking place right before their eyes: the reform of corporate balance sheets.

The present recession in Japan, therefore, has been caused by changes in corporate, rather than consumer, behavior. Consumers, to a large extent, have not changed their behavior over the last 12 years.

NO ECONOMIC TEXTBOOK COVERS THE PRESENT SITUATION IN JAPAN

An examination of the behaviors of individual companies reveals that nearly 2,000 firms out of the 3,500 listed companies in Japan are currently paying down their debts, while just under 1,000 companies have been increasing their borrowings. (The amounts of debt have remained unchanged for the remaining 500 firms.[2]) Listed companies are companies that have access to both banks and the capital market. The fact that the majority of them are repaying debts despite the zero-interest environment suggests that their concern over their balance sheets is a serious one indeed. The fact that these companies admit that bankers are willing lenders, as indicated in the Bank of Japan *Tankan* survey mentioned above, shows that their concern is serious. The ratio of those paying down debts grows even higher when non-listed companies are included.

The sheer number of companies rushing to repay debts despite the zero-interest environment suggests that this is an extremely unusual situation under a capitalist economy, whose major premise is that companies are always seeking to expand business. Indeed, no economics textbook has ever dealt with a situation where the vast majority of companies are paying down their debts at a 0% interest rate. As such, the current situation in Japan has to be dealt with from a completely new perspective. This is because conventional economics is built on the assumption that businesses are always engaged in maximizing profits, and virtually no consideration has been given to the situation where the top priority for businesses is to minimize debts.

In other words, what is happening throughout Japan is completely alien to the very foundations of conventional economics and management theories. However, in recent years, this alien world is emerging not just in Japan but also in the United States, Taiwan, and Thailand, just to name a few countries. In the United States, the asset side of the balance sheets of a large number of companies has been damaged by the bursting of the IT bubble, only to see the liability side come under suspicion due to the uncovering of the Enron debacle. The outcome of all this is that many, if not most, corporate executives in the U.S. today are very much occupied with the need to produce clean balance sheets. With so few companies in the mood to increase debt, corporate demand for funds has continued to decline in the U.S. despite a succession of interest rate cuts by the Federal Reserve, as shown in Exhibit 1.4.

Coming back to Japan, the lack of corporate demand is exacerbated by the fact that the high savings rate of the household sector, one of the two wheels that had supported the growth of the Japanese economy through the 1980s, is still very much in place. In other words, people are saving as enthusiastically as before. Yet, businesses are in no mood to borrow, which means that the other wheel has broken down.

In the past, money circulated in Japan because businesses borrowed and used the funds the households saved. Today, even though households are saving, businesses are not borrowing. Not only that, businesses are doing all they can to repay their debts. As a result, compared with the days when businesses were eagerly borrowing money to invest, there has emerged the risk that the entire savings of the household sector will immediately translate into a deflation gap.

Exhibit 1.4   U.S. corporate sector also showing signs of balance sheet recession

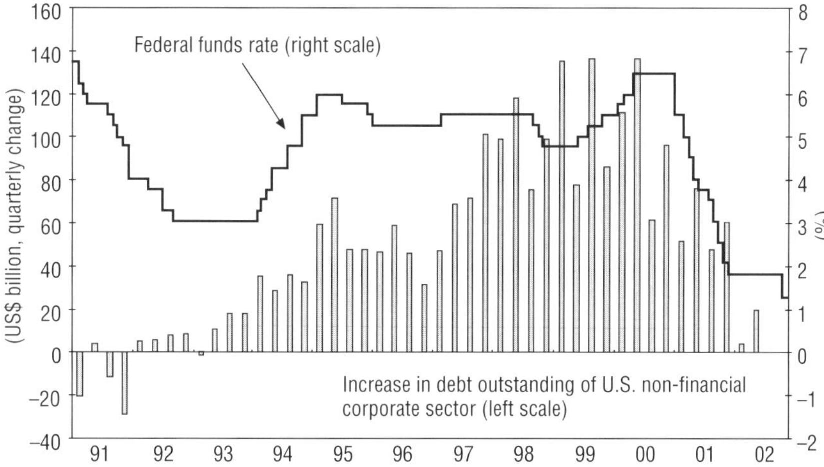

Source: Board of Governors of the Federal Reserve, "Flow of Funds in the United States."

BALANCE SHEET RECESSION LEADS TO GREAT DEPRESSION

To put this deflationary gap into numbers, let us say that a person with an income of ¥1,000 normally spends ¥900 and saves ¥100 with a bank. The ¥900 portion will become someone else's income, and the remaining ¥100 will be lent to someone by the bank to be spent. If the bank has trouble placing the entire ¥100, all it has to do is to lower the interest rate a little. With a lower rate, there will always be someone willing to take up the money. As a result, there will be ¥900 plus ¥100 worth of spending that is equal to the initial income of ¥1,000, and the economy moves forward.

In a balance sheet recession, the person with an income of ¥1,000 still spends ¥900 and saves ¥100. The ¥900 portion will enter the income stream, but the ¥100 portion cannot find borrowers because the corporate sector is busy paying down debts in spite of zero interest rates. This will make the financial institution awash with money, because it now has the ¥100 from the household sector plus the funds repaid by the corporate sector. This lack of borrowers explains why interest rates fall sharply in a balance sheet recession. (This point will be discussed in detail in Chapter 3.) It also means that in the overall economy, only ¥900 worth of demand is generated. Since one person's spending is the next person's income, in this case, the total economy shrinks from the initial ¥1,000 to ¥900. Then, if the household which now has an income of only ¥900 again saves 10% of income and spends only ¥810, and if the bank is still unable to lend this money, an income of only ¥810 will be generated at the next stage.

The drop in income from ¥1,000 to ¥810 also means the economy has deteriorated sharply, which probably means further declines in asset prices. This, in turn, will make businesses work still harder to pay down their debts, while reducing the demand for funds. This vicious cycle is the pernicious characteristic peculiar to a balance sheet recession.

When does this vicious cycle end? If the government does nothing to rectify this situation, the cycle will end when the private sector becomes so impoverished that, as a whole, it can no longer save any money.

Let us assume that the person's income falls from ¥1,000 to ¥500 as a result of the vicious cycle. At this level, he can no longer save any money because of the rent and other obligations contracted earlier on the assumption that his income will remain at ¥1,000. This means that he might have to spend the entire ¥500, or all of his income, just to make ends meet. This means that the income of the next person is also ¥500. If the second person also has to spend all of his income to maintain his standard of living, the third person's income will also be ¥500, and so on. That is, the economy will reach a new equilibrium when the private sector (that is, the household sector plus the corporate sector) becomes so impoverished that people can no longer save any money. In other words, the economy stabilizes when there is no more leakage from the income stream in the form of saved but uninvested funds. And it is this ¥500 world that is typically called the "Great Depression."

THE JAPANESE ECONOMY HAS EERIE SIMILARITIES TO THE U.S. IN THE 1930s

In fact, the above mechanism brought the Great Depression to the U.S. in the 1930s. Until 1929, many Americans bought shares on margin (= debts). The crash of the New York stock market in 1929 left those investors with massive debts. People tried to pay down their debts by curbing consumption and investment, which in turn depressed the economy. The weak economy pushed share prices down further, which made people even more eager to pay down debts, resulting in a truly vicious cycle.

President Herbert Hoover, however, refused to adopt measures to support the economy, on the grounds that the deterioration of the economy was due to the existence of rotten elements in the economy that had fanned the bubble and that these elements had to be done away with first. Because of his refusal to move away from the balanced-budget principle, the above vicious cycle was allowed to continue until the economy reached the contractionary equilibrium. At that point, U.S. GDP fell to about half, and share prices fell to one-tenth of their peak values, while the unemployment rate climbed to well over 20%.

The situation that Japan finds itself in today is, in many ways, similar to that in the United States between 1929 and 1933, including the magnitude of the wealth lost and its implications for private-sector balance sheets. As mentioned earlier, the amount of wealth lost as a result of the asset-price collapse in Japan is equivalent to 2.7 years worth of GDP in the year of peak asset prices – that is, 1989. In contrast, the amount of wealth lost in the U.S. as a result of the fall in asset prices during the Great Depression is said to be US$108.9 billion, which is about the size of the U.S. gross national product (GNP) in 1929 (US$101.5 billion), when share prices reached a peak, or around twice GNP in 1933 (US$50.9 billion), when it had fallen to half the 1929 levels. Meanwhile, seen as a whole, U.S. national wealth in 1933 was 75% of 1929 levels.[3]

By contrast, in Japan the amount of wealth lost from the point at which share prices peaked in 1989 to recently (end-2001) is estimated at around ¥1,200 trillion, which is 2.7 times the 1989 GDP, or 2.3 times the recent levels of GDP. Meanwhile, national wealth as a whole is now 59% of 1989 levels.[4] This means the wealth destruction was far bigger in Japan this time around than in the U.S. during the Great Depression, with most of the Japanese wealth lost concentrated in the real estate sector.

Although Japanese share prices, which were largely supported by foreign investors during the last 12 years, did not fall to one-tenth of their peak values as in the U.S. in the 1930s, those assets where foreign investors did not show interest did fall to nearly one-tenth of their value. These included golf club memberships and commercial real estate, as seen earlier.

In fact, almost all economic statistics, including flow of funds statistics mentioned earlier and market indicators such as interest rates and stock prices, show that Japan is never too far away from falling into a vicious cycle. As long as nationwide balance sheet adjustments continue, the economy can fall into a vicious cycle anytime, anywhere.

ENDNOTES

1 Bank of Japan, *Tankan Short-term Economic Survey of Enterprises in Japan*, "Lending Attitude of Financial Institutions." The figures are for principal enterprises and small enterprises.

2 *The Japan Company Handbook* (Toyo Keizai, various years).

3 Raymond W. Goldsmith, *The National Wealth of the United States in the Postwar Period* (Princeton, N.J.: Princeton University Press, 1962), cited in *Historical Statistics of the United States, Colonial Times to 1970* (New York: National Bureau of Economic Research); Department of Commerce, "Economic Report of the President 1996."

4 Cabinet Office, "Annual Report on National Accounts of FY2001."

2

FISCAL STIMULUS ESSENTIAL IN OVERCOMING BALANCE SHEET RECESSION

ZERO GROWTH MAINTAINED ONLY BECAUSE OF FISCAL STIMULUS

The balance sheet recession the Japanese economy finds itself in is as rare as the nationwide asset bubble that occurs perhaps once in half a century. However, when the bubble bursts and people realize that the asset prices they had been chasing were wrong, they are forced to alter their behavior from the usual profit or utility maximization to restoring financial soundness. That, in turn, through the fallacy of composition, plunges the economy into a pernicious vicious cycle.

Why, then, against such odds, has the Japanese economy been able to come this far without plunging into a depression? The answer to this question was shown in Exhibit 1.2 in Chapter 1. The exhibit showed that while the corporate sector moved dramatically from negative to positive territory, causing a huge loss in demand, the government sector moved in the exact opposite direction, from positive to negative territory. In other words, instead of running a budget surplus, the government began running large budget deficits by borrowing and spending money. By doing so, the government was basically borrowing and spending the funds that the household sector saved but the corporate sector did not borrow. In other words, the government made up for the demand lost in the corporate sector. And as long as someone makes up for the lost demand, there is no reason for the contractionary cycle to start.

The Japanese economy, therefore, managed to stay away from depression only because the government's fiscal spending closed the demand-and-supply gap resulting from the shift of corporate behavior and kept it that way year after year. In other words, the government was borrowing and spending the ¥100 the bankers could not lend in the previous example.

The curve for general government in Exhibit 1.2 shows that Japan's fiscal balance was in surplus between 1990 and 1992 due to the after-effects of the "bubble" — that is, large tax revenue. It was in surplus for the same reason the U.S. budget was in surplus during and immediately after the IT bubble. Starting around 1992–93, however, a wide gap developed between demand and supply when private businesses switched to balance sheet repair mode en masse. If left alone, this gap would have resulted in a massive contraction of the Japanese economy.

Fortunately, the fundamental instinct of the Liberal Democratic Party (LDP), the ruling party in Japan, has been to put in more public works whenever the economy turns sour. Thus, from the beginning of the 1990s, and in a typical pork-barrel fashion, the ruling party has pumped up spending packages whenever the economy has shown signs of weakness. These pork-barrel politics in effect, and in retrospect, prompted the government to borrow and spend the household savings that the corporate sector was no longer borrowing. This action, in turn, filled the huge deflationary gap that had developed within the private sector, and prevented the onset of a vicious cycle.

Unfortunately, the magnitude of the decline in asset prices was huge, as indicated earlier. Commercial real estate prices, for example, plunged 85% on average, leaving a huge hole in the balance sheets of thousands of companies throughout the country. Such a huge hole cannot be filled in a year or two of debt repayments. It will take many years, if not decades (especially for those who bought at the peak), to fill the hole by paying down debt. The amount involved is just too large.

Furthermore, as noted earlier, the household sector continued to save during this entire period. With businesses no longer borrowing money, this meant that a large demand-and-supply gap developed within the private sector year after year.

All of this suggests that, even under the best of circumstances, recovery from a balance sheet recession of this magnitude will take many years. Unless an extremely large fiscal stimulus is put in place all at once (this point will be discussed further in Chapter 4), there are no quick fixes to this problem.

With the government filling the deflationary gap with fiscal stimulus each year, its debt increased sharply, as shown by the government's line plunging deeply into negative territory in Exhibit 1.2. But it is only because of the government's actions that the Japanese economy, which should have entered a vicious cycle long ago, has managed to maintain stability.

Not realizing what might have happened in the absence of fiscal stimulus, many media commentators have said, "The government has implemented stimulus packages worth ¥140 trillion over the past 10 years, but the economy has not turned upward, so staying on this course is meaningless." Although this view is widely held in Japan and abroad, it is one of the most misguided and dangerous of consensuses. These commentators do not realize that, over the past decade, Japan has lost wealth equivalent to 2.7 times its annual GDP. In terms of the amount of national wealth lost, present-day Japan outstrips the United States' Great Depression of the 1930s by a healthy margin.

The only reason the Japanese economy has been able to avoid falling into a depression and has managed to sustain its stability despite this massive loss of wealth and subsequent contraction in corporate demand was that the ¥140 trillion in stimulus packages kept the deflationary spiral from starting. Had there been no fiscal stimulus, the Japanese economy today would have contracted by 40–50%, if the U.S. experience during the 1930s is any guide.

Contrary to popular belief, therefore, Japan's fiscal spending was extremely effective in preventing the economy from entering the vicious cycle that would lead to a depression. By filling the deflationary gaps as soon as they appeared each year, the government managed to maintain the level of activity throughout this period in spite of the devastating loss of wealth. Indeed, the policy worked so well for so long that the general public, including most commentators on the economy, never learned that the economy was actually on the verge of entering a depression throughout this period.

CALLING FISCAL STIMULUS "CAMPHOR SHOTS" IS INAPPROPRIATE

The opponents of Japan's fiscal stimulus policy, however, argue that, even if the stimulus has the effect of keeping the economy going, it is still nothing more than "camphor injections," in the sense that such spending leaves nothing changed for the better in the medium to long term. They maintain that a temporary shot in the arm is no cure for the massive structural problems that Japan must overcome in order to enter a period of self-sustaining growth.

What these commentators have failed to see, however, is that thanks to the government's fiscal stimulus, large numbers of firms have successfully compressed their debts. And their success in repairing their balance sheets is the necessary condition for the economy to enter a period of self-sustaining growth.

As Exhibit 2.1 shows, the outstanding balance of interest-bearing corporate debts declined by ¥113 trillion between its peak in 1995 and the year 2001. Since this figure is net of forward-looking loans taken out by firms with clean balance sheets, the actual reduction of debt overhang by

Exhibit 2.1 Interest-bearing debt returning to the pre-bubble trend line

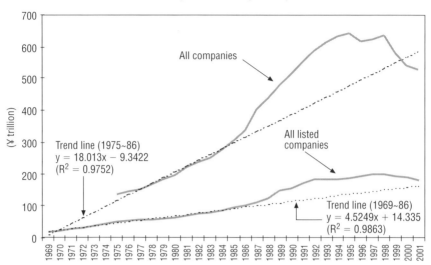

Sources: Ministry of Finance, "Financial Statements Statistics of Corporations by Industry, Yearly"; Toyo Keizai, *The Japan Company Handbook.*

troubled companies is much larger. This improvement in corporate balance sheets, made possible by the fiscal stimulus, will remain even after such stimuli are terminated.

Japanese banks have not been idle, either. They have disposed of ¥90 trillion, or nearly US$800 billion, in NPLs already.[1] No other banking system in the world has written off this much in NPLs. Criticism should be directed, therefore, at those inept commentators who fail to notice such efforts and improvement at the micro level and carelessly label stimulus packages as "camphor shots." The government's fiscal stimulus packages were by no means camphor shots with only temporary effects.

The necessary condition for an economy to enter a period of self-sustaining growth is to have most of its companies looking forward with reasonably clean balance sheets. Viewed from this perspective, in a situation like Japan today, where the vast majority of companies are still looking backward and trying to repair their balance sheets, the success of fiscal stimulus should be judged on the basis of how much such stimulus has helped those companies reduce their debt. The fact that Japanese companies were able to compress so much debt, as shown in Exhibit 2.1, means that fiscal stimulus over the years has indeed been highly successful. It is the cure that goes directly to the root of the problem by helping companies reduce their debt overhang.

ONE PERSON'S DEBT IS ANOTHER PERSON'S ASSETS

In this respect, one should not forget that balance sheet recession is a problem that exists largely within the private sector. A lender believes that his loans are sound because borrowers are repaying on schedule. If repayment stops, they become non-performing loans. In other words, one person's debt is another person's assets. As such, a nationwide balance sheet problem cannot be repaired by a blanket debt forgiveness, because such a policy will simply shift the problem from one part of the society to another.

Furthermore, if the flow of income is allowed to stop due to business failures or unemployment, payments on debts will also come to a halt. Such a stoppage will suddenly saddle lenders with more NPLs. If the lender — for example, a bank — decides to call in other loans so as to maintain capital ratios in the face of a sudden increase in NPLs, the chain of troubles can quickly grow bigger.

When there are damaged balance sheets everywhere in the private sector, therefore, the only solution is for the government to maintain the level of economic activity so that companies and households will have the income to pay down their debts. In this way, the overall balance sheet of the economy can improve, if only slowly, while the danger of entering a chain reaction of defaults and bankruptcies, which will push the economy into depression, can be kept to a minimum.

Viewed in this light, what the government has done so far is to maintain people's total income through fiscal spending. Even if the project is to dig a ditch and fill it up, if it closes the ¥100 gap described in the previous chapter, it will maintain people's income because all of the initial income of ¥1,000 will be spent and become the next person's income. And as long as income is maintained, companies will have the income to pay down debt, which in turn repairs their balance sheets.

THE LOW MULTIPLIER ARGUMENT ASSUMES A WRONG MODEL

As fiscal spending does not appear to have improved the Japanese economy, some economists have claimed that fiscal outlay in Japan has an extremely small multiplier effect. The multiplier is the amount of economic activity created in addition to that created by the initial stimulus.

Indeed, a large number of commentators are opposed to the fiscal stimulus, on the grounds that it has a very low multiplier effect. Although this kind of argument sounds plausible on the surface, it is actually totally wrong and irrelevant for present-day Japan.

It is wrong, because the fiscal policy was working in repairing corporate balance sheets. It is irrelevant, because the very concept of the multiplier effect assumes that the economy is initially in a stable equilibrium requiring no outside support. With the economy in a stable equilibrium before the stimulus is applied, one can meaningfully talk about and actually measure the multiplier effect of a fiscal stimulus by calculating how much growth the stimulus has added to the economy. Put differently, those who claim that the multiplier effect on Japan's fiscal spending is low are implicitly assuming that the economy is in a stable equilibrium (or not too far from it).

The Japanese economy today, however, is as far from stable equilibrium as any economy can possibly get. After all, this economy needs a budget deficit of over 6% of GDP just to stay at 0% growth. Without the massive fiscal support from the government, this economy will collapse into a deflationary spiral any minute, as explained earlier. In such an economy, it is absolutely meaningless to talk about the multiplier effect of a fiscal stimulus, because it cannot be meaningfully measured.

This is because, in order to measure the multiplier effect, one must first visualize the shape of the Japanese economy without the fiscal support. Such an economy is likely to be in the midst of a massive deflationary spiral or already at the end of that process — that is, in the midst of a depression where as much as 50% of GDP might have disappeared.

The multiplier effect of fiscal spending is, then, the difference between this depressed level and the present level of GDP. Since the gap between the two will be massive, so will be the multiplier. Thus, instead of numbers like 1.1 or 1.2, which one often hears about, the actual number could be so large as to be totally ridiculous. It is for this reason that it makes little sense to talk about the multiplier effect in present-day Japan.

Unfortunately, many econometric models in research institutions are built on the assumption that the Japanese economy is at or near a stable equilibrium. As such, they are ill-equipped to handle situations where the economy itself is far removed from a stable equilibrium. The predictions of most econometric models do not make any sense if the economy initially is not in a stable equilibrium. Not realizing these limitations of the model, many economists end up arguing against the seemingly "useless and ineffective fiscal stimulus."

Back in 1997, for example, both the International Monetary Fund (IMF) and the Organization for Economic Cooperation and Development (OECD) had asked Japan to reduce its "ineffective" fiscal stimulus, implicitly assuming that a reduction in ineffective government spending would not have a large negative impact on the economy. At that time, both institutions sent teams to Japan and actually interviewed the author, among others, before making their recommendations. The author's strong warnings against reducing government spending or raising taxes, however, were ignored in their final recommendations to the Japanese government. Furthermore, the

Japanese government, under the then prime minister Ryutaro Hashimoto, accepted the recommendations to reduce the budget deficit and so slashed spending while raising taxes.

The result was an unmitigated disaster, with the Japanese economy experiencing an unprecedented five quarters of negative growth — about the worst economic performance of any major industrialized country since World War II. The devastation was so large that even today, six years later, most economic indicators have not recovered their level of 1996, the year before the fiscal rehabilitation was implemented. All of this went to prove that the amount of economic activity fiscal spending had been supporting — that is, the multiplier — was indeed very large.

THE SAME MISTAKE MADE BY PRESIDENT ROOSEVELT IN 1937

It is interesting to note that exactly 60 years earlier, President Franklin D. Roosevelt made the same mistake that Prime Minister Hashimoto made in Japan in 1997. After the mismanagement of the economy by President Herbert Hoover, the newly elected President Roosevelt launched the reconstruction of the U.S. economy in 1933 by adopting an aggressive fiscal policy by the name of the "New Deal." Although the policy was haphazardly applied and was not always consistent, Roosevelt almost doubled the federal expenditure from 1933 to 1936.[2] By 1937, four years later, some of the economic indicators had more or less recovered to their levels of the 1920s, even though unemployment remained very high.

Believing that the economy was well on its way to recovery, and that a budget deficit is a bad thing, Roosevelt made the mistake of trying to reduce the deficit for fiscal 1937. The effect was immediate: the economy collapsed, with share prices again falling to half their former levels, industrial production plunging 30%, and the jobless rate skyrocketing.

Shocked, Roosevelt immediately turned his fiscal policy around, but the damage was done. Indeed, it took an enormous amount of time and energy to heal the wound for the second time, and the U.S. economy did not begin its recovery in earnest until 1941, when the Japanese attack on Pearl Harbor and World War II pushed the U.S. government to increase its spending several-fold.

In February 1997, two months before the Hashimoto government launched its fiscal rehabilitation, I pointed out, in an article co-authored with Shigeru Fujita, the risks of premature fiscal contraction by examining the U.S. experience in 1937.[3] Even though the article failed to stop the Hashimoto government from raising taxes and cutting spending starting in April 1997, the fact that the economy collapsed, exactly as I predicted in the article, was noted by many, including those in the media and government.

That, in turn, catapulted me into the very center of policymaking circles within the LDP, and allowed me to make several policy proposals in the areas of both fiscal policy and banking reform.

CUTTING FISCAL STIMULUS WILL FURTHER INCREASE BUDGET DEFICITS

In Japan, there is an enormous number of "fiscal rehabilitation first" advocates, including former officials of the Ministry of Finance (MOF). They call for fiscal rehabilitation without regard to the state of the real economy, so much so that one suspects perhaps they cannot get a lucrative private-sector or semi-private-sector post-retirement job from their ministry unless they keep saying so. (Why this may be so is discussed in Chapter 4.)

However, the amount of the 1996 budget deficit which Prime Minister Hashimoto attempted to slash through his fiscal rehabilitation measures starting in 1997 was ¥22 trillion. This was only two-thirds of the present deficit of ¥30–35 trillion, yet the Hashimoto government felt that the fiscal 1996 budget deficit of ¥22 trillion was too large.

The outcome of the government's bold attempt was a major economic catastrophe, with GDP growth rates falling from 4.4% in 1996 to five quarters of negative growth in 1997 and 1998. The collapsing economy resulted in plummeting tax revenues. By 1999, the deficit had swollen to ¥37 trillion as a result of both the fall in tax revenue and the need to increase spending in order to save the economy. The increases in the consumption tax and people's burden of social security premiums, the abolition of special tax cuts, and the refusal to put in a major supplementary budget only resulted in a 68% *increase* in the budget deficit instead of the planned reduction of ¥15 trillion. The "pain" and "sacrifices" imposed on the people then only reopened the wound further and made no contribution to the rehabilitation of either the economy or the fiscal balance. The fall in growth and the increase in the budget deficit are shown in Exhibit 2.2.

Meanwhile, MOF officials, who refuse to admit their mistakes in 1997, continue to claim that, the second quarter of 1997 (when the Hashimoto government raised the consumption tax rate) aside, consumption in the third quarter rose year-on-year and that the deterioration of the economy was due to other factors, such as the Asian currency crisis. However, as Professor Tatsuo Hatta of the University of Tokyo points out,[4] a closer examination of consumption statistics for the third quarter of 1997 shows that a large gain was registered in food only. And this was in reaction to a major drop in this segment in the same quarter of the previous year resulting from the O-157 coliform bacillus scare. Sales of consumer durables, which were directly hit by the boost in the consumption tax, declined in the third quarter as

Exhibit 2.2   Poorly timed fiscal reform in 1997 actually increased budget deficit

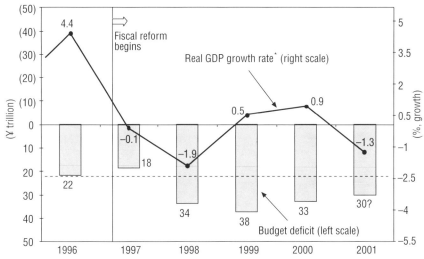

* The figures before 2001 are based on the System of National Accounts with the base year of 1968.
Sources: Ministry of Finance; Cabinet Office.

expected, proving that the fiscal rehabilitation measures then adopted pulled the economy down.

Attempts at fiscal rehabilitation amid a balance sheet recession are bound to put the economy in a vicious cycle, as explained earlier. Such an attempt would enlarge the wound by causing the economy to deteriorate and weakening the financial system, resulting in a larger instead of smaller budget deficit.

Even in the U.S. during the 1930s, the largest budget deficit as a percentage of federal expenditure was not recorded during Roosevelt's New Deal years but in 1932, when Hoover was still the president. In that year, 60% of federal expenditure had to be financed with deficit because of collapsing tax receipts.[5] And the tax receipts were collapsing because Hoover, a staunch believer in a balanced budget, refused to contemplate a large fiscal stimulus to stabilize the economy. All these experiences in both Japan and the U.S. go to prove that, in a balance sheet recession, fiscal measures that provide critical underpinnings to the economy should not be withdrawn carelessly.

PROACTIVE FISCAL POLICY IS BETTER THAN FALLING BEHIND THE CURVE

In a balance sheet recession, the sooner the fiscal measures are mobilized, the smaller will be the ultimate budget deficit. If the fiscal stimulus is delayed, the recession will become deeper, and the stock market might collapse in the meantime. Resorting to a fiscal stimulus after the economy and stock market have collapsed would require massive spending, because the wounds will be so much larger. In the earlier example, where the economy contracts from ¥1,000 to ¥900, and then to ¥810 and so forth, if the government puts in the stimulus worth ¥100 from the beginning, the level of economic activity will remain at ¥1,000. Two years of that will mean a budget deficit of ¥200 for the total economic activity of ¥2,000.

If the government waited a year before taking action, the economy would have collapsed to ¥810 in size. This means that the stimulus needed to return the economy to the original level of economic activity will be ¥190, while the total economic activity for the two-year period will be ¥1,900. This means ¥100 worth of economic activity would have been lost forever. In other words, the sum of the budget deficit and economic activity lost will be ¥290. This is ¥90, or 45%, more than the case where the government put in fiscal stimulus from the very beginning in a proactive fashion. Even though one may argue that the second case incurs ¥10 less budget deficit, in the real world, chances are high that the budget deficit will be greater in the second case as well, because a weaker economy almost always results in reduced tax receipts.

Even though the Japanese fiscal stimulus successfully helped companies repair their balance sheets while keeping the economy going, except during the first year of the Obuchi Cabinet (July 1998 to April 2000), it was never applied in a proactive manner. Indeed, each time the fiscal policy was applied, it was always "behind the curve" in the sense that it was mobilized only after the economy showed significant weakness. This means that a lot of unnecessary deficit was incurred, while economic activities that could have been saved were lost forever. In a balance sheet recession, where the economy could fall into a vicious cycle from any deflationary gap that remained unfilled, reactionary fiscal policy is always inefficient and wasteful.

In this kind of recession, a proactive fiscal policy is essential in both keeping the economy going and in minimizing the medical bill — that is, the deficit. The last thing a policymaker should do in a balance sheet recession is prematurely withdraw the fiscal stimulus. As amply observed in 1997 (and in 1937 in the U.S.), such a withdrawal can result in an instant collapse of the economy while enlarging the deficit by decimating the tax receipts.

Once asset prices have fallen to a reasonable level, a proactive fiscal policy applied consistently can put the economy in a virtuous cycle and significantly shorten the time needed to repair private-sector balance sheets. Although Japan actually entered such virtuous cycles on two previous occasions, in 1996 and 2000, both were torpedoed by the MOF, which is hell-bent on reducing the budget deficit regardless of economic conditions. This point will be discussed further in Chapter 4.

It is regrettable that Japanese policymakers are not flexible enough to realize that, had they moved sooner, they would have assuaged people's fears and the market's apprehension that much sooner and could also have saved some of the spending (= the budget deficit).

WOULD FISCAL STIMULUS BRING ON A MARKET CRASH?

Recently, academics who do not understand anything about the marketplace, as well as former officials of the MOF, who have routinely refused to listen to the voice of the market and ordered interventions, have been arguing that the market will crash if the fiscal stimulus is increased. Their arguments can be classified into several categories.

The first is that if fiscal measures are mobilized, those investors who have bought shares betting on Koizumi's structural reform agenda would be disappointed because they would assume that the government has abandoned structural reform. However, ever since Koizumi took office, share prices have been falling, not rising. In fact, during the four months between the inauguration of the Koizumi government and just before the terrorist attacks in New York and Washington on September 11, 2001, stock prices in Japan had already lost more than ¥100 trillion in market capitalization, or 26.4% of their value. Unlike the media and those analysts who liked Koizumi's reformist agenda, investors — who actually had their money in the Japanese stock market — fled the market because they knew that Japan was in a balance sheet recession and that the policies of the Koizumi government would only make the situation worse. This means that not too many investors are betting their money on Koizumi's structural reform agenda.

More importantly, these academics do not realize that, if the economy heads toward a meltdown as it did during the 1997 fiscal reform, the market reaction would be "dump Japan" no matter how vehemently the government pushes for structural reform. This is entirely natural, because no one will buy Japanese assets when the bottom is falling out of the economy itself and the future earnings of Japanese assets have become impossible to forecast with any degree of accuracy.

That is exactly what happened in 1997 when Prime Minister Hashimoto tried to reduce the budget deficit. The exodus of investment funds from Japan, which resulted in a simultaneous fall of both the stock market and the yen, was so shocking that a new term, "dump Japan (*nihon uri*)" was added to the market jargon. The market showed an identical reaction when Koizumi came to power and insisted on fiscal reform. With both the yen and the stock market falling simultaneously in 2001, the market was again full of "dump Japan" comments, just as in 1997.

The major premise required for investors, particularly foreign investors, to buy Japanese assets is that the economy is either stable or expanding, because otherwise it would be impossible to forecast returns from those assets appropriately. Only after a degree of stability is assured for the economy will investors examine which companies have made headway in restructuring or have exciting new products. Thus, in a balance sheet recession, fiscal measures are needed to stabilize not only the macroeconomy, but also asset prices.

PROACTIVE FISCAL POLICY BOOSTS MARKET CAPITALIZATION BY ¥200 TRILLION

Another argument against fiscal stimulus is that if such measures are taken again, long-term bond yields in Japan would rise sharply and cause massive capital losses to Japanese financial institutions, who hold an enormous amount of Japanese government bonds (JGBs). They argue that capital losses on their bond holdings will deal a fatal blow to Japanese financial institutions that are already severely weakened by the last 10 years of recession and asset price declines.

It is natural, however, for interest rates to rise when the economy turns around. It is putting the cart before the horse to claim that the economy should remain depressed because higher interest rates would hurt financial institutions. Moreover, this argument ignores the fact that stock and other asset prices will rise when fiscal measures successfully buoy the economy. A stronger economy will strengthen the banks and reduce the incidence of NPLs as well.

The Obuchi Cabinet came into power in July 1998 with the slogan, "I will not run after two hares," meaning that Obuchi would not try to balance the budget and stimulate the economy at the same time. The Cabinet compiled a large supplementary budget immediately after share prices reached their lowest post-bubble level on October 15, 1998. Between that day and Obuchi's death on April 2, 2000, total market capitalization increased by a whopping ¥213 trillion. Since financial institutions held 14.5% of all issued shares as of October 1998, banks' capital gains during the period could have reached as much as 14.5% of ¥213 trillion, or ¥31 trillion.

During the same interval, yields on JGBs rose from 0.845% to 1.775%. Since financial institutions held ¥43.7 trillion in JGBs in October 1998, their capital losses resulting from higher interest rates amounted to approximately ¥3 trillion. In other words, Japanese financial institutions made a capital gain of ¥28 trillion after subtracting the capital loss resulting from higher bond yields thanks to the Obuchi government's proactive fiscal policy. The gain from the healthier economy, therefore, was 10 times larger than the capital loss the financial institutions incurred on their bond holdings. The healthier economy also reduced the frequencies of non-performing loans and stabilized real estate prices.

In total, it is obvious that the improved economy through positive fiscal policy is far better for the Japanese economy and the banks than otherwise. It simply does not make any sense to focus attention just on the capital loss on bond holdings of financial institutions when the same institutions hold so many other assets that actually gain in value from an improved economy.

ANDREW MELLON AND HEIZO TAKENAKA

So far, it has been shown that it is reckless to attempt fiscal rehabilitation when the economy is in a balance sheet recession. This thinking directly contradicts the stance of the Koizumi government, which is: "No economic recovery without structural reform."

In the United States, the share-price bubble burst in 1929 and the economy rapidly deteriorated toward the Great Depression. However, President Hoover remained on the sidelines and did not provide fiscal stimulus on the grounds that inept management was responsible for the succession of bank and corporate failures. Hoover not only believed in a balanced budget, but he was also what we call a "structural reformist."

Hoover was backed by his Treasury secretary, Andrew Mellon, who advocated, "Liquidate labor, liquidate stocks, liquidate real estate ... It will purge the rottenness of the system ... Values will be adjusted, and enterprising people will pick up the wrecks... ."[6] Mellon had the same idea as Heizo Takenaka, state minister in charge of both the Financial Service Agency (FSA) and economic and fiscal policy in the Koizumi government. That idea is that structural reform should be pressed ahead by thoroughly purging the rotten part of the economy, namely NPLs and inefficient segments of the corporate sector.

Everyone knows what happened to the United States as a result of President Hoover's insistence on a balanced budget and acquiescence to the failures of troubled businesses and banks. The economy got into deeper and deeper trouble, to the extent that stock prices plummeted to one-tenth of their peak levels, the unemployment rate shot up to 22% with many major cities experiencing an unemployment rate up to 50%, and half of the GDP was lost. Mellon's advice only opened the wound wider and did nothing to solve the problem. The Hoover administration did not realize that people were actually doing the right and responsible things, but was caught in a massive fallacy of composition.

Moreover, as banks were allowed to fail, the credit-creation mechanism failed, plunging the entire economy into a depression. Even Milton Friedman, a leading monetarist and a strong opponent of fiscal activism, pointed out that it was a great mistake for the monetary authorities at the time to allow the shakeout of banks.[7]

I find it hard to understand why the recent crop of reformists, including Heizo Takenaka, have single-mindedly pursued a policy of "pain" that would only open the wound wider and called for a bank and corporate shakeout despite the bitter experience of the United States seven decades ago.

Moreover, it is already proven that structural reform cannot replace fiscal policy in propping up the economy. In 1997, Lawrence Summers, then the deputy secretary of the U.S. Treasury, pointed out to the Hashimoto administration just before it embarked on fiscal rehabilitation that even though structural reform is important, it is no substitute for macroeconomic policy. Summers made a thorough analysis of the Japanese economy and by the summer of 1996 diagnosed its condition as balance sheet recession, though he used the phrase "classical (= pre-1930s) credit cycle." Based on this analysis, he argued in 1997 that the attempt to reduce the budget deficit will totally wreck the Japanese economy.

However, Hashimoto and officials at the Ministry of Finance ignored his warning, saying that the Japanese economy would not buckle under even if fiscal spending was cut and that there was no cause for worry because they would increase demand through structural reform and deregulation. The IMF also backed Hashimoto. Unfortunately, Summers' fears were realized.

Summers knew from his own country's experience of Reaganomics that it takes a long time — anywhere from five to 15 years — for structural reforms to bear fruit. After all, it was President Bill Clinton, who came to power 10 years after Reaganomics, who benefited most from the supply-side reforms of the Reagan administration. Summers also knew that in the 1930s, the U.S. media were also full of calls for structural reform, just like in Japan today, when the real problem lay in the balance sheets and the lack of aggregate demand.

Paul Krugman of Princeton University has begun to voice a similar view. In a paper written in April 2001, Professor Krugman cited the example of the United States in the 1930s and questioned the wisdom of the "structural reform first" argument, saying that he could not see how the Japanese economy would improve through a policy that would increase joblessness and bankruptcies in the name of structural reform when the economy was already suffering from a shortage of aggregate demand.[8]

Despite these warnings based on lessons from history, the current Koizumi government is repeating the same mistakes made by the Hashimoto government four years ago and by the Hoover administration in the United States 70 years ago, by trying to limit fiscal stimulus in the middle of a balance sheet recession.

RIGHT POLICIES, WRONG PROMISES

Why is it, then, that the fiscal stimulus in Japan is so unpopular? There are two possible reasons. First, it is said that "he who prevents a crisis never becomes a hero." The LDP's fiscal policies of the last 10 years, apart from the period of fiscal retrenchment between 1997 and 1998, have had the effect of steering the economy away from danger. As a result, the Japanese public were unaware of how close they were to economic catastrophe during that period.

Furthermore, after 10 years of crisis prevention, people began to take the situation for granted. In other words, people started saying that since nothing happened after spending ¥140 trillion, the money must have been wasted on some of the most useless projects on earth. However, as mentioned earlier, the truth of the matter is that without that ¥140 trillion being spent, the economy would have fallen into depression long ago.

It is a sad fact of life that a crisis must happen before a hero can be created. In Hollywood movies, a hero emerges *after* a catastrophic event has occurred, not before. Someone who averts a crisis before it happens does not appear to others as a hero, because they are unaware of his actions and of how close they came to disaster. It is the responsibility of journalists and analysts to provide proper background information to the public so that they will appreciate the work of non-heroes. Unfortunately, none of this analysis was forthcoming. As a result, the general public in Japan did not know how fortunate they really were.

The second reason for the poor image of fiscal stimulus programs, however, has to do with the problem of politicians themselves. Not realizing that the economy is in a balance sheet recession, many politicians facing elections have said that the economy would improve once their next stimulus measures were put in place. Needless to say, the economy turns upward when stimulus measures are taken, but it deteriorates again as soon as their effects wear off, as long as businesses continue to pay down their debts. Thus, another stimulus package becomes necessary, and politicians once more promise that their package will put the economy in an autonomous recovery — and so it goes on ….

Since this has been going on for such a long time with no autonomous recovery in sight, the people now have the impression that they have been cheated all along, and that the money was spent by politicians on some of the most useless projects on earth, just so that they could secure political support. The economy did not budge, despite repeated stimuli, for the obvious reason that the fall in asset prices was so large that one or two years of paying down debts was not sufficient to repair the majority of corporate balance sheets. Not realizing what might have happened in the absence of fiscal stimulus, the public began to believe that the economy would not improve no matter what stimulus measures were taken.

The truth of the matter is that, except for the fact that they were always behind the curve, the fiscal policies themselves were all correct, but the election promises were all wrong. It ended up this way because most of the politicians and the mass media did not realize that the Japanese economy was in a balance sheet recession. Although this lack of understanding was unfortunate, this situation is much better than one where the promises were correct, but the actual policies were wrong, for in that case, there would not be any economy left.

If the government had explained from the beginning that the recovery would take at least five if not 10 years, because much time would be needed to repair the balance sheets across the nation, people would have understood. After all, it is they who are paying down the debt. When they realized that if everybody tries to pay down debt at the same time, there will be a fall in the demand for goods and services and the economy will contract, they would have understood the need for fiscal stimulus. Once people realized that it would take years to repair corporate balance sheets damaged by an 85% fall in commercial real estate prices, they would have formed their expectations accordingly.

Unfortunately, the above was never explained by those in power to the general public. This lack of understanding has generated a strong sense of distrust among a large part of the public toward conventional political techniques and economic measures. The distrust made them put their bets on the Koizumi government, which has tried to do things differently from the past. For example, the reform-minded government of Junichiro Koizumi has imposed a limit on the issue of new government bonds of ¥30 trillion a year, a figure that is totally meaningless in terms of economics. In effect, Koizumi has tried to limit the size of the fiscal deficit to ¥30 trillion a year.

It goes without saying that if the amount of savings the household sector generated but the corporate sector refused to borrow happened to be less than ¥30 trillion, Koizumi's issuance limit would have caused no problem. Unfortunately, that has not been the case, especially in the face of the global slowdown in economic activity. As a result, this limitation in fiscal mobility allowed ¥5 to ¥10 trillion of deflationary gap to remain unfilled, and again plunged the Japanese economy into a vicious cycle.

Minister Takenaka, who was one of those who had strongly supported the Hashimoto government's fiscal rehabilitation policy in 1997, admitted in a panel discussion in which I was also a participant that Hashimoto's policy had been premature. Yet, recently, Takenaka has been aggressively arguing that he would increase aggregate demand through structural reform and deregulation rather than fiscal spending. He is about to take the same road that led the economy into disaster six years ago. There is a saying, "Danger past, God forgotten," but it is difficult to understand — and sad to see — that Takenaka is about to repeat the grave mistakes of six years ago.

RICARDIAN EQUIVALENCE NOT TRUE IN JAPAN

Reformists, including Economics Minister Takenaka, continue to argue that the economy is weak because Japanese people are worried about the future and, as a result, are saving rather than spending money. They argue that since people's worries include the huge budget deficit, by removing the deficit, they would start spending money and the economy would recover. In economics, this possibility is called Ricardian equivalence, which states that since a government's deficit financing increases people's worries about a future increase in taxes, they will not spend as much as otherwise. That, in turn, will negate the effectiveness of fiscal policy.

Based on this argument, they claim that reforms with considerable accompanying pain are necessary to remove people's worries about their future and that is precisely what the Koizumi government has set out to achieve. Even though the data (Exhibit 1.2) show that it is the corporate sector rather than the household sector that is responsible for the dramatic change in the economy since 1990, the Koizumi government, and Minister Takenaka in particular, have chosen to ignore the facts and continue to argue that the behavior of households is more to blame.

Everyone would admit to having some worries about the future, if asked. Nevertheless, Exhibit 1.2 showed that corporate efforts to repair balance sheets have resulted in a loss of corporate fund demand, equivalent to 14% of GDP compared with 10 years ago, while personal savings remained virtually unchanged throughout this period. (In 2000 and 2001, savings actually declined.)

If the arguments of the fiscal reformists, including Takenaka, are correct and the Japanese people are really worried about the budget deficit, their savings should have increased sharply between 1990, a year when there was a large budget surplus, and the present, when the fiscal balance is deeply in the red. However, the saving behavior of individuals, who should be worrying about future tax increases, has not changed at all during the past 10 years; whereas businesses, which have no reason to worry about budget deficits, have dramatically changed their behavior.

If household-sector savings have increased in line with the expansion of budget deficits because of people's fears of future tax increases, the reduction in the budget deficit would bring savings down and may increase consumption. The fact that people's saving behavior has not changed at all between a budget surplus period and a deficit period suggests that Ricardian equivalence does not hold in present-day Japan. Thus, a reduction in the budget deficit would not reduce savings and increase consumption.

FIVE TO 10 TRILLION YEN IN ADDITIONAL SPENDING REQUIRED

What people are really worried about is not the budget deficit, but their own job security as their employers try to repair their corporate balance sheets. If this is the case, in order to allay people's fears and improve the economy, the authorities should help businesses repair their balance sheets as quickly as possible so that they can start taking forward-looking actions again.

The truth of the matter is that the need for fiscal stimulus today has nothing to do with morality or anti-reform sentiment. The need comes purely from the fact that the household sector is saving, but the corporate sector is not borrowing. This fact must be explained to everyone within and outside Japan. If the government fails to share this truth with the people and gives the impression that it is putting in fiscal stimulus reluctantly, anti-deficit camps will have a field day bashing the government as anti-reformist and reactionary. Such bashing will reduce the effectiveness of the fiscal stimulus, especially its announcement effect. It is absolutely essential, therefore, that the government explain fully to the people that its fiscal policy is based on a correct understanding of the economy, and that it is not buckling under the pressure of construction companies and the like. Failure to do so could cost the government and the economy dearly.

In a sense, the Japanese economy had been very lucky until 2001. The IT bubble in the United States had helped Japan increase exports to that country. Japan also benefited much from sales of parts to other Asian countries that exported to the United States. Exports are welcome because they help fill the gap between the household and corporate sectors. Indeed, as Exhibit 1.2 showed, the foreign sector consistently borrowed equivalent to 2–3% of GDP throughout the post-bubble period in the form of current account deficits which these countries ran vis-à-vis Japan.

However, the U.S. economy today is quite exhausted, with symptoms of balance sheet recession cropping up here and there. As indicated earlier, the Federal Reserve, America's central bank, has reduced interest rates 12 times since early in 2001 and the present levels of short-term rates have not been seen since the 1950s. Yet, there has been no increase in the corporate demand for funds.

If the U.S. economy suffers from the after-effects of the IT bubble, Japan will no longer be able to depend on external demand (that is, exports to the United States) to fill its deflationary gap. Thus, stimulus packages must be increased to offset this factor in order to keep the bottom from falling out of the Japanese economy. This means that a substantial supplementary budget in the order of ¥5–10 trillion in additional spending may be necessary, since it will have to offset the weak domestic demand as well as the decline in U.S. demand.

ANOTHER BALANCE SHEET CORRECTION ARISING FROM LOW GROWTH

Recently, because the economy has been in the doldrums for such a long time, a different kind of balance sheet correction is emerging at the corporate level. To be more precise, companies have been teaching themselves to operate in such a way that they stay afloat even when growth is nil or negative for years at a time. One way to survive in a zero or negative growth environment is to have as little debt as possible.

Up to the 1980s, the finances of many Japanese companies were predicated on high growth, which allowed for high leveraging compared to companies in the U.S. and Europe. (In other words, borrowings were well in excess of equity capital.) Back in the 1980s, whereas many management theorists around the world praised Japanese-style management, others criticized the finances of Japanese companies for their massive borrowings relative to equity capital. Indeed, during the early 1980s, Japanese companies were leveraged almost five times as highly as their U.S. counterparts. This is shown in Exhibit 2.3.

However, the Japanese economy continued to grow strongly over this period, and domestic asset values also continued to rise. As a result, Moody's and Standard & Poor's awarded Japanese companies extremely high credit ratings. In other words, high leveraging was not a problem, because asset values were rising even faster.

However, the collapse of the asset price bubble blew major holes in balance sheets, and the ensuing fallacy of composition from companies trying to repair their balance sheets meant that the Japanese economy moved from high growth to zero growth (and even then it only managed zero growth thanks to fiscal support). Furthermore, this low growth has continued for more than a decade due to the stop-and-go nature of fiscal policies.

When growth remains this low for this long, corporate executives have to restructure their companies so that they can survive even with low growth, rather than running them on the assumption that high growth will return soon, as they have in the past. When this happens, high leveraging becomes a problem. It becomes extremely dangerous to be highly leveraged when the economy as a whole is experiencing low or zero growth. After all, companies with borrowings do go bust much more frequently than companies without borrowings.

Exhibit 2.3 Japanese companies are still more leveraged than U.S. companies

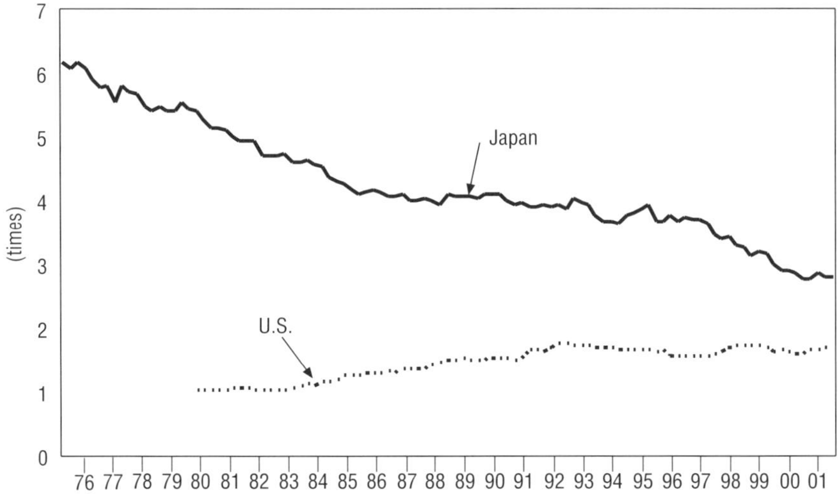

Sources: Ministry of Finance, "Financial Statements Statistics of Corporations by Industry, Quarterly";
U.S. Department of Commerce, "Quarterly Financial Report for Manufacturing, Mining, and
Trade Corporations."

CHANGING DEFINITION OF WHAT CONSTITUTES A HEALTHY BALANCE SHEET

As a result of prolonged slow growth, therefore, the people's perception of what constitutes a healthy balance sheet is changing. The implications of this are that companies will not stop repaying loans once their balance sheets have regained their pre-bubble health, but will keep on paying down debt until leveraging is lowered to meet the requirements of a slow- or no-growth environment. This may be called the "Second Balance Sheet Recession."

The average leveraging of Japanese companies has fallen considerably compared to what it was at one stage, but is still 1.7 times higher than that of U.S. companies, which for their part have increased their leveraging over the past few years.

Of course, the leveraging of companies in any country is affected substantially by the history of direct and indirect financing in that country, tax laws, and even levels of interest rates. Even so, few Japanese companies are looking to return to the sort of leveraging levels that they had during the period of high growth. This is another reason why it looks as though Japanese companies will remain under pressure to repay their loans for some considerable time yet.

Now that the Japanese economy has matured and its latent growth rate has declined, it is inevitable in some sense that Japanese companies should be attempting to lower their leveraging. Furthermore, it is unlikely that we will see again the sort of rapid growth that took place after the war, when there was an absolute shortage of capital. In this respect, it is inevitable that Japanese companies should be looking to adjust their balance sheets to match the needs of a new era, and it would be fair to say that Japan is currently in the middle of that transition process.

The danger is that, like so many fads in the business world, this can also go too far. It could go too far in the sense that companies may decide on a leverage ratio based on today's zero-growth economy. But the Japanese economy today, where everyone is paying down debt, is far from normal in the sense that when corporate debt repayment is finished, the fallacy of the composition problem will go away. That means a higher growth may return once the balance sheet problems are corrected.

If companies assume that zero or negative growth is here to stay, they will miss the opportunities presented when the fallacy of composition problem is resolved and a higher growth rate returns. In order to keep companies from de-leveraging too far, therefore, it is urgent that reasonable growth is brought back as soon as possible. Otherwise, the excessive de-leveraging itself can cause the fallacy of composition and make economic recovery that much more difficult to attain.

WHEN WILL THE BALANCE SHEET RECESSION END?

Exhibit 2.1 showed where Japanese companies stand today in terms of debt levels vis-à-vis past trends. The past trend lines on interest-bearing debt shown there reflect the rate of growth of interest-bearing debt of Japanese companies prior to the bubble years. Thus, the trend lines are extensions of the trend between 1969 and 1986 for all listed companies and between 1975 and 1986 for all companies.

The chart showed that for both listed companies and all companies, the temporary swelling of debts has come to a complete stop and businesses are trying to reduce debts to their former levels. In fact, on the all-company basis, the interest-bearing debt outstanding has fully returned to the past trend line. This means that Japanese companies have already succeeded in removing the debt overhang created during the bubble days, and that their debt levels are already back to their pre-bubble norm.

Although this result suggests that their debt repayment should soon be coming to an end, one must note that the past trends shown here also incorporate the rate of increase in asset prices during the pre-bubble days. This means that if the rate of increase in asset prices from 1986 to the present were the same as the rate of increase between 1969 and 1986, then repayments of debts by businesses should be coming to an end.

Unfortunately, actual asset prices have fallen to levels that are well below the trend line. Some of them have fallen to the levels of the early 1980s. This means that even though debt levels have been compressed, since asset prices have fallen even lower, companies should still be uncomfortable with their balance sheets. In other words, without explicitly including the trend in asset prices, it is difficult to say from Exhibit 2.1 when businesses will stop paying down their debts.

The published GDP statistics actually include figures on assets and liabilities by sector in current prices, although these are made available many years after the usual GDP growth numbers are announced. Using the 2000 data, which is the latest data available, an indicator of financial health defined in terms of a ratio between net assets and total liabilities for the business sector was obtained. This ratio, called the net wealth ratio here, was then compared with its own pre-bubble average. The result is shown in Exhibit 2.4. It shows that significant progress has been made by the corporate sector in regaining its financial health. Since the calculation was based on 2000 figures, the above result suggests that if the income level and asset prices have not changed in the meantime, the debt overhang should soon be eliminated.[9] By then, businesses should have stopped looking backward and started looking forward.

For this to happen, however, fiscal policy must provide firm underpinnings to the economy so that income and asset prices do not deteriorate beyond their 2000 levels. It also assumes that the desirable leverage ratio of Japanese companies has not changed since the pre-bubble days.

Unfortunately, the above-mentioned attempt by the Hashimoto government to cut the budget deficit prematurely, starting in April 1997, was repeated four years later under the Koizumi government, resulting in three consecutive quarters of negative growth in 2001 coupled with a massive fall in asset prices. In the share market alone, over ¥120 trillion in market capitalization has been lost since the inauguration of the Koizumi government.

Furthermore, because of persistent slow growth, Japanese companies are now trying to reduce leverage, as mentioned earlier. This factor makes it difficult to forecast when companies will really feel comfortable with their balance sheets.

Even though significant progress has been made, because of the much weaker economy and asset prices acquiesced to by the Koizumi government, the debt overhang may not be eliminated for a few more years beyond 2003. In a sense, the Koizumi government has been forcing a sick person to run a marathon, instead of giving him the rest needed for recovery. The patient's recovery will naturally be delayed.

Exhibit 2.4　Net wealth ratio of Japanese companies

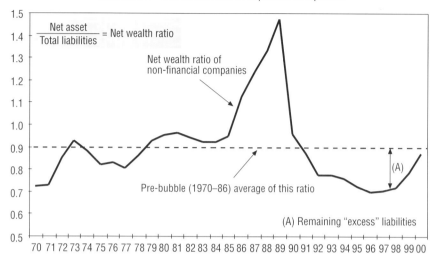

Source: Cabinet Office, "Annual Report on National Accounts of 2002."

JAPAN IS CONDUCTING A HISTORIC EXPERIMENT

In modern history, Japan is the only country that has not fallen into a depression despite a loss of wealth greater than the loss experienced by the U.S. during its Great Depression.

Losing this much wealth and still maintaining zero growth is a remarkable achievement, by any stretch of the imagination. In this sense, Japan is conducting a historic experiment to see whether or not it is possible to keep the economy going and help its companies restore their balance sheets with prompt and persistent fiscal actions in the face of a gigantic collapse in asset values.

Granted, in the 1930s Germany and then the United States overcame the Great Depression with fiscal measures, and these cases have been discussed as Keynesian economics. But Japan is the first nation to avoid falling into a depression in the first place by mobilizing fiscal measures from the very beginning. Though unintended, Japan has demonstrated that even if a bubble grows and bursts, the economy will be able to avoid a depression, and the private sector can concentrate on repairing its balance sheets, if fiscal countermeasures are mobilized from the beginning.

As the fall in asset prices has been so massive, there still is a large debt overhang that needs to be reduced. But the experiment the Japanese are conducting in applying fiscal stimulus from the very beginning in order to maintain income which, in turn, helps businesses to restore their balance sheets, should be of great interest to the United States and many other countries which have fallen into balance sheet recession recently.

Although there are many formidable hurdles that Japan must overcome before the country can claim that the experiment has been a success (these hurdles will be discussed later in the book), its track record so far has been impressive. Furthermore, it should be in the interests of the world economy to ensure that the experiment is not abandoned prematurely.

ENDNOTES

1 Bank of Japan, "Japan's Nonperforming Loan Problem," October 11, 2002, p. 1.

2 Executive Office of the President, *Budget of the United States Government, Fiscal Year 2003*, Historical Tables, Section 1, "Overview of Federal Government Finances," Table 1.1: Summary of Receipts, Outlays, and Surpluses or Deficits: 1789–2007. http://w3.access.gpo.gov/usbudget/fy2003/hist.html.

3 Richard C. Koo and Shigeru Fujita, "Listen to the Bond Market for the Timing of Fiscal Reform (*Zaisei Saiken no Jiki wa Shijyo ni Kike*)," *Shukan Toyo Keizai*, February 8, 1997, pp. 52–59.

4 Tatsuo Hatta, "Book Review: A Study on Current Japanese Economic Policy (*Gendai Nihon Keizai Seisaku-ron*, by Kazuhide Uekusa," *Shukan Toyo Keizai*, December 15, 2001, p. 58.

5 Executive Office of the President, *op. cit.*

6 Paul Krugman, "Purging the Rottenness," *The New York Times*, April 25, 2001.

7 Milton Friedman and Anna Jacobson Schwartz, *The Great Contraction 1929–1933* (First Princeton Paperback Edition, 1965), pp. 61–63.

8 Krugman, *op. cit.*

9 See Richard Koo, "Good Budget Deficits vs. Bad Budget Deficits (*Yoi zaisei akaji, warui zaisei akaji*)," pp. 93–99, for details of the calculation. Richard C. Koo and Shinya Nakamura, "The Japanese Economy Entering the Second Stage of Balance Sheet Recession (*Dai2 dankai ni haitta Balance Sheet Fukyo Nihon no Yoake wa Chikai*)," *Shukan Toyo Keizai*, December 25, 1999, pp. 66–71.

3

MONETARY POLICY INEFFECTIVE IN TODAY'S JAPAN

BANK OF JAPAN'S QUANTITATIVE EASING WILL NOT IMPROVE THE ECONOMY

In an ordinary world, stimulus measures available to the government are by no means limited to fiscal policy. Indeed, in most modern economics literature, it is argued that monetary policy, instead of fiscal policy, should be the main tool of the government in dealing with fluctuations in economic conditions. On today's college campuses, where memories of the Great Depression of the 1930s are fading rapidly, the monetarist idea that monetary policy is the most effective means of countering business cycles is in the mainstream.

Monetarists are those people who believe that monetary policy is most effective in controlling economic fluctuations and that fiscal policy, with its attendant increase in future tax liability, is largely ineffective. Since the Koizumi Cabinet started out with the announcement that fiscal policy had been ineffective and the budget deficit must be reduced, it is pinning great hopes on monetary policy to turn the economy around.

For example, the "bold economic policy" released by the Advisory Council on the Economy and Finance in October 2001, an advisory panel to Prime Minister Koizumi, demanded that the Bank of Japan "take appropriate measures" and made frequent reference to "quantitative easing."[1] Heizo Takenaka has frequently attended the policy meetings of the Bank of Japan and has been asking the bank to ease monetary policy even further. He has even threatened that if the central bank did not do the government's bidding, the bank would be stripped of its independence. Many commentators, both within and outside Japan, have also repeatedly remarked that if the Bank of Japan took a more aggressive policy, the economy would improve faster.

However, putting blame on the Bank of Japan for the anemic performance of the economy stems from the failure to truly understand balance sheet recession. This is because very little can be expected from monetary policy in this rare type of recession, which happens perhaps once in half a century.

Since I started my career as an economist for the Federal Reserve Bank of New York, which is America's central bank, I am reluctant to admit that the central bank is powerless. Yet, in the situation in which Japan finds itself today, monetary policy is almost totally ineffective. During the last decade, for example, the economy failed to show any sign of response to monetary policy changes, no matter how deeply interest rates were cut or how much liquidity was injected into the financial system. Since this issue is directly related to solving the problem of non-performing loans, I would like to discuss this problem in detail.

NO FUND DEMAND DESPITE THE LOWEST INTEREST RATE IN HISTORY

There is a good reason why monetary policy is not effective. For monetary policy to be effective, there must be many people in the private sector who respond to the central bank's cuts in interest rates. In other words, there should be many people who are induced to save less, to buy a home, or to invest in plant and equipment in response to the lowering of interest rates by the central bank. It is only when the reduced savings or newly borrowed money is spent that income is generated for the next person and the economy moves forward. In other words, it is not lower interest rates *per se* that improve the economy rather, it is the people's reaction to lower interest rates (that is, borrowing money to spend or saving less) that improves the economy.

When the balance sheets of corporations are impaired, however, they are likely to make paying down debts their top priority. They feel that they have to pay down their debts as quickly and quietly as possible before journalists or analysts from the outside begin to suspect that their balance sheets are actually under water. From the perspective of individual companies, they are behaving appropriately and responsibly. But it also means that, for those companies, borrowing money is the last thing on their mind. When the vast majority of the companies in an economy are in this category, however, the whole economy ceases to respond to the lowering of interest rates by the central bank.

Even so, the Bank of Japan has reduced interest rates as low as possible in order to induce people to borrow and spend. As a result, the present interest rates in Japan are the lowest ever recorded in human history. The benchmark 10-year Japanese government bond is now (mid-January, 2003) yielding 0.8%. This is significantly lower than the lowest-yield U.S. treasury bond reached during the Depression, which was 1.85%. Human beings have been engaged in economic activities for a long, long time. But they have never before witnessed the levels of interest rates found in Japan today.

Although interest rates are as low as they could possibly be, 70–80% of companies in the country are still rushing to pay down their debts. As a result, the corporate sector as a whole is now a net supplier of funds to the banking system and capital markets to the tune of ¥20 trillion, or 4% of GDP, a year. Furthermore, companies paying down debt include many exporters who enjoy robust foreign markets and are not affected by deflation or by what some economists call "high real interest rates" (more on this topic in Chapter 4) in Japan. The fact that companies from all walks of life are paying down debt even when interest rates are near zero indicates how serious their balance sheet concerns are. Under such a balance sheet environment, demand for funds is not likely to rise no matter how low interest rates sink.

JAPAN'S BOTTLENECK IS DEMAND FOR FUNDS, RATHER THAN SUPPLY OF FUNDS

The extraordinarily low interest rates in Japan stem from the same fact that has rendered monetary policy powerless — namely, that businesses across the nation are rushing to pay down debts, resulting in a flood of money in financial institutions and the capital markets. With the household sector still saving money as before, while companies are paying down debt to the tune of ¥20 trillion a year, the financial institutions are awash with money but are unable to find borrowers. As a result, competition among lenders for the few remaining borrowers is absolutely fierce, resulting in the lowest bank lending rates in the history of mankind.

It is true that the banks' capacity to lend is lower than it once was. Compared with the 1980s, when most Japanese banks were rated triple A and had both ample funds and capital, their capacity to lend has declined considerably. However, what is often overlooked is that businesses' demand for funds has fallen earlier and faster. In other words, even though the banks' capacity to supply funds has declined, corporate demand for funds has declined more deeply. This is why the market is awash with money and interest rates have fallen as far as they have.

That the banks are eager to lend is clearly demonstrated in the Bank of Japan's *Tankan Short-term Economic Survey of Enterprises in Japan*, commonly known as the *Tankan* survey. Exhibit 3.1 shows the results of the central bank's quarterly surveys of more than 5,000 corporate borrowers regarding the lending attitudes of banks. In this series of surveys, the Bank of Japan asks borrower companies whether the banks are eager to lend or are eager to recover funds.

The results are that, with the exception of the 1997–98 period (and the post-2000 period, which will be discussed in Chapter 7) when the banks across the nation were mired in a credit crunch, since the beginning of the 1990s the banks have been quite eager to lend. During the 1993–97 period, for example, their willingness to lend was almost equal to their willingness to lend during the bubble days of the late 1980s. In fact, they have been queuing up at creditworthy corporations in order to lend. It is no wonder that interest rates have come down so much.

The fact that borrowers are not borrowing, while admitting that the banks are eager to lend, shows that the true bottleneck is on the demand side. If supply is not the bottleneck, no matter how far the supply problem is solved via monetary easing or quick disposal of NPLs, the economy will not turn around unless demand returns.

Even though those who are advocating additional monetary easing and quick resolution of the NPL problem argue that bankers cannot lend because their funds are frozen in unpromising businesses in the form of NPLs, the extremely low interest rates and the results of the Bank of Japan's surveys both show conclusively that the problem is on the demand side, not the supply side.

Exhibit 3.1 Bankers were willing lenders except on two occasions

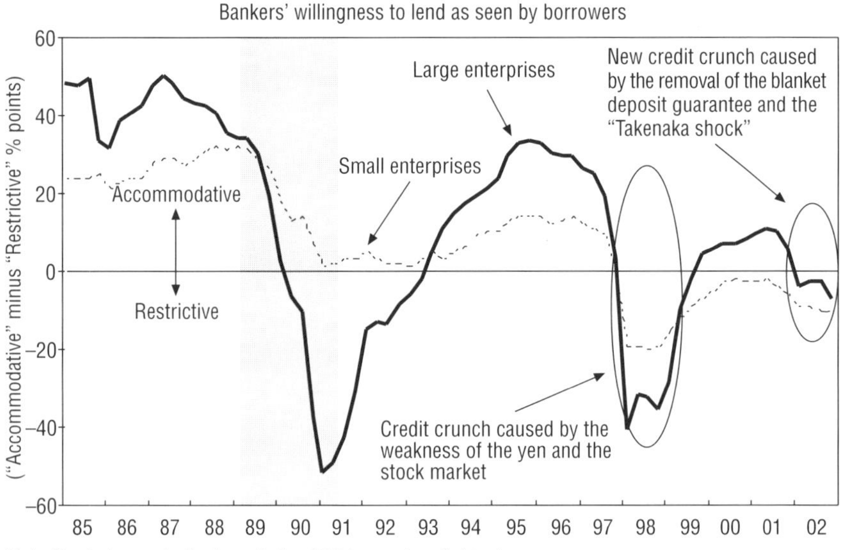

Bankers' willingness to lend as seen by borrowers

Note: Shaded areas indicate periods of BOJ monetary tightening.

Source: Bank of Japan, *Tankan* survey.

Additional monetary easing or quick disposal of banks' NPLs, however, are solutions to the *supply* problem. The ultimate goal of monetary easing by the Bank of Japan or of the disposal of NPLs is to enable the banks to lend more. However, if the bottleneck is on the demand side, no matter how well the supply problem is resolved, the economy will not recover unless the demand problem is resolved.

Unfortunately, this perspective is totally missing in most discussions of this problem. Or, more precisely, this perspective is missing in those discussions that do not include Japanese market participants who face the problem of lack of demand in their line of business every day. As a result, most people outside Japanese financial circles end up arguing that the economy would turn around if only the banks could lend more. The present interest rate levels and market conditions show that that is not the case at all.

RELUCTANCE TO LEND IN 1997–98 DUE TO SUPPLY FACTORS

In contrast, the banks' reluctance to lend between 1997 and 1998 was without doubt due to supply factors. At that time, the Japanese economy was in shambles because of the Hashimoto government's fiscal reform policy. As the economy collapsed, investors at home and abroad who knew that the Japanese economy had been supported by fiscal stimulus dumped their holdings of Japanese equities and exchanged their yen proceeds from sales of equities into U.S. dollars. This "dump Japan" phenomenon resulted in a synchronous weakness of both the yen and stock prices, which dramatically worsened the capital ratios of Japanese banks. Their numerator was hit by the weakness of the stock market, and their denominator was hit by the weakness of the yen.

An OECD report of November 1998[2] reported that a ¥1 decline in the yen–dollar exchange rate at that time forced Japanese banks to reduce their assets by ¥1 trillion. Thus, a ¥5 depreciation against the dollar would have forced Japanese banks to wipe ¥5 trillion, or an amount equivalent to 1% of Japan's GDP, from their books.[3] The situation was so horrendous that by early 1998, the whole country was engulfed in a credit crunch, as shown in Exhibit 3.1. It was only at this time that the economy worsened due to the problems on the supply side of funds.

Although the banks' reluctance to lend in 1998 was due to the fact that fund supply declined faster than fund demand did, the problem was solved by the subsequent injection of capital into the banking system. As Exhibit 3.1 shows, once the injection was made, the lending attitudes of the banks improved sharply.

Except for the above-mentioned 1997–98 period, the fact that lending is not increasing at all while borrowers admit that the banks are eager to lend, shows that the problem is with demand factors rather than supply factors. Under these circumstances, easing of the supply factor even more through additional monetary easing or disposal of NPLs will not improve the economy. Additional monetary easing or rapid disposal of NPLs are neither the necessary nor sufficient conditions for economic recovery. NPLs are not the cause of the poor economic conditions; rather, it is the other way around.

Exhibit 3.1 also shows that the banks' lending attitude was very tight in the 1990–91 period. This was because at that time, the Bank of Japan was tightening monetary policy in an attempt to crush the land price bubble. As can be seen in Exhibit 3.2, short-term rates were raised to over 8% when the inflation rate was only 2%, making borrowers feel that banks have been very tight with their lending. Since then, however, as the Bank of Japan has eased its monetary policy, bankers' willingness to lend has also improved dramatically. But the borrowers still refused to borrow, indicating that the problem is on the demand side and not on the supply side.

THE KEY MONETARY TRANSMISSION MECHANISM ALSO DESTROYED

The monetary tightening of the 1989–91 period did leave a scar on the economy, however. The fact that Japanese monetary policy was mobilized to crush the real estate bubble meant that the most important sector for monetary transmission in the economy was the first sector that was hit and

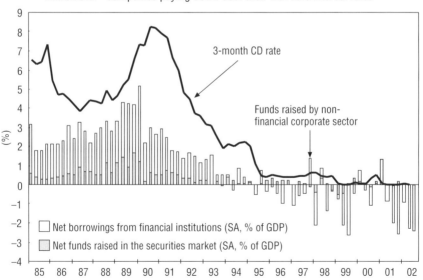

Exhibit 3.2 Companies paying down debt even with zero interest rates

Note: Figures after third quarter 1998 are based on a new flow of funds series.

Source: Bank of Japan, *Tankan* survey.

destroyed. Of all the transmission mechanisms between the monetary authorities and the real economy, the role of the construction and real estate sector is the most important. After all, monetary policy works only through the interest-sensitive sectors of the economy, and this is the most interest-sensitive sector in any economy. Furthermore, the construction and real estate sectors have huge spill-over effects to all other industries. The construction of new buildings, for example, increases the demand for everything from steel and cement to curtains and carpets.

By targeting and torpedoing this sector, the Bank of Japan ended up destroying the key component of the monetary policy transmission mechanism. Even though bankers were willing lenders during most of the 1990s up until 1997, construction and real estate was a notable exception, as Exhibit 3.3 shows. Since banks' problem loans are concentrated in the real estate sector (or the collateral for the loan was real estate), they were in no mood to increase their exposure to this sector either.

What this means is that, even though most economists implicitly assume that the monetary transmission mechanism is always there, in the real world the transmission only goes through a limited number of channels; when those channels are blocked or destroyed, the effectiveness of monetary policy drops off sharply. After losing the real estate sector, therefore, there was not much left in the Japanese economy that the monetary authority could affect through the lowering of interest rates.

Exhibit 3.3   Financing difficulty of the real estate sector

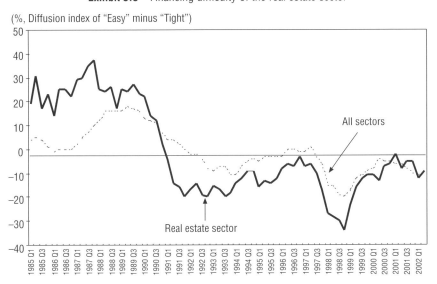

(%, Diffusion index of "Easy" minus "Tight")

Source: Bank of Japan, *Tankan* survey.

INFLATION TARGETING USELESS WHEN FUND DEMAND IS NEGATIVE

Loud opposition has been voiced by monetarists from around the world to the above conclusion that monetary policy is not effective under the present circumstances. Since monetarists believe that *any* macroeconomic problem can be solved as long as the central bank's monetary policy is correct, they could never accept the argument that monetary policy is powerless in present-day Japan. According to their theory, such a situation could never happen.

In order to counter the notion that there is nothing more the Bank of Japan can do, they have come up with inflation targeting and quantitative easing as the means for the bank to regain control of the economy.[4] Inflation targeting means the central bank will target a level of inflation rate as its monetary policy target. For example, if the Bank of Japan sets a 2% annual inflation rate as its policy target and eases monetary policy until that target is reached, this is inflation targeting. Quantitative easing means the central bank continues to add liquidity to the banking system even if interest rates have no more room to go down.

Those economists claim that if the Bank of Japan sets an inflation target and then makes a commitment to supply liquidity through quantitative easing in order to reach this target, people would expect inflation rather than deflation and start borrowing money to spend. Because the value of money decreases in inflation, they claim that this policy would boost consumption and lead to an economic recovery. They also claim that inflation will ease the balance sheet problem by raising the price of assets. According to this argument, therefore, the Bank of Japan still has some tools at its disposal and should not be saying it has exhausted all the available means just because interest rates have fallen to zero.

Because of the simplicity of this argument, both the Western and Japanese mass media got on the bandwagon and, since around the middle of 1999, a great deal of time and energy has been spent on supporting this argument. Many politicians who had been at a loss as to what to do with the 10-year-old recession also got on the bandwagon. As a result, the debate has grown into a major political issue involving the Diet and the Bank of Japan.

Even though the above monetarist counter-arguments are both simple and persuasive, there are major problems in applying them to present-day Japan. As the Bank of Japan has pointed out, inflation targeting was introduced by countries that were trying to bring a virulent inflation rate down. It was never used to bring on or accelerate inflation.

This is because the fact that an economy is suffering from inflation means that there is a robust demand for funds. If this is the case, the central bank can and should break the back of inflation by making its intentions known and by tightening the supply of liquidity.

The central bank can achieve its goal because it is the only supplier of liquidity in the economy. The curb on liquidity by the central bank will make it impossible for the private sector to borrow money beyond that supplied by the central bank. The subsequent bidding war for funds among the potential borrowers will push the interest rate higher and break the back of inflation. In such a world, therefore, the restraint on liquidity supply by the central bank acts as an effective constraint on private-sector economic activities and achieves the goal of controlling inflation.

In a balance sheet recession, however, businesses and individuals are saddled with excess liabilities and are forced to pay down debts by curbing consumption and investment. The last thing they are interested in is *increasing* their borrowings.

Exhibit 1.2 in Chapter 1 indicated that corporate-sector demand for funds in Japan has been negative since 1998. Negative fund demand means that there are more businesses paying down debts than there are those that are raising funds. With so many businesses paying down debts at the same time, the capital markets and financial institutions are awash with money, depressing interest rates to the abnormally low levels we see today. Under these circumstances, supply of liquidity by the Bank of Japan does not act as a constraint on anything. In other words, the Bank of Japan hardly has any influence.

If fund demand is negative when the interest rate is 6%, lowering the interest rate to 3% may generate positive fund demand. However, negative fund demand at zero interest rates means that there is no more room for monetary policy because the interest rate cannot be cut any further. Forcing the Bank of Japan to adopt inflation targeting is meaningless under the present circumstances, because the central bank does not have any tools to achieve the target.

WHAT PROFESSOR KRUGMAN HAS MISSED

Advocates of inflation targeting have rebuffed the above argument by saying, "It may be so, but if the Bank of Japan announced a target and showed its strong resolve to attain it through quantitative easing, the number of people with inflationary expectations would increase. When these people move to borrow money to spend, the economy should get better."

Professor Paul Krugman of Princeton University, for example, had strongly advocated "quantitative easing" in order to attain an inflation target.[5] He argued that the Bank of Japan should print money as quickly as possible and supply it to the market through quantitative easing. By force feeding the private sector with liquidity, the money supply should grow, and if money supply grows, so will the level of prices.

At a first glance, this opinion seems to be correct in terms of macroeconomics. Most people will probably agree with Krugman when told that increasing money supply would raise prices and solve the problem of deflation.

Unfortunately, the real world of balance sheet recession is not so kind to Krugman. What he has missed is the fact that in 1993, when the Japanese economy fell into balance sheet recession, Japan still had a positive inflation rate. At that time, the Consumer Price Index (CPI) inflation rate in Japan was 1.3% annually. But that did not prevent companies from embarking on a massive effort to reduce borrowings and pay down debt. Hence, even if a mild inflation is induced somehow, it will not be able to end the recession for the same reason that the inflation in 1993 could not prevent the economy from falling into a balance sheet recession in the first place.

In fact, Japan's deflation began in earnest in 1998 as a result of economic deterioration stemming from the ill-advised fiscal reform in the midst of a balance sheet recession. In other words, even though Krugman and others believe that the cause of Japan's recession is deflation, deflation is actually a result, rather than the cause, of balance sheet recession.

Moreover, starting in 1999, the Bank of Japan, if only to prove the monetarists wrong, started a campaign of quantitative easing, and a massive amount of liquidity has been added as a result. However, absolutely nothing happened, both in the real economy and the financial markets. Indeed, the economy continued to weaken, and share prices continued to fall, leaving those investors who bet on the monetarist argument with huge losses. In the end, even Krugman admitted in his *New York Times* column of July 8, 2001,[6] that there is no demand for funds in Japan and that ordinary monetary easing is not going to be effective.

IRRESPONSIBLE BORROWERS NEEDED TO MAKE INFLATION TARGET WORK

But why? Why did the monetarist argument, which is so widely accepted in the economics profession, fail so miserably in Japan? The answer lies in the problem of sequencing.

To begin with, the present zero interest rate environment is an extremely favorable environment for borrowers. For those who are creditworthy and are thinking of investing in new projects, this may be a once-in-a-lifetime opportunity to do so. Now that the zero interest rate environment has lasted for so long, however, it is probably safe to assume that those creditworthy borrowers with interesting projects have already borrowed funds in order to expand their businesses.

What this means is that in order to make the economy better than it is today by means of an inflation target or quantitative easing, these measures must change the behavior of those who are *not* borrowing and spending money today. The key question therefore is: will businesses and individuals who do not borrow today because of their balance sheet concerns change their mind and borrow money tomorrow if the Bank of Japan announced an inflation target and tried to attain that target with aggressive quantitative easing?

Krugman's earlier recommendation is, in essence, equal to the Bank of Japan calling on Japanese businesses and saying, "There is going to be an inflation, so forget about your balance sheet problems and start borrowing money. Forget your excess liabilities and past mistakes and borrow to spend, because the borrower will always win in an inflation."

If most Japanese businesses responded by saying, "I am tired of paying down debts, which I have been doing for the last 10 years. Let's bet on inflation and borrow freely to spend," Krugman's idea would succeed without any problem.

The problem is that, although the Japanese people's morality might have declined somewhat during the past 10 years, it has not fallen anywhere near those levels that would make it possible for Krugman's idea to succeed. This is because those who are trying to clean up their balance sheets are behaving appropriately and responsibly. They are by no means behaving incorrectly. For those with debt overhang, improving their financial health by reducing debts is a very appropriate and responsible behavior.

To urge them to forget about their balance sheet problems and bet on inflation when the inflation itself has not materialized is to urge them to take a very irresponsible action. Building an entire policy on the assumption that people will act irresponsibly is not realistic.

They may behave differently when their balance sheets are already cleaned up, or when inflation is already visible to everyone. But it is unrealistic to assume that these businesses, which have been pursuing the right and responsible actions, will suddenly abandon all their morality *before* inflation is actually in place, just because the central bank began talking about inflation targets.

A much more likely scenario is that they would respond to the urging of Krugman and the Bank of Japan by saying, "Inflation targeting is a very interesting suggestion, but let us clean up our balance sheets first. After our clean-up is complete, we will join you." In fact, many Japanese business executives have told me exactly this when I have asked them about inflation targeting. That means they are not going to change their behavior until their balance sheets are clean. But if these companies do not change their behavior, nothing will be changed in the economy and no inflation will materialize.

It is a sequencing problem in the sense that inflation must happen *before* people will change their behavior. But unless people change their behavior first, inflation will not happen.

IS THE IMPERIAL PALACE WORTH THE ENTIRE STATE OF CALIFORNIA?

Of course, if the Bank of Japan were to set an inflation target that would clean up corporate balance sheets immediately, people might change their behavior. But that would require an inflation rate that would bring back the asset prices of the bubble days, when the land on which stands the Imperial Palace, in the center of Tokyo, was worth as much as the entire state of California. If asset prices are boosted to those levels, Japan's balance sheet problems will be solved overnight.

Even if such a target is announced, however, no one will believe it. If the leaders of the Bank of Japan announced that they would boost the value of land in Japan so that the Imperial Palace was worth as much as the entire state of California, people would simply think that they had gone crazy. The Japanese people already know that the bubble prices were wrong.

The same applies to the monetarists' criticism of the Federal Reserve Bank of New York for its behavior in 1931. They claim that the rate hikes by the Federal Reserve at that time, which were designed to stem the outflow of gold from the United States, were the direct cause of the Great Depression and that without those rate hikes the Great Depression could have been avoided. However, the behavior of the people at that time stemmed from their realization that stock prices in 1929 had been wrong. They would not have changed their effort to repair their balance sheets unless stock prices returned to their 1929 levels or they had repaid their debts in full. There is a good possibility, therefore, that the U.S. economy would have plunged into depression even if the Federal Reserve Bank of New York had not raised interest rates in 1931.

Even if it were possible to restore asset prices to the levels that prevailed during the bubble, those levels would need to be sustained permanently in order to prevent people from reverting to debt repayment mode. If people thought the bubble prices were good only for a short period of time, they would sell off their assets for safer cash. However, if everyone tried to sell assets at the same time, there would be no buyers and it would be totally impossible to maintain asset prices at bubble levels unless the government or the Bank of Japan became the buyer. This shows how difficult it is to overcome balance sheet recession with monetary policy.

CRIMINAL BANKERS NEEDED FOR QUANTITATIVE EASING TO WORK

The monetarists would counter the above by saying that the central bank will not just be talking about inflation; it will be pumping huge amounts of liquidity through quantitative easing. When people see that for themselves, they will change their mind. But will they?

In order to attain an inflation target, not only borrowers but also lending institutions (that is, banks) must change their behavior and lend more aggressively. After all, they are the first institutions to receive increased liquidity from the Bank of Japan's quantitative easing. The question, therefore, is whether the banks' lending behavior will change with quantitative easing.

Let us suppose that you, the reader, are the president of a bank in Japan. Facing the horrendous shrinkage in loan demand in your region, you take the following actions. First, you bring in the absolute state-of-the-art credit screening techniques from, say, the U.S. Then you order your credit department to lower lending standards to the lowest level that is acceptable to bank regulators. And finally, you drop the basic lending rate to the level that is just enough to cover your operating costs. Armed with these decisions, you then ask all your loan officers to do everything humanly possible to unearth all possible loan demand in your business region.

Suppose that, after two weeks, your loan officers have come up with a figure of ¥100 billion-worth of possible new borrowers based on the conditions specified above. They tell you that this is the absolute maximum before going afoul of the bank regulators.

Just as you are looking at the report from your loan department, the Bank of Japan suddenly places a deposit of ¥1 trillion with your bank as a part of its aggressive quantitative easing program. The Bank of Japan also tells you that it expects no interest payment from your bank on this deposit.

What will be the increase in lending from your bank which now has ¥1 trillion in deposit to lend? Based on the above conditions, the answer has to be ¥100 billion, even though the bank has ¥1 trillion to lend. This is because, for your bank to lend more than ¥100 billion, its lending standards will have to be relaxed far beyond those that are minimally acceptable to the authorities. In other words, you could be liable for criminal prosecution if you try to lend more than ¥100 billion.

In fact, today's banks are under tremendous pressure to keep their lending standards high so as not to produce any more NPLs. The FSA, Minister Takenaka and most Western commentators are all demanding that banks screen their borrowers thoroughly and lend only to those who are both creditworthy and willing to pay high interest rates. Indeed, most banks today are trying desperately to reduce their NPLs in order to recover the trust of depositors and rating agencies. Asking them to make loans by drastically lowering their lending standards is an impossible proposition. Such a relaxation of lending standards will also be unacceptable to the shareholders and rating agencies.

But if individual banks do not change their behavior, there is no reason for the additional liquidity from the Bank of Japan to circulate outside the banking system. And if the additional liquidity from the quantitative easing is all bottled up within the banking system, there is no reason for the inflation to accelerate. In other words, unless the banks change their behavior at the micro level, there is no possibility of the inflation rate rising beyond the present level at the macro level.

If inflation actually materializes, some borrowers who have not qualified for loans may qualify because their balance sheets will look much better. But, this will happen only after consumer prices and asset prices have begun to rise and the existence of inflation has been confirmed. To ask the banks to ease lending standards on the assumption that there will be inflation, when in fact there is none, is extremely irresponsible and reckless.

This is not a situation unique to Japan. In the United States during the 1930s, monetary policy also became ineffective, giving birth to the expression "liquidity trap." More recently, historically low interest rates in the U.S., Taiwan, and Thailand all failed to produce recovery in corporate demand for funds. And in all these cases, balance sheet problems arose after the crash of asset prices.

These events indicate that, when businesses are looking backward instead of forward, monetary policy becomes largely ineffective. Neither quantitative easing nor inflation targeting is effective in a balance sheet recession, unless one assumes irresponsible, if not criminal behavior, on the part of banks and corporate borrowers. It is no wonder the Bank of Japan is not willing to go along with such policy recommendations.

FISCAL POLICY DETERMINES MONEY SUPPLY IN BALANCE SHEET RECESSION

The next question then is: what will happen to the remaining ¥900 million sitting in your bank, as described earlier? If the private sector's demand for funds is limited, as described, this ¥900 million can circulate in the economy only if the public sector borrowed it and spent it. Thus, when the government runs a budget deficit and finances it through the issuance of government bonds that are purchased by banks, the ¥900 million will be able to leave the banking system and enter general circulation via government spending. When the government spends proceeds from the sale of bonds to the banks, a new cycle of income stream and money supply growth begins.

This means that during the times of severe shortages of private-sector demand for funds, the deficit spending by the government and the subsequent purchases of government bonds by financial institutions play a critical role in propping up the economy as well as maintaining the money supply. The present level of money supply in Japan is maintained to a large extent because the government has been running large deficits and issuing large amounts of bonds to finance the deficits. Had there been no issuance of government bonds, the level of the money supply would have contracted to a fraction of where it is today.

In fact, between 1929 and 1932, the U.S. money supply declined by 40%. As indicated earlier, Milton Friedman wrote that this decline was caused by the fact that the Hoover administration allowed bank shakeouts, which resulted in the failures of a large number of banks in the United States. I suspect, however, that another reason for this decline is the fact that President Hoover, a staunch believer in a balanced budget, refused to offset the decline in private-sector demand for funds with government borrowings. The government's failure to offset the decline thus resulted in the collapse of both the real economy and the money supply.

What this means is that the present monetary policy and money supply in Japan are both heavily dependent on the government's fiscal policy. In the absence of private-sector demand for funds, it has been the large borrowings by the public sector which have kept the money supply in Japan from collapsing altogether.

During balance sheet recession, therefore, the effectiveness of monetary policy is heavily dependent on the state of fiscal policy. If the latter is expansionary, the liquidity provided by the central bank will be able to enter general circulation. However, if the latter is contractionary, the money supply has no reason to expand no matter how much liquidity is provided by the central bank. Contrary to the belief of monetarists, therefore, monetary policy is not only *not* almighty, but also becomes heavily dependent on fiscal policy during a balance sheet recession.

The preceding section also shows that it is impossible in today's Japan for the central bank to offset, through monetary easing, the loss in demand stemming from the government's fiscal retrenchment. It also means that those officials of the Bank of Japan are making an empty promise when they say, "If the government presses ahead with structural reform, we will ease monetary policy further to provide underpinnings to the economy." If the government, which currently is the only major borrower, abandons its role, no matter how much liquidity the central bank supplies to the financial institutions, the mechanism through which such funds circulate outside of the financial institutions will be lost.

QUANTITATIVE EASING DOES NOT MAKE THE PRIVATE SECTOR RICH

Many commentators who do not know how monetary policy works assume that if the Bank of Japan supplies ample liquidity, the economy will improve because additional liquidity will make the private sector "rich." Nothing is further from the truth.

Central banks, including the Bank of Japan, usually supply liquidity by purchasing government bonds, corporate bonds, or other financial assets from the private sector and paying cash for them. Since it is usually the financial institutions that own these assets that qualify for purchases by the central bank, monetary easing typically means the purchases of government bonds by the central bank from banks in exchange for cash. This means that private financial institutions merely exchange their government bonds for cash with the same value. It does not mean that the private sector as a whole will get richer through monetary easing. (Strictly speaking, when the Bank of Japan presents itself as a buyer of those assets, the demand for those assets increases relative to the world where the bank did not present itself as a buyer. This should result in a higher price for those assets than before, thus making the private sector somewhat richer than before. But such an increase in wealth is usually minuscule.)

More importantly, central banks can supply liquidity to the private sector only through purchases of financial assets; it is unable to buy any goods or services other than those that it consumes itself. In other words, it cannot just go out and buy washing machines and pianos as a means to supply liquidity.

The power to buy those items rests with the government as a representative of the people, not with the central bank. It is the government, not the central bank, which can buy anything from washing machines to fighter planes. Thus, those monetarists who are arguing that the Bank of Japan should go out and buy up everything from washing machines to land are basically admitting that what is really needed is more fiscal stimulus. In other words, the government can add liquidity directly to the real economy through fiscal expenditure, whereas the central bank can add liquidity only to the financial sector. This is one reason why fiscal policy of government spending is more effective than monetary policy in stimulating the economy during a balance sheet recession when private-sector demand for funds is weak or non-existent.

Minister Takenaka has argued on numerous occasions, including in a one-to-one debate with me on television, that (1) companies have borrowed too much in the 1980s and therefore must reduce their borrowings, (2) the government has borrowed too much and therefore must reduce its debt, but (3) the Bank of Japan must increase the money supply. However, anyone who has studied economics will note that not even God could accomplish all three at the same time. Although the central bank can supply the liquidity to the banking sector, for this liquidity to circulate in the economy and to become money supply, someone from the private or public sector must borrow that liquidity from the bank and use it. With no one borrowing money, the liquidity supplied by the Bank of Japan will simply sit in the banking system and will add nothing to the economy's income stream.

In fact, when the Bank of Japan tries to supply funds through its open market operations today, fund demand is so stagnant that frequently the offers from the banks fail to reach the levels planned by the central bank. This is evidence that monetary easing has completely reached its limits. It therefore does not make any sense to expect more from the Bank of Japan. Borrowers are behaving correctly. So are the lenders. Everyone is behaving appropriately. Yet, when this is all put together, it results in the fallacy of composition. This is why monetary policy is ineffective and the economy is getting deeper and deeper into trouble without proper fiscal policy.

"HELICOPTER MONEY" WILL MAKE MATTERS WORSE

The monetarists, who cannot stand the above views, would say: "That said, since experiments with inflation targeting and quantitative easing do not cost anybody anything, the Bank of Japan should adopt them anyway and see what happens." Others may argue that the claim that monetary policy can be ineffective is nonsense, because one can always scatter bank notes from a helicopter; such "helicopter money" would surely turn the economy around.

Although the term "helicopter money" is very frequently used in economics, it is doubtful whether such a policy will bring the results people really want. The following example shows why.

Let us assume that the Bank of Japan one day mailed ¥1 million in new bank notes to every Japanese citizen. The person who finds ¥1 million in his mailbox will probably feel very happy at that moment, because he thinks he is richer by that amount. The problem is what happens next.

When the person finds out that every other Japanese person has also received ¥1 million, he would turn pale. Because at that instant he would realize that what he can buy with that amount has just shrunk dramatically. After all, no one in their right mind would sell goods or services in exchange for ¥1 million that came down from the sky.

Today's currencies are not backed by gold or silver. Their value is maintained solely by the trust people have in their central banks. Those of us who live in Japan, for example, keep the Japanese yen in our wallets, because we trust its guardian, the Bank of Japan, and trust that it will not do anything reckless. Like air, the trust people have in the Bank of Japan is so complete that no one is really conscious of it. They are not conscious of it because the

Bank of Japan has been an effective guardian of the yen for the past 50 years, and the yen has been one of the strongest currencies in the world.

However, if the Bank of Japan should take such a reckless action as to send everyone in the country ¥1 million, the people's trust in the central bank will be lost instantly. Once that trust is lost, there will be a mad exodus of Japanese funds into the U.S. dollar or the Euro, because that is the most efficient way of protecting the value of one's assets.

Unlike in the U.S., where the Federal Reserve had in the past discouraged member banks from offering foreign currency deposits, foreign currency deposits are readily available anywhere in Japan. In the days before Japan liberalized capital movement, money could have flowed into other domestic assets, such as real estate. However, foreign deposits and foreign remittances have been liberalized so extensively since the financial "Big Bang" of 1997 that the flight away from the yen will certainly go to the dollar or the Euro.

At the same time, the number of people who are willing to accept the yen as a medium of exchange will decline dramatically, because no one can be certain about the value of the yen. They will all want their payments in dollars or Euros. Such a development would plunge Japan into a world of bartering and hyperinflation in no time.

THE CURE IS WORSE THAN THE DISEASE

Hyperinflation, in turn, will certainly end the balance sheet recession in one stroke, because people will no longer have to worry about repaying debts denominated in the worthless yen. In this sense, it is not absolutely impossible to end the balance sheet recession with monetary policy. However, the economy will then face a world of foreign currencies and bartering, which would be several times worse than the present balance sheet recession.

Even though "helicopter money" may end the balance sheet recession, it does so by creating an even more serious problem than the present deflation. By creating a more serious problem than the present balance sheet recession, "helicopter money" forces people to change their priorities and end their debt repayment activities. And for this to happen, the Bank of Japan must go "mad" enough so that people will not trust it any longer. In fact, Krugman has repeatedly argued that the Bank of Japan should declare that it will turn itself into an "irresponsible" central bank.[7]

However, it is absolutely impossible for an economy to improve when the currency people relied on is taken away from them. No economy has enjoyed a better growth rate with bartering and foreign currencies than when it had its own stable currency. It is, indeed, the case of "the cure is worse than the disease."

Moreover, even though hyperinflation will make life easier for businesses that have debt overhang, those who have been lenders (for example, depositors) will suffer losses in the same amounts as the gains felt by the debtors. This means that those who have been saving for the future will lose their savings, making them more cautious than before in their spending. Indeed, for the economy as a whole, inflation and deflation are simply a transfer of income between the borrowers and the lenders, and there will be no increase or decrease in the wealth of a nation.

By contrast, the devastating effect on the economy of losing a trustworthy national currency is immeasurable. After all, an economy that has to depend on bartering and foreign currencies will be lucky if it can survive, let alone grow.

THERE IS EITHER TRUST OR NO TRUST: NO IN-BETWEEN

When an extreme case such as the one cited above is presented, most monetarists will argue back by saying that there is no need to go that far, that the central bank should pursue a much milder inflation of a few percent. For example, Krugman had advocated that Japan should guide the inflation rate to about 4%.[8]

The problem with this argument is that such a moderate inflation target will not result in a loss of trust in the Bank of Japan. But if the people's trust in the central bank is not lost, there is no reason for them to change their behavior. And if their behavior is not changed, even an inflation of only a few percent will not come about. The fact that so much quantitative easing during the last few years has failed to change people's behavior suggests that the trust is still intact. And as long as the trust is there, nothing will happen to inflation because people have no reason to abandon their right and responsible behavior of paying down their debts.

Fundamentally, there is either trust or no trust, and there is no position in-between. As mentioned earlier, modern currencies are not backed by gold or silver. Their values depend entirely on the trust the people have in their central bank.

Some monetarists might argue that there has to be a way for a central bank to engineer a soft-landing by changing its stance once again right after losing the trust of the people. The reality, however, is not so simple. This is because, by then, the central bank has already lost its credibility. Although trust can be lost in one day, rebuilding trust after losing it can take years, if not decades. So, even if it tries to act responsibly in order to ensure that inflation does not get out of control, no one will believe it. This means that there is no such thing as a Bank of Japan-induced mild inflation.

Even if a mild inflation is somehow created, the experience of "balance sheet scare syndrome" since 1993 shows that it will not be sufficient to prevent companies from paying down debt, as mentioned earlier. And until companies finish paying down their debts, balance sheet recession will not go away.

TRY "MAD EXPERIMENT" IN THE NEVADA DESERT, NOT IN JAPAN

Although there is no instance where what economists call "helicopter money" was actually used, there are some episodes of its nearly happening. It has been said that during World War II, both Germany and the United Kingdom printed massive amounts of counterfeits of their enemy country's bank notes. Since both countries mobilized their national resources to make these counterfeits, they must have been extremely well made. These counterfeits were the "weapons" intended to destroy the enemy's economy, yet neither side ever used them because the use by one party was certain to bring on retaliation. Both sides wanted to avoid the damage such a disaster will cause.

Although some economists use the term "helicopter money" without thinking it through thoroughly, those people who came closest to using it were aware of the devastation it can bring about. A monetary policy which functions only by destroying the trust the people have in their central bank will also destroy the infrastructure that is the major premise of economic activities in modern societies. It will bring about nothing but the destruction of the economy.

Foreign monetarists who have come to Japan are known to have said to the Bank of Japan, "Try dramatic monetary easing. Even if it doesn't work, it will cost you nothing." The Bank of Japan has reportedly replied, "Try your experiment in the Nevada Desert, where no one lives. We cannot conduct such an experiment in densely-populated Japan." The Bank of Japan has all its senses.

Of course, now that the U.S. economy is also in a balance sheet recession, those monetarists can try out their ideas in the U.S. However, it is doubtful that the Federal Reserve will buy such ideas when it is its turn to decide. This is because the more one thinks about the issues and problems involved, the more cautious people invariably become.

This experiment may not cost anything if it does not work, but if it works, the Japanese economy will in one stroke plunge into a world of barters and foreign currencies, which would be hundreds of times worse than the present balance sheet recession.

MARKET PARTICIPANTS ALSO DISCARD MONETARISM

The Bank of Japan, in fact, has stepped up aggressive quantitative easing since 2001, but its effect has hardly been felt either on the market or the real economy. Moreover, the yen has appreciated further, while stock prices have recorded new lows. This is because a large number of investors and market participants in Japan and abroad have realized that there is no private-sector fund demand in Japan today; that even if the Bank of Japan eased monetary policy, the mechanism through which such a policy had an effect on the real economy is missing.

In the last few years, everyone who has invested in Japanese stocks in the belief that the Bank of Japan's monetary easing would turn the economy around has lost money. If the monetarists had been right a few years ago, the Japanese economy by now would have recovered vigorously and be on its way to expansion. The economy has actually moved in the opposite direction. In this sense, one can say that a learning effect is taking place among a large number of investors and market participants.

This is a major change compared with the second half of the 1990s. In those days, a large number of foreigners still believed that the economy would improve if only the Bank of Japan stepped up its monetary easing. The reason I am referring only to foreign investors here is that since Japanese institutional investors and banks were intimately aware of the lack of private-sector fund demand from their daily contact with their domestic corporate clients, they never saw any reason to get on the monetarist bandwagon. They had known from their daily personal experiences that there was absolutely no reason for additional monetary easing to work. Hence, they have been managing their funds in the bond rather than stock market, in stark contrast to foreign investors who invested in the stock market, thinking that recovery would come soon enough with additional Bank of Japan easing.

In practice, even in the absence of a mechanism through which monetary easing has its effect on the economy, if there were enough people in the market who believed in the theory that monetary easing would be effective, one could still move stock prices and exchange rates by monetary easing. However, even those investors who once believed in such ideas are now aware of the real status of the Japanese economy and are no longer persuaded by such arguments.

CHAIRMAN GREENSPAN INDICATES THE LIMITS OF MONETARY POLICY

It must have been a great shock for those who believed in monetarism when, despite the reduction of 525 basis points in interest rates implemented by the

Federal Reserve chairman Alan Greenspan since the beginning of 2001, the U.S. corporate demand for funds not only failed to recover, it kept on declining. The reason for this failure was precisely because U.S. businesses have been busy repairing their balance sheets since the bursting of the IT bubble and the Enron affair. This evidence in the U.S. has also helped change the stance of those who had believed that the Japanese economy would improve if only the Bank of Japan took additional action.

Furthermore, in October 2001, Greenspan recommended to the U.S. Congress and the White House that a fiscal stimulus package equivalent to 1–1.5% of GDP be implemented. Although this recommendation was made right after the terrorist attacks on September 11 when the U.S. economy was on the verge of stalling, it was still a bold decision on the part of the Fed's chairman because it is an admission by him that monetary policy alone will not be sufficient to deal with the crisis. Although there were many occasions in the past when the Fed asked Congress and the White House to reduce its budget deficit, this was the first time that the Fed had asked for an *increase* in the deficit. It shows that the Federal Reserve chairman had become aware of the limits of monetary policy.

It appears that Greenspan, who is said to have studied the Japanese experience of the past decade very carefully, was becoming worried about the deflationary impact stemming from the collapse of the IT bubble. This was first shown in a dramatic shift in his position toward the tax cut at the end of 2000.

Until that time, Greenspan had voiced strong opposition to fiscal stimulus, including tax cuts. However, he suddenly agreed to the tax cut (that is, mobilization of fiscal policy) at the end of 2000. At that time, the bubble in the U.S. share market was already losing steam, and Greenspan's very close examination of Japan's recession probably prompted him to prepare for similar consequences in the U.S. He must have realized that in a balance sheet recession, monetary policy alone is not sufficient and that mobilization of fiscal measures is essential.

In this sense, the Bank of Japan governor, Masaru Hayami, should go beyond presenting counter-arguments to such unreasonable demands from the Koizumi government as inflation targeting. He should publicly urge the government to take appropriate fiscal measures in order to make the monetary policy work more effectively. Unless public-sector fund demand is increased to make up for the absence of private-sector fund demand, there is no way for the liquidity supplied by the Bank of Japan to move out of financial institutions and enter the income stream of the real economy.

WEAK CURRENCY POLICY NOT AN OPTION FOR SURPLUS COUNTRY

There is an argument, however, that if the Bank of Japan would purchase the U.S. dollar or U.S. treasury bonds instead of Japanese government bonds in order to strengthen the dollar vis-à-vis the yen, it would have a positive impact on the Japanese economy through both imported inflation and an increase in exports. While finally admitting in April 2001 that there is no fund demand and that conventional monetary policy is ineffective in Japan, Krugman still claims that the Bank of Japan can turn the economy around through massive foreign exchange market intervention.[9]

We should note, however, that just as in the U.S., intervention in the foreign exchange market is under the jurisdiction of the government (= Ministry of Finance) and not under the power of the central bank (= Bank of Japan). Thus, strictly speaking, because of its budget implications, intervention in the foreign exchange market is more a part of fiscal policy than of monetary policy.

The legal issues aside, the greatest problem with the weak-yen policy is whether the United States and other trading partners would condone Japan's weakening its currency, when the country already has the largest trade surplus in the world. If the country with the largest trade surplus were to adopt a weak-yen policy and increase its exports to the United States, it would exacerbate not only its trade imbalance, but also the already alarming size of the U.S. trade deficit, which is the worst in history.

Furthermore, the United States itself is in a balance sheet recession, with its manufacturing sector particularly badly hit. With the U.S. capacity utilization ratio down to levels last seen in the early 1980s, many in the U.S. Congress are in no mood to take in more imports that could ignite a protectionist sentiment. In fact, there has been no dearth of anti-dumping and other actions by the U.S. government aimed at keeping imports, especially steel imports, from growing faster.

What this means is that the U.S. reaction to an overt effort by the Japanese authorities to weaken the yen is likely to be negative. More precisely, even if the U.S. administration does not object strongly, the Congress will. After all, the United States is already running the worst trade deficit in history and its economy is not all that strong either. Indeed, there were already some such protests in the U.S. Congress in July 2002 against the Japanese efforts to keep the yen from appreciating. Many of those congressmen who were involved in the protest indicated that they would rather see a weaker dollar, which would help increase U.S. exports.

Japan can, of course, carry out intervention even if the United States does not agree with it. But, what will happen then is obvious if we only look at the result of Japan's unilateral attempt to weaken the yen through the purchase of the dollar at the end of June 1999. Immediately before his retirement from the government, Eisuke Sakakibara, the then vice minister of finance in charge of international affairs, suddenly departed from his long-held stance of cooperation with the United States and carried out massive and unilateral foreign exchange intervention in order to weaken the yen. Thus, for the first time, he went out and sold over ¥3 trillion so as to push the yen lower without first obtaining consent from Secretary Summers of the U.S. Treasury. Not only that, Sakakibara publicly stated that he would cut the value of the yen from the prevailing rate of around ¥117 to the dollar to more than ¥122 to the dollar.[10]

In the U.S., the newly appointed secretary of the Treasury, Lawrence Summers, was speaking out loud on the United States' need to increase savings and exports. He was concerned that a lack of prompt action on these imbalances would eventually come to haunt the U.S. economy. At the same time, he was greatly concerned that Japan was not doing enough to stimulate its domestic demand. Although the Japanese economy was obviously losing the forward momentum it obtained from the massive fiscal stimulus ordered by Prime Minister Obuchi a year earlier, the then finance minister, Kiichi Miyazawa, was in no hurry to act. In June 1999, for example, he was still saying, "We will decide on the supplementary budget after we have examined the second quarter GDP, which will be released in September." Although the subsequent GDP figures would indicate that Japan was again courting with negative growth, exactly as feared by the U.S. government, the Japanese government at that time was totally confident as well as complacent.

When the Japanese unilaterally embarked on the policy of pushing the yen lower, which would only exacerbate trade imbalances for the U.S., Secretary Summers was visibly furious. He openly criticized the Japanese foreign exchange intervention, saying that the U.S. would have none of it.

The sudden confrontation between the U.S. and Japanese monetary authorities took the foreign exchange market by surprise. The market participants had thought that since May 1995, there was an agreement between the U.S. and Japanese authorities to cooperate in the foreign exchange markets. When they realized that that was no longer the case, and that the U.S. secretary of the Treasury was talking about the need to increase savings and exports in the U.S., they rushed to buy yen and sell dollars. The result was a massive appreciation of the yen, which almost reached ¥100 = US$1, instead of the depreciation expected by Sakakibara.

THE ANATOMY OF A STRONG YEN

This reaction of the market participants was not at all abnormal. This is because the large trade deficit on the part of the U.S. means that the dollar is constantly under pressure from those transactions that relate to trade. The only way to keep the dollar from falling under such circumstances is to invite foreign capital into the country to offset the foreign selling of dollars stemming from the U.S. trade deficit.

The fact that the U.S. is running a large trade deficit means that Toyota has earned more dollars in the U.S. from selling Lexuses than Chrysler has earned yen in Japan from selling Jeeps. This means that the dollar-selling pressure from Toyota in trying to pay its workers and suppliers at home in yen is greater than the yen-selling pressure from Chrysler in trying to pay its workers and suppliers in Detroit in dollars. Since, at the end of the day, both parties will have to convert their entire foreign exchange earnings back to their domestic currencies, if those two were the only participants in the foreign exchange market, the dollar would be falling and the yen would be rising in order to clear the market.

In order to keep the dollar from falling, therefore, foreign investors must fill the gap between the dollars Toyota wants to sell and the dollars Chrysler wants to buy. It has to be foreign investors, because domestic U.S. investors do not have the yen to sell in exchange for the dollar.

Over the years, foreign investors did provide the huge support needed to keep the dollar from collapsing under the weight of the U.S. trade deficit. Through their appetite for everything from U.S. treasuries to the Rockefeller Center (although this one was eventually sold back), foreign investors kept the dollar up.

But these foreign investors are also extremely sensitive to trade issues. This is because they are taking a large foreign exchange risk by holding on to dollars when the U.S. is running a huge trade deficit. Indeed, Japanese investors have incurred literally astronomical losses by investing in U.S. assets as a result of depreciation of the dollar since the early 1970s. After all, the dollar fell from ¥360 = US$1 in the early 1970s all the way down to ¥80 = US$1 in the spring of 1995.

More importantly, those bouts of dollar depreciation almost always followed trade friction or the trade imbalance becoming a major political issue. Thus, there was a Plaza Accord in September 1985 when the dollar was pushed from ¥240 all the way down to ¥120. At that time, the whole of the United States was engulfed in protectionism. The difficulties with semiconductor agreements and "numerical targets" for imports pushed the dollar down in the early 1990s, and the emotionally charged auto talks in the mid-1990s finally pushed it all the way down to ¥80 to the dollar. Any investor who remembers this sorry history, therefore, cannot be immune to trade matters.

Although many commentators on the foreign exchange market have argued that since the investment-related foreign exchange transactions are nearly 100 times larger than the trade-related transactions, it is silly to pay much attention to the trade developments, nothing could be farther from the truth. Even though the ratio of 100 to 1 is probably correct, most investors, especially Japanese investors, do pay close attention to trade developments, among other factors, when they make their investment decisions to buy dollars. This is to be expected given that they had lost so much money by investing in dollars. If all those investors who have the yen to sell are paying attention to trade issues, those issues will affect the foreign exchange rate. In fact, this is the key reason why the Japanese yen has remained such a strong currency despite the very weak economy and very low interest rates in Japan.

Furthermore, these investors have the freedom both to buy dollars and not buy dollars. They even have the freedom to sell dollars if that appears to be appropriate. This is in sharp contrast to exporters, who must convert all their foreign currency earnings into domestic currency in order to pay their workers and suppliers at home. In other words, exporters have no choice but to sell all their foreign currency earnings at the end of the day, while investors can change sides at will.

What all of this means is that, whenever trade problems become an issue, or whenever there seems to be a big dispute developing between the U.S. and Japan on the economic front, the first instinct of most Japanese investors is to get the hell out of the dollar, either by outright selling or putting a hedge on their dollar investments. They are worried that trade problems might prompt the U.S. to seek a weaker dollar in order to solve them. They are also aware that, even if the administration is publicly opposed to the idea of a weaker dollar, it may do little to stop the dollar from falling, especially when the Congress is not happy with the United States' trade performance.

Once investors take the above action, Japanese exporters to the U.S. will suddenly find that there are no buyers for their dollars in the foreign exchange market. But unlike the investors, these exporters have no choice but to continue selling their dollars for yen in order to pay their liabilities at home in yen. And that usually results in a sharp upward movement of the yen relative to the dollar.

CONSENT OF THE CONGRESS AND U.S. TRADE REPRESENTATIVE REQUIRED FIRST

In late June 1999, when Japan's market intervention to the tune of ¥3 trillion outraged Secretary Summers, the market was stunned that the disharmony between the United States and Japan had become public. It was clear that the U.S. was not happy with Japan using the beggar-thy-neighbor policy of increasing exports instead of doing something about its own domestic demand. After all, Japan did not fall into recession because foreigners stopped buying Japanese exports. As the "overseas" line in Exhibit 1.2 in Chapter 1 indicates, Japan's current account surplus has remained virtually unchanged since the early 1990s. Japan is in recession because of its domestic problems with corporate balance sheets.

At the minimum, the dispute spelled the end of the U.S.–Japan cooperation and coordination in the foreign exchange market that had existed since May 1995. With all of this taking place against the backdrop of a massive U.S. trade deficit and a huge Japanese trade surplus, the Japanese investors ran for cover, thus pushing the yen from ¥120 to the dollar to nearly ¥100 to the dollar. The dollar-buying intervention by Sakakibara, therefore, was totally counterproductive.

Sakakibara's successor, Makoto Kuroda, had an excellent sense of balance and again cooperated with the United States. When Japan finally adopted a supplementary budget in November 1999, the United States softened its stance, and the yen–dollar rate gradually regained stability.

This example demonstrates how bilateral cooperation and coordination are essential to the stability of the yen–dollar rate when the two countries have such a large trade imbalance between them. The exchange rate cannot be determined at the discretion of one party only.

Krugman, however, still claims that the Bank of Japan should adopt a weak-yen policy, even if it means purchasing the dollar. When I had a chance to debate with him for the Japanese magazine *Bungeishunju*[11] in late 1999, I said to him,

> You are always calling for weak yen. But those of us in Japan all remember what happened in July 1999 when that was tried. The yen actually went sky high. So before recommending a weak-yen policy to the Japanese, I would like you to visit the USTR [United States Trade Representative] and Congress in Washington, D.C. and get their support for your weak-yen proposal first. If such a support is forthcoming from the US, Japan would be happy to consider the weak-yen as a viable policy option.

Krugman replied by saying that, had the Bank of Japan also eased monetary policy in conjunction with the foreign exchange intervention, Secretary Summers would have acquiesced to the Japanese intervention. But no such conditions were ever made known by Summers, certainly not in public. In fact, Summers made it very clear on numerous occasions that Japan must do more to increase domestic demand and not rely on the United States when the U.S. itself must do something about its record trade deficit. That was the end of my exchange rate policy discussions with Professor Krugman.

What the June 1999 episode showed was that for the country with the largest trade surplus in the world, the option of pushing its currency low and exporting its way out of its balance sheet recession was non-existent. Moreover, if Japan had unilaterally carried out foreign exchange market intervention that was against the interests of its trading partners such as the United States, the intervention might have had the effect of calling the attention of the foreign exchange market participants to the magnitude of the trade imbalance, which in turn would have boosted the value of the yen. And that is exactly what happened in the summer of 1999.

COMPETITIVE DEVALUATION MUST BE AVOIDED

On looking back at history, one can see that when balance sheet recession hit the global economy in the 1930s, every nation devalued its currency in order to get out of the recession on the strength of external demand. In other words, they were all doing what Krugman is now advising Japan to do. The result was an ugly competitive devaluation, followed by the massive erection of trade barriers through higher tariffs. As a result, world trade plummeted and global depression followed. This is an example of the fallacy of composition on a global scale.

This bitter historical experience shows that when so many economies — ranging from the United States to Japan, Taiwan to Thailand — are in a synchronous balance sheet recession, a beggar-thy-neighbor policy via competitive devaluation is something those nations must avoid at any cost.

It was no coincidence that John Maynard Keynes spearheaded the efforts to create the International Monetary Fund in 1945 in order to prevent the recurrence of such a tragedy. Even though domestic fallacy of composition problems can be countered by government's fiscal actions, in the absence of a world government, there is no entity that can counter an international fallacy of composition. It is for this reason that Keynes put together the IMF. The same IMF has been recommending to Japan since March 2002 that it adopt a more positive fiscal policy that includes a supplementary budget. It has even stated that the mistakes of 1997 should not be repeated.[1 2]

ENDNOTES

1 Council on Economic and Fiscal Policy (CEFP), "Basic Policies for Macroeconomic Management and Structural Reform of the Japanese Economy," June 21, 2001. http://www5.cao.go.jp/shimon/index-e.html.

2 *OECD Economic Survey 1997–98, Japan*, November 1998, p. 66.

3 Richard C. Koo and Koichi Iwai, "The Weakening Yen and Japan's Credit Crunch Problem (*En-yasu ga Maneku Kuzen Zetsugo no Kashishiburi*)," *Shukan Toyo Keizai*, September 12, 1998, pp. 36–43.

4 Paul Krugman, "It's Baaack: Japan's Slump and the Return of the Liquidity Trap," *Brookings Papers on Economic Activities*, No. 2, 1998, pp. 137–205.

5 *Ibid.*

6 Paul Krugman, "A Leap in the Dark," *The New York Times*, July 8, 2001.

7 Krugman, *Brookings Papers on Economic Activities, op. cit.*

8 *Ibid.*

9 Krugman, "A Leap in the Dark," *op. cit.*

10 *Nihon Keizai Shimbun*, June 27, 1999.

11 Richard C. Koo, Debate with Paul Krugman, "Is a Strong Yen an Evil? (*Nihon Keizai En-daka wa Akuma k*a)," *Bungeishunju*, November 1999, pp. 130–43.

12 IMF, *World Economic Outlook*, April 2002, Chapter 1, p. 21. http://www.imf.org/external/pubs/ft/weo/2002/01/pdf/chapter1.pdf.

4

Conditions For Recovery

SUSTAINABILITY OF FISCAL STIMULUS

Even if the importance of fiscal stimulus in balance sheet recession is understood, many people are rightfully cautious about its use because of the already large size of government debt outstanding, which is said to be approaching 150% of GDP.

One can sum up the whole issue of fiscal spending and balance sheet repairs as a question of which will come first — the collapse of state finances due to the ongoing fiscal deficit, or healthy balance sheets at the majority of Japanese companies. Everything will turn out right in the end if companies repair their balance sheets and start making forward-looking investments before state finances collapse. However, it could all end in tears if state finances collapse first.

At the moment, there are no signs that Japanese companies are starting to ease up on loan repayments, even though interest-bearing liabilities within the private sector are much lower than in the past. This is because asset prices, as exemplified by share prices, are continuing to fall. In other words, the goal of a clean balance sheet is moving further and further away. At the same time, there are no signs either that the market is getting fed up with too much government debt. Quite the contrary, the price of government bonds keeps increasing and the yield keeps falling. This means that the demand for Japanese government bonds is greater than the supply — that is, the market is more than happy to absorb JGBs.

When one talks about the sustainability of fiscal deficit, one has to be careful that it is an issue that is determined by the market, not by academics or lawyers. If the market accepts it, the deficit financing can go on for a long time. For example, the U.K. had government debt outstanding equal to over 250% of its GDP at the end of World War II, but the country called the

United Kingdom is still around. More importantly, if the U.K. government had not fought the Nazis during that war because of the large size of its fiscal deficit, the United Kingdom might have disappeared in the 1940s.

Furthermore, once the economy begins to recover with fiscal stimulus, tax receipts can grow quickly from their present depressed levels. Under the New Deal policy of President Roosevelt, the U.S. federal government expenditure was doubled, but during the same period, government revenue tripled, thus keeping the budget deficit from growing. Indeed, the deficit as a percentage of government expenditure was biggest in 1932, when Hoover was still the president. Thus, once the economy starts to recover, the budget deficit could shrink quickly through increases in tax revenues.

The role of fiscal policy in a balance sheet recession is to maintain the income of the people, including that of business corporations. As long as they have income, businesses will have the revenue to pay down debts, while individuals can pay their home loans as long as they have a job. When the income dries up, businesses will fail, while individuals will become jobless and insolvent. When the number of businesses and households with balance sheet problems is in the millions, once the wave of bankruptcies begins, there is the risk of starting an endless chain of bankruptcies that will lead directly to depression.

If Japan helps its businesses repair their balance sheets by adopting a proactive fiscal policy, and then moves on to fiscal rehabilitation only after the corporate balance sheets are repaired and the private sector resumes forward-looking investments, Japan will have succeeded in one of the greatest economic experiments history has ever witnessed. What Japan will have proven is that even if an asset-price bubble emerges and bursts, if the right policy is implemented from the beginning with patience, the problem can be solved without plunging the entire economy into a depression.

The voices of both the stock and bond markets are loudly encouraging the government to continue this great experiment. The ultra-low interest rates, in particular, are saying that this is the time to boost fiscal stimulus, not reduce it. The weak stock market is also a warning about the state of the economy: this is not the time to ignore macroeconomic reality in favor of structural reform policies that produce results only after many years of incubation. The fact that interest-bearing debts of businesses have declined substantially, as seen in Exhibit 2.1 in Chapter 2, shows that the efforts of both the public and private sectors thus far have not been in vain.

Since Japan is the first country to have applied fiscal stimulus from the very beginning and to have kept the economy going in spite of what has happened to asset prices, the absence of any precedent makes some people skeptical about the outcome of this experiment. However, there are no other alternatives.

The success of the experiment will be truly celebrated when the government will be able to slash the budget deficits once the health of the corporate balance sheets is restored and the companies begin to borrow again. For the experiment to be truly successful, the government must demonstrate that it is able to slash expenditure when that moment comes, against the wishes of many vested interests. Therefore, many challenges still remain before Japan reaches its ultimate goal. However, the fact that an embankment of only ¥140 trillion has been able to prevent a flood of ¥1,200 trillion is a great feat and should not be underestimated.

HISTORIC OPPORTUNITY FOR INFRASTRUCTURE BUILDING

The magnitude of the budget deficit is raising the fear that at some point the absorption of large amounts of government bonds will become impossible. I have long argued that the sign of problems in the absorption of government bonds will appear as higher interest rates. At the same time, the increase in interest rates stemming from a recovery in private-sector fund demand will mean the end of the balance sheet recession and the resumption of autonomous recovery. When such a point is reached, policies will have to be changed toward fiscal retrenchment in order to avoid crowding out of the long-sought-after private investments.

The present condition of the economy, however, is that private-sector fund demand has declined by as much as ¥35 trillion compared with its level of only four or five years ago. Reflecting this shrinkage, interest rates have fallen sharply. This means that the economy is moving further and further away from the condition that would cause the fear of government bonds not being bought.

The sharp decline in government bond yields and the sharp increase in government bond prices during this period mean that the demand for government bonds is far greater than the supply. Indeed, Japanese institutional investors and banks are rushing to buy government bonds because there are no other borrowers who will take their funds. These market signals suggest that debating whether or not government bonds can be absorbed is a waste of time.

On the contrary, these exceptionally low interest rates are the market's way of telling policymakers that now is a historic opportunity to build any infrastructure that is in short supply. After all, if there is anything still needing to be constructed in Japan, doing it now will significantly lower both the present and future burden on taxpayers. For example, if a ¥1 trillion project is financed with a 10-year bond issuance, the interest cost to taxpayers over the 10-year period will be ¥100 billion at the current JGB yield of around 1.0%. In a pre-bubble "normal" world, JGB yield averaged 5–6%. This means that, if the same project is implemented after the balance sheet recession is over and when the yield on JGBs has returned to normal levels, the interest cost to taxpayers will be ¥500–600 billion for the same project.

In other words, the total cost to taxpayers (principal and interest) for the same project will be 50% more if construction is postponed until the balance sheet problems are over. Since Japan still has a lot to do, now is the historic opportunity to put all those projects in place. Putting in the necessary infrastructure now will both help the economy fight the balance sheet recession now and lower the tax burden in the future.

SOUND STATE OF JGB SUBSCRIPTIONS

In addition to interest rates, there are other clues as to the levels of difficulty faced by the government in placing its bonds. One clue is the currency denomination of such bonds; another is the nationality of the people who are buying them. There are three stages of government bonds placements:

1   The bonds are denominated in the currency of the issuing country and are purchased by the country's nationals.
2   The bonds are denominated in the currency of the issuing country and are purchased by foreign nationals.
3   The bonds are denominated in foreign currencies and are purchased by foreign nationals.

Among these categories, the safest stage is (1), followed by (2) and then (3), which involves the greatest risk. In fact, most of the countries that defaulted on their debts, including Russia and the Latin American countries, were in category (3).

The United States, although its budget deficits are not so large at the moment, has a very large current account deficit and foreigners hold nearly 40% of all U.S. treasury bonds issued in the past.

If those foreign holders lose their confidence in the management of the U.S. economy, they may sell off their huge holdings of U.S. bonds all at the same time. That could put highly unwelcome pressure on the U.S. financial markets in the form of skyrocketing interest rates. Therefore, the nation is basically in category (2).

That foreigners might dump their U.S. treasury holdings is not purely a theoretical possibility, either. It actually happened in March 1987, two-and-half years after the Plaza Accord where G5 countries agreed to push the dollar down. At that time, the dollar was inadvertently allowed to fall below ¥150 for the first time. Since this was only four weeks after the Louvre Accord, which assured the world that the dollar had fallen enough and that its stability (above ¥150) was in the interests of all concerned, the market was shocked. In the ensuing panic, the dollar fell dramatically to as low as

¥137, while U.S. bond yields skyrocketed from 7.5% to 9.0% in only six weeks as foreign investors fled the U.S. markets in a hurry (Exhibit 4.1). The dollar regained its stability, and bond yields came down, only after massive efforts on the part of the U.S. and Japanese monetary authorities to

Exhibit 4.1   Fall in the dollar pushing U.S. interest rates higher in 1987

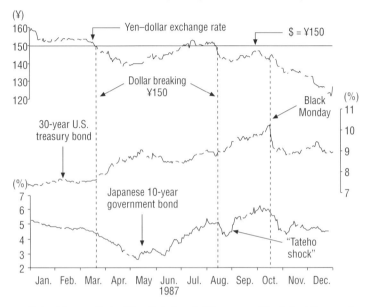

Sources: Federal Reserve Bank of New York; Board of Governors of the Federal Reserve; Japan Bond Trading Company.

stabilize the exchange rate. The dollar fell below the ¥150 level again in August, and the U.S. bond yield resumed its climb until the stock market crashed on the infamous "Black Monday" in October 1987. With so much of its bonds held by foreigners, the United States is rightfully concerned about the "dump America" phenomenon by foreign investors and manages its foreign exchange policy with the utmost care.

In contrast, Japan's current account balance is in huge surplus and, because its bonds are denominated in domestic currency and purchased primarily by its own nationals, it is in category (1). Although there is a problem in that its stock market is supported primarily by foreign investors, Japanese nationals make up 95% of its government bond market. And they are the same investors who understand the seriousness of the balance sheet recession from their day-to-day contact with their corporate clients. Such a market, based on a clear understanding of balance sheet recession, is not likely to go out of whack any time soon.

WORRIES ABOUT THE PLACEMENT OF JGBs A LUXURY

The JGB market is not only being supported almost exclusively by Japanese nationals, but is also enjoying record price levels while yields are at their lowest levels in history. In this sense, the JGB market is in a category better than (1), which we might call category (0). That is, JGBs are denominated in the currency of the issuing country and are enthusiastically grabbed by its own nationals.

Therefore, it will be a long time before the problem of the placement of government bonds emerges. First, the yields will have to return to normal levels (5–6% on average for 10-year instruments before the bubble days) and the category has to shift from (1), (2), and then (3) before the placement problem arises. Even after the warning signals appear (that is, a shift to category (2)), it is likely to take a long time before the actual absorption problem arises.

As indicated earlier, worrying about the default of the Japanese government while it is still in category (0) is a luxury. The responsibility of the policymakers under such circumstances would be to address more urgent problems before worrying about a situation that may or may not arise in the distant future.

Of course, the fact that the prices of JGBs are at record levels suggests that investors who hold such bonds may have a very severe "altitude phobia." If there is any news that might be considered even remotely negative for bond prices, the reflexes of these investors would be to sell the bonds while prices are still high. That means the market has a very large downside risk.

However, there have been several shocks that have sharply depressed JGB prices during the last few years, but each time the market has recovered quickly. This means that those people who sold according to their reflexes suffered heavy losses. These lessons have taught them that unless private-sector demand for funds materializes, any selloff in the bond market will be short-lived. This is because, for interest rates to stay high, there has to be demand for funds at those higher rates of interest. Since 95% of investors in JGBs are Japanese nationals who are fully aware of what is happening to the private-sector demand for funds, the market is not likely to act irrationally for long.

This has been proven most clearly when reports of repeated downgrading of JGBs have appeared. Initially, there was a major uproar each time downgrading was reported, but as prices have remained firm despite this news of downgradings, people are no longer alarmed by such news. They have also realized that the stated explanations for downgrades issued by the foreign rating agencies are not consistent with the reality of the Japanese financial market that these investors face every day.

RATING AGENCIES ARE NO GODS

In particular, it is clear from their statements that the rating agencies (Moody's, Standard & Poor's, and Fitch) themselves are not aware of the fact that Japan is in a balance sheet recession. They have not realized that the vast majority of companies in Japan are paying down debt, while the household sector is still saving as before. They have not grasped the point that the deflationary pressure stems not from the lack of reform (however it is defined), but from the fact that the corporate sector is no longer borrowing the funds that the household sector has saved.

If they understood that household savings are turning into a deflation gap because of the fallacy of composition problem within the corporate sector, they would see the budget deficit in a different light. Since the government cannot instruct companies not to repair their balance sheets, the only choice left for the government is to take action to offset what is happening to the private sector. That is the lesson the world learned in the 1930s. Furthermore, since it is the budget deficit that is closing the deflation gap and keeping the money supply from shrinking, the economy will become much worse if fiscal spending is reduced or withdrawn.

In fact, when Japan implemented fiscal rehabilitation in 1997 at the urging of the IMF and the OECD, not only did the economy collapse, but the budget deficit also increased 68%, or from ¥22 trillion to ¥37 trillion, instead of diminishing as noted earlier.

Freedom of expression allows rating agencies to say whatever they like, but the Japanese people must judge for themselves if their analyses or prescriptions for Japan suit the actual conditions in Japan. If the analyses made by such agencies are problematic, then their ratings also would be problematic.

The advocates of "fiscal rehabilitation first" in Japan and other countries make a big commotion, as if they have heard the voices of gods, every time Japan is downgraded. However, there is ample evidence that the rating agencies are no gods. A recent example is their total failure to predict the Asian currency crisis.

The rating agencies' opinions should be heard but not taken as absolute truth. Like other people, they can make mistakes. Regarding the recent situation in Japan, in particular, the market's judgment has been more accurate than that of the agencies.

LESSONS FROM THE BOND MARKET

It is the yields on government bonds (that is, long-term interest rates — hereinafter to be referred to as "interest rates") and the strength of private-sector fund demand that send the signals as to whether the fiscal stimulus should be increased or decreased.

The budget deficit should be reduced if interest rates are high and there is ample demand for funds from the private sector. Allowing a budget deficit to continue under such circumstances runs the risk of crowding out private-sector investments or of igniting inflation. However, at the opposite pole where interest rates are ultra-low and private-sector borrowers are nowhere to be seen, as in present-day Japan, increasing the budget deficit can raise the growth rate and income levels in both the medium and long term.

However, when interest rates are mentioned as an important signal for policy, bureaucrats or academics who do not understand the markets would say, "Interest rates may rise or fall at any minute. The government policy cannot depend on something that is so volatile." It is true that interest rates often fluctuate sharply in a short period of time due to technical or other factors in the market. But it should not be forgotten that the average level of interest rates over some length of time reflects an important judgment of the people who actually buy and sell government bonds.

In particular, interest rates reflect the following views of the market participants:

1   Whether or not the share of government bonds held in their overall portfolio (assets under management) is appropriate.
2   Forecasts of future inflation.
3   Forecasts of future private-sector demand for funds.
4   Forecasts of future supply of government bonds.

With respect to item (1), if investors feel that the weight of the JGBs in their portfolio is too high, they will sell off the bonds, which means that JGB prices will fall (= interest rates will rise). Therefore, government bond yields will not be able to maintain the present ultra-low level of 1.0% if investors really think that there are too many JGBs in their portfolios.

Concerning item (2), if inflation is forecast, holding 10-year JGBs with yields of 1.0% will run the risk of incurring a huge capital loss. Therefore, if inflation fears become real, the investors will sell off the low-yield government bonds in a hurry, which will result in higher interest rates and plummeting government bond prices.

Similarly, with respect to item (3), if there are signs of recovery in the demand for funds from private enterprises, since they typically pay a higher interest rate than the government, investors will also sell off the government bonds and redirect their funds to private-sector borrowers. For example, if an investor knows that Sony is going to issue bonds with yields that are higher than those of JGBs, he will either refrain from purchasing government bonds or sell off those bonds in order to buy the bonds to be issued by Sony. This will worsen the demand-and-supply balance of the government bonds, which will result in lower government bond prices and higher yields.

However, this rise in interest rates resulting from the new vigor of private enterprises is a very healthy development and should be welcomed. Indeed, this type of interest rate increase should be called a "good interest rate increase." After all, the ultimate goal of economic policy is to restore the health of the economy and, in the case of balance sheet recession, that means restoring the private sector's demand for funds.

If the private sector is willing to borrow in order to invest, there is no need for the government to offset the shortfall in demand through its deficit spending. In other words, when private-sector companies are coming back to borrow money, the government should cut its deficit spending as fast as possible. Moreover, if the government continues its deficit spending under such an environment, crowding out will result. The rise in interest rates under this environment is a signal that the budget deficit should be reduced.

Before the emergence of the asset bubble in the 1987–88 period, 10-year JGBs yielded 5–6% a year. Therefore, if the present yield of 1.0% begins to rise to those levels, that means private-sector demand for funds has returned to normal levels and it is time to implement fiscal rehabilitation.

GOVERNMENT BONDS: A VERY PRECIOUS INVESTMENT VEHICLE

What we are most concerned with is item (4), or the forecasts of the demand-and-supply balance of JGBs. As the Japanese tabloids write about the horrendous size of the budget deficit almost on a daily basis, this subject has become the greatest matter of concern for market participants. If they believe that the issuance of government bonds will sharply exceed the past forecasts, they will naturally become cautious about purchasing government bonds. Some may actually try to sell off their holding before the demand-and-supply balance really deteriorates. This should bring down the prices of government bonds and raise their yields.

However, the fact that the ultra-low interest rates have persisted, despite the horrendous magnitude of the budget deficit being pointed out almost daily in the media, means that investors feel the present volume of government bond issues will not become a big burden to the market in the foreseeable future. If this were not the case, it would be impossible for the government bond yields to stay so low. In other words, for interest rates to rise sharply, some event or development must occur that is totally unforeseen at the present moment. The possibility of such a development occurring is not zero, but at the present time it is considered to be very remote. If everyone feels that the future supply of government bonds will exceed the market's capacity to digest them, interest rates would have to be much higher than they are now.

The present level of government bond yields is the result of all of the above-mentioned judgments of the investors, including their fear of future JGB supply. That is to say that the market has already discounted for all of these factors and fears. Hence, the view that interest rates may suddenly rise sharply tomorrow and stay high for an extended period of time thereafter cannot be justified unless one assumes that the present market participants are fools and are missing something very important.

Needless to say, interest rates may surge in the short term due to some exogenous shocks, but there must be sufficient demand for funds in order to maintain that high level of interest rates. An examination of the Japanese bond market for the last few years shows that interest rates surged a number of times due to short-term shocks, but, as mentioned earlier, since there was a shortage of fund demand at those high levels, the rates have returned to their former levels.

There are many critics of the budget deficit and government bonds. But how many of those people would agree to have their pension or life insurance premiums managed without an investment in government bonds? Managing funds without investing in JGBs today would mean that their pension benefits would decline sharply and their life insurance premiums would increase several-fold.

Under the present conditions, JGBs are a very precious investment vehicle for institutional investors that are managing the pensions or life insurance of the general public. The advocates of fiscal rehabilitation keep asking whether or not the government can repay its debts, but the actual flow of the Japanese people's money is sending another message. By pushing the price of government bonds higher and higher, it is saying the people would like the government to borrow more, not less. It is the Japanese people who would suffer the most if the government were to decide to pay down debt while there is such a paucity of private-sector borrowers for funds. And that was the disaster of the 1997–98 fiscal reform effort.

BOND MARKET AS A POLICEMAN FOR THE ECONOMY

Needless to say, the market is not always right. Sometimes, a stock market may crash suddenly, or the exchange rate may fluctuate by as much as ¥20 to the dollar over a couple of days. Because of the nature of the instrument, however, the bond market tends to attract the most cautious investors. This is because stocks tend to fall into self-perpetuating benign (or vicious) cycles once their prices assume a rising (declining) trend, because the rising share prices bring positive (negative) wealth effects, which makes people richer (poorer) and prompts them to spend more (less), which in turn increases (decreases) corporate earnings, which further pushes up (down) stock prices. A typical example of such a benign (vicious) cycle is a bubble (market crash). In contrast, the bond market is free from this characteristic.

This is because when inflation fears rise as the business condition improves, investors sell their bondholding because of the fear of higher interest rates and consequent capital loss on their bondholdings (item 2). The resultant decline in bond prices (increase in interest rates) has the effect of cooling the economy. Conversely, when inflation fears turn into deflation fears because of the deterioration in the economy, bonds are purchased and their prices rise (interest rates decline), which provides the underpinnings to the economy.

Thus, the bond market has a stabilizer or counter-cyclical effect on the economy. As such, it never gets carried away for too long. This counter-cyclical effect is why the bond market is often referred to as the "policeman of the economy."

Furthermore, while stock prices fluctuate depending on the management efforts and earnings prospects of individual firms, the bond market — the government bond market, in particular — basically reacts only to the economic performance of the nation as a whole. Therefore, it is most suited for taking the "body temperature" of the economy.

The message from the foreign exchange market is inherently the result of a comparative evaluation of the two economies. Therefore, it is not determined on the basis of factors in only one country.

Unfortunately, the bond market in Japan has not gained the kind of citizenship the same market enjoys in the U.S. When people talk about the markets in Japan, they typically mean the stock and foreign exchange markets. But this omission is particularly dangerous in the world of balance sheet recession, since the bond market is where the most critical life signs are observed. The Japanese policymakers would do much better if they paid more attention to the voice of the bond market.

The yields on JGBs stood at 2.3% when fiscal rehabilitation was launched in fiscal 1997. At present, they stand at 1.0%, which is 57% below the pre-fiscal rehabilitation level even though the current budget deficit of over ¥30 trillion is 40% greater than at the beginning of 1997. The current yield is about the lowest long-term interest rate ever recorded. This should be interpreted as a call from the Japanese economy to the government, via a messenger (that is, the bond market), that now is the time to follow a positive fiscal policy rather than launch fiscal rehabilitation.

Had Prime Minister Hashimoto paid more attention to the bond market, he could have avoided the grave mistake of launching fiscal rehabilitation in 1997, when interest rates were already at record-low levels. By ignoring the message from the bond market, Hashimoto's fiscal reform efforts only wrecked the economy and swelled the budget deficit. Similarly, policymakers could have avoided the needless caution on the fiscal stimulus had they noticed that, even with large deficits, the bond yield remained at record-low levels.

The fact that the budget deficits have increased by 40% since fiscal 1996 while interest rates have declined by 57% during the same period suggests that the decline in private-sector demand for funds has been greater than the increase in the budget deficit. In fact, the budget deficit increased by ¥15 trillion from 1996 to reach ¥37 trillion in 1999, while private-sector fund demand shrank by ¥35 trillion during the same period. In other words, the demand for funds from the private sector was falling faster than the supply of government bonds.

The fact that the present yields on JGBs remain at record-low levels despite the loud fears voiced by the media about the magnitude of the budget deficit should be considered as the conclusion reached by the actual investors (as opposed to no-action, talk-only commentators) after careful examination of the four points described earlier.

Although commentators at home and abroad who are not paying attention to the sorry state of the private-sector fund demand in Japan are making a big issue out of the magnitude of the budget deficit, the message from the bond market is the opposite. Through a record-low long-term interest rate, the market is saying that the economy could worsen further unless a more aggressive fiscal policy is adopted.

Perhaps there are limits to the size of the budget deficit at some point, but the behavior of the Japanese people thus far suggests that such limits are still far in the distance and that this is not a matter the policymakers should be worrying about at the present moment.

GLOBALIZATION AND REAL INTEREST RATES

Throughout this book, it has been argued that the disposal of non-performing loans and fiscal rehabilitation are not urgent issues for the present Japanese economy and that they should be implemented slowly. Both of these arguments are based on the ultra-low levels of Japanese interest rates. If the placement of JGBs were such a major problem, interest rates would not be so low. Likewise, if the banks' NPLs were a constraint on economic recovery, bank lending rates would not be so low.

When these points are raised, commentators at home and abroad counter by saying, "But real interest rates in Japan are high." Since prices in Japan have been declining, real interest rates are higher than nominal interest rates. However, while the discussion of real interest rates has some significance for those households and individuals whose economic activities are basically confined to Japan, for the corporate sector, which is struggling to survive in a global economy, it is doubtful that the discussion of real interest rates calculated only on the basis of domestic prices has any significance.

This is because if there is no domestic demand and prices are falling, the companies can choose to sell their products overseas, where there is demand and prices are increasing. In fact, in the last few years, Japanese enterprises have been intensively investing their management resources in the buoyant overseas markets, especially the U.S. market, rather than in the stagnant domestic market.

Furthermore, when deflation was considered a serious problem in Japan in 2001, the yen rate against the dollar was considerably below the previous year's ¥100-to-the-dollar levels. This meant that many Japanese companies were able to set their overseas prices at levels much more favorable to them than a year earlier when the yen was much stronger. The real interest rates, taking this factor into account, could have been much lower than the nominal interest rates.

Even while they enjoyed the benefits of the weaker yen and increasing external demand, most Japanese companies were still paying down debt. This is because they believed that they had to compress their debt overhang and lower their high leverage ratios as quickly as possible, regardless of the level of interest rates. As indicated earlier, the nationwide rush to repair balance sheets started in around 1993 when Japan still had inflation. Since people have already realized that they were chasing wrong asset prices in the 1980s and that those prices are not likely to come back anytime soon, it is pointless to assume that, at some level of interest rates, these people will stop repairing their balance sheets and start borrowing money again.

Although real interest rates have been a popular analytical tool among some economists, businessmen in Japan and abroad seldom talk about real interest rates. Furthermore, over the past 10 years, prices have fallen most sharply for semiconductor and personal computer products. In other words, the real interest rates in that sector were the highest. But these were also the sectors that have invested most heavily in plant and equipment during the last 10 years.

The fact that even those companies with a large export business are paying down debt as fast as possible suggests that the real interest rate argument as a constraint on growth seems misplaced. When an executive with a top Japanese electronics firm said that "even we will be blown away in the next storm if we do not reduce our debt levels now," he was referring to the balance sheet concerns, not the level of real interest rates.

More importantly, it should be remembered that the real rates are high because the economy is weak. And the economy is weak because so many companies are paying down debt all at the same time. Thus, the causality is from the balance sheet problems to the real interest rates, not the other way around. In this environment, to think that somehow lowering the real interest rate can turn the tide of recession seems thoroughly unrealistic. One does not cure a sick patient with a high fever by throwing him into a freezer.

TWO TYPES OF DEFLATION

Furthermore, even though prices are falling due to the weak economy, those prices that are falling are doing so from very high levels compared to prices available outside the country. In talking about deflation and high real interest rates in Japan, therefore, one has to take into account the massive structural changes taking place in the retail and distribution sectors of the Japanese economy. To be more precise, until around 1995, the Japanese market was still largely closed to foreign goods. As a result, there was a huge differential between Japanese and foreign prices.

Around 1995, however, with the yen–dollar exchange rate hitting ¥79.75 = US$1, and more and more Japanese manufacturers moving offshore, both the official and non-official barriers to trade began to crumble. The barriers began to break down because it was no longer just foreigners trying to sell in Japan, but also the Japanese companies producing abroad trying to sell in Japan. The newer establishments such as 100-yen shops and Uniqlo also began the process of so-called price destruction — in effect, bringing down domestic prices to international levels.

Even though this process means lower prices and "deflation" for those businesses that have never previously faced this kind of competition, it is not a deflation that is caused by the lack of money supply or aggregate demand. Indeed, this is a very healthy adjustment in prices that is long overdue.

Put differently, there seem to be two price declines: those to the level of global prices, and those that go beyond the level of global prices. The former represents healthy structural change, while the latter represents a worrisome contraction in aggregate demand or an incorrect monetary policy.

In Japan today, the vast majority of price declines are in the former category, with very few in the latter category. After all, Japanese prices are still very high compared to international levels. But if the price declines are mostly of the former category, there is little that the central bank should be concerned about, since there is very little that it can do to turn the tide of globalization.

The seemingly excessive emphasis which foreign economists place on Japan's "deflation problem" and "high real interest rates" probably comes from the fact that they do not live in Japan and are not aware of the fact that most of the deflation is actually a belated adjustment to global prices. In comparison, both the U.S. and Europe had opened their markets for low-cost imports long ago. As a result, the marginal effect of additional low-cost imports on their price levels is likely to be limited.

On the other hand, most Japanese can still remember the days when beef and oranges were prohibitively expensive, since those days were not so long ago. As recently as 2001, when gasoline prices were rising sharply all over the world, the Japanese were rejoicing over the sharply *falling* gasoline prices. Prices were falling because, at around that time, the Japanese government deregulated the gasoline market, resulting in much increased competition among gasoline suppliers. This market-opening factor more than offset the higher cost of crude oil, and resulted in lower gasoline prices at the pumps.

These perverse price movements can happen because Japan is still in a transition between a fully opened market and a closed one. For economists and policymakers, therefore, it is essential that they know what is behind the Japanese deflation numbers when they talk about high real interest rates and their monetary policy implications.

Although many economists typically blame deflation for Japan's stagnating economy, the country with the highest economic growth today, China, also has deflation. Its CPI has been falling 1–2% a year since the middle of 1997, whereas Japan's CPI has been falling 0–1% since the middle of 1998, as shown in Exhibit 4.2 According to a Chinese official I spoke to, "The prices are falling simply to international levels." And such price declines do not necessarily impede economic growth, as the Chinese case has amply proven.

NEW YORK ASSET STRIPPERS FLOODED TOKYO HOTELS IN 1996

Up to now, the discussion has been mostly about how to avoid falling into a vicious cycle. Since the danger of falling into such a cycle is always present in a balance sheet recession, the policymakers must remain vigilant about that risk at all times. However, the possible paths for the Japanese economy are by no means limited to the current stagnation or falling into a vicious cycle. There is, in fact, also the possibility of putting the Japanese economy into a virtuous cycle where a growing economy and rising asset prices go hand in hand.

This talk of a virtuous cycle may sound odd when the danger is everywhere in the other direction. However, during the last 12 years, there

Exhibit 4.2 Deflation in both Japan and China

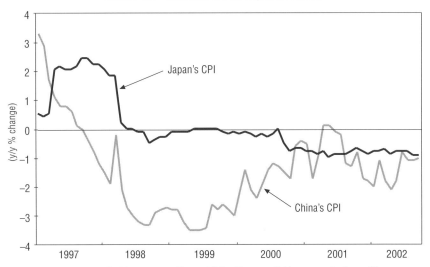

Sources: Ministry of Public Management, Home Affairs, Posts and Telecommunications, "Consumer Price Index"; National Bureau of Statistics of China, "Consumer Price Index."

were at least two occasions when the economy was actually in a virtuous cycle of rising asset prices and rapid economic growth happening at the same time. The first occasion was the 1995–96 period (Japan recorded 4.4% real GDP growth in 1996, which was the highest among the G7 countries); and the second was the 1999–2000 period, when the stock market went up so much that market capitalization increased a whopping ¥213 trillion, which is nearly half of Japan's yearly GDP.

Both times, however, the Japanese Ministry of Finance slammed on the fiscal brakes, killing the virtuous cycle dead in its tracks. On the first occasion, the MOF convinced Prime Minister Hashimoto to reduce the budget deficit by raising taxes and cutting spending, which in no time pushed the economy into five consecutive quarters of negative growth. The subsequent fall in asset prices also led to a massive banking crisis. In the second case, the momentum of the virtuous cycle was allowed to dissipate when the MOF resisted the quick introduction of the needed supplementary budget, thus allowing the deflationary pressures to creep back in again. This was followed by Prime Minister Koizumi's ill-advised pledge to keep the issuance of JGBs to below ¥30 trillion a year, which resulted in both a massive fall in asset prices and three consecutive quarters of negative growth for the economy.

The failure to maintain the forward momentum on both of these occasions was truly unfortunate in that if the brakes were not applied so soon, Japan could have climbed out of its balance sheet recession by now.

In particular, the 1995–96 opportunity was truly missed in that, during that period, a large number of asset strippers from the U.S. as well as overseas Chinese investors were flooding Tokyo hotels looking for commercial properties to buy. The fact that these international investors were coming to Japan meant that property prices had already fallen to levels that made international sense. In other words, the relationship between the rent and property prices was already back to international standards. If these investors had kept on buying assets, they would have provided a floor for property values and made the subsequent repairs of Japan's corporate balance sheets far easier.

Unfortunately, it was precisely at that moment that Prime Minister Hashimoto, at the urging of the MOF, decided to embark on fiscal reform by raising taxes and cutting spending. The subsequent collapse of both the economy and asset prices was so severe that all those foreigners who had come to Japan to buy assets quickly fled, making the crash of property values that much worse. The fact that most economic indicators together with asset prices today are so far below their 1996 levels suggests that seven years later, Japan still has not recovered from the damage wrought by the ill-fated attempt to reduce the budget deficit in 1997. Put differently, if Prime Minister Hashimoto had not embarked on fiscal reform in 1997 and instead had maintained the same level of fiscal stimulus as in previous years, it is highly likely that the Japanese balance sheet problem would have been a thing of the past long before this book was published.

In other words, although I have argued that the Japanese fiscal policy has been one of the most successful in history, it could have done even better had it not fallen back into a stop-and-go mode so often. Even though the medicine was correct, it was applied in the least effective manner.

Both the 1995–96 and 1999–2000 cycles were started with a strong fiscal stimulus. In the case of the former, it was the U.S. government that forced Japan to put in place strong domestic demand stimulus measures in exchange for the U.S. government helping the Japanese to fight the strong yen. In the latter case, it was Prime Minister Keizo Obuchi's determination to pull the Japanese economy out of the 1997–98 fiasco that prompted the strong fiscal response.

CONDITIONS FOR STARTING A VIRTUOUS CYCLE

The above suggests that the key to starting and maintaining a virtuous cycle is to put in a big fiscal stimulus and keep that stimulus in place for the time being. The government must also pledge — both domestically and overseas — that it will not step on the brakes prematurely. In other words, it will not step on the brakes until the majority of Japanese companies are comfortable with their balance sheets. The government must also explain to the people why fiscal stimulus is needed in a balance sheet recession.

The pledge is necessary because too many Japanese business people and overseas investors were burned when they decided to bet on the two previous virtuous cycles, only to see the economy and the stock market collapse soon afterwards as a result of the senseless removal of the fiscal stimulus. As a result, Japanese businessmen as well as overseas investors are now extremely skeptical of any announcement of "anti-deflation measures" by the Japanese government. They are not likely to respond quickly even if a substantial stimulus is put in place, because they will be afraid that there will be no follow-up, and that the fiscal reformists at the MOF will raise their ugly heads again and torpedo the economic recovery. In order to calm their fears, therefore, the government must make a pledge up-front that the past mistakes will not be repeated.

The justification for fiscal stimulus is necessary because so few people, both within and outside Japan, are aware of the fact that Japan is in a full-blown balance sheet recession where everybody is trying to improve their balance sheets by paying down debt. They do not realize that the vast majority of Japanese companies today are paying down debt even at 0% interest rates. But since the companies are doing the right and responsible thing, the government must take actions to offset the deflationary pressure stemming from the private sector. If this point is not fully explained, ignorant media will characterize the fiscal stimulus simply as pork-barrel politics of the worst kind, thus making the public even more skeptical about the government's intentions.

Over the past 10 years, Japanese corporations have succeeded in sharply reducing their interest-bearing debt. But during this time, when governments — such as the Hashimoto administration and the current Koizumi administration — did not do enough to fill the deflationary gap, the economy deteriorated and asset prices plunged. In effect, such mismanagement has caused the goal of a healthy balance sheet to recede even further into the distance, creating a vicious cycle of debt repayment and falling asset prices. And all this time, the fiscal deficit has continued to mount.

SHORTENING THE TIME IT TAKES TO REACH THE GOAL

As mentioned in Chapter 2, the economy will not be able to enter a path of self-sustaining recovery until such time as the majority of companies have repaired their balance sheets. In this respect, there are two questions to be asked:

1 How much fiscal support will still be needed in the future?
2 Are there ways of speeding up the process?

In answer to the first question, as I have indicated in Exhibit 2.4 in Chapter 2 using the GDP statistics of fiscal year 2000, companies' balance sheets should have recovered to pre-bubble levels by now. However, the subsequent fall in asset prices and the weakness in the economy are pushing this goal further and further away.

The goal will become closer to being achieved if the economy enters a virtuous cycle. In other words, there is no constant answer to the first question — it is organically linked to the health of the economy. At present, because the government of Prime Minister Koizumi is not interested in fiscal stimulus, it is in effect allowing the economy to deteriorate and asset prices to fall, thus putting the goal of carrying out balance sheet repairs further away for most corporations.

Moreover, if the economy remains depressed, then companies will tend to become even more cautious and speed up their loan repayments. As indicated earlier, Japanese companies are still 1.7 times more leveraged compared to their U.S. counterparts. Although high corporate leverage ratios are acceptable during periods of high economic growth, during periods of low economic growth they could prove fatal for companies. This very fact alone, at a time of low economic growth, is stimulating loan repayments at Japanese companies.

If we accept that (1) is determined by the results of (2), then the policymakers should be diverting all their energies to finding ways of shortening the repair process. In other words, policymakers must find ways to put the Japanese economy back in a virtuous cycle as quickly as possible.

WAR — WHAT IS IT GOOD FOR?

In the past, it is wars that have solved serious balance sheet recessions, including the Great Depression of the 1930s. This is a well-known fact, but the mechanism by which wars solve balance sheet recessions has not received much explanation. In other words, many critics simply say that war represents an exceptional state of affairs and think no more about it.

However, that does not mean that balance sheet recessions cannot be overcome *without* war and its attendant death and destruction. War overcomes balance sheet recessions not because it kills and destroys, but because it forces governments to respond to the existential threat by placing huge orders for military wares with very strict delivery times.

In other words, when war comes, governments place orders for thousands of fighter planes and dozens of destroyers. Moreover, there is no time for slacking, because delayed deliveries invariably mean lost battles, if not lost wars. In other words, the delivery time is just as important as the size of the order. These massive orders are even placed at companies with balance sheet problems, because the key consideration in a war is productive capacity and technological strength, not financial soundness.

The huge orders with extremely short delivery times invariably strain companies' existing production capacity. These orders force the companies to engage in capital investment and to take on additional workers to meet the deadlines. Thus, suddenly they are forced to act in a forward-looking fashion in a way that they would never have considered during peacetime.

If companies are to engage in capital investment, they need cash. Those companies with balance sheet problems, however, are unlikely to have plentiful funds at hand. However, financial institutions will be more than happy to lend money if the company already has a huge order to fill, and the source of the order is the government — the most trustworthy customer of all.

Once that happens, money that had been sitting in financial institutions is suddenly reintroduced back into the real economy, creating additional income streams. Thus, even if many companies still have balance sheet problems, the economy surges forward toward recovery as production and incomes expand rapidly.

Moreover, when production and incomes recover, people feel better, and they tend to spend more money, which soon creates new demand outside the government, where the demand first originated. Eventually, this leads to a virtuous cycle of a healthier economy and rising asset prices, which brings closer the goal of balance sheet adjustment.

In other words, it is not war that overcomes the balance sheet recession; it is the huge orders with extremely short delivery times coming from the government that pull the economy out of the vicious cycle and away from the fallacy of composition.

Even if the central banks were to target inflation and encourage companies to borrow more on the basis that the debt would eventually be eroded by inflation, those firms beset by balance sheet problems are unlikely to respond until they have resolved their balance sheet problems. However, even those companies saddled with considerable balance sheet problems would probably borrow money in order to expand their capacity to handle orders from the government if such orders actually materialized. It is for this reason that during balance sheet recession, it is the fiscal policy, not monetary policy, which can make an impact.

GOVERNMENT SPENDING OVER THE LAST 12 YEARS HAS BEEN TOO CAUTIOUS

If we look at the current problems facing Japan from that perspective, it is obvious that even though government spending over the last decade has not been insignificant, it was never put in in such a way as to create excess demand and shortages. Indeed, there has been no sign of companies battling to meet strict delivery times. On the contrary, companies have more commonly had the idea of trying to live on a limited order for as long as possible. Because it was offered only in dribs and drabs, even ¥140 trillion of fiscal stimulus was barely enough to stop the vicious cycle. Moreover, as mentioned earlier, as the economic slump continued, people became steadily more pessimistic. This prompted businesses to lower their leverage, which added to the already considerable momentum toward debt repayment, and worsened the fallacy of composition problems throughout the country.

Moreover, since the Koizumi administration took office, there has been nothing but talk of freezing public spending. In other words, the government has been moving further and further away from what it should be doing in a time of balance sheet recession. As a result, even those companies existing on government orders are giving no thought to increasing capital spending or adding more workers. The government and the MOF, therefore, are conducting all spending at present in a way that will have the least impact. The result is that the fiscal deficit mounts, while the economy fails to move into a virtuous cycle.

LEARNING FROM THE QIN DYNASTY

In thinking about how to prevent the economy from becoming steadily poorer, it might be worth looking at an example from ancient China. Emperor Ying Zheng of the Qin dynasty is credited with being the first emperor to unify China and with building the Great Wall. Before he embarked on unifying China, he asked Cheng Guo, an accomplished civil engineer, to design a great canal in order to extend the irrigation system and boost agricultural production.

However, the canal was not ready after three years, and upon investigation it became clear that engineer Cheng Guo was actually a spy from a rival kingdom. By directing all of Qin's energies into building the canal, Cheng Guo was trying to prevent Qin from attacking other countries. When the truth was uncovered, everyone believed that Emperor Zheng would instantly put Cheng Guo to death. However, Zheng instead told Cheng Guo that he would spare his life if the engineering works were completed within one year — not the five years he had originally been promised. As a result, Cheng Guo completed the project the following year. Completion of the canal became a vital part of Qin's efforts to unify China.

If Emperor Zheng had been a narrow-minded leader, he would have put Cheng Guo to death upon discovering the truth, the project would have been abandoned, and work which had taken up the country's efforts for several years would have been lost. Naturally, the unification project would probably also have been rendered impossible.

I wonder whether this story might not also have some bearing on the current situation in Japan. When it comes to Japanese public works, the road lobbyists and the dam lobbyists lurk behind the scenes, some of whom are working only to secure works budgets for their own constituencies, rather than aiming for what public works are meant to achieve.

After decades of such pork-barrel politics, the Japanese population is having an allergic reaction to all the nonsense occurring in the country at large, which in turn is placing all public works spending in jeopardy.

However, if all public works spending were frozen, that would generate a huge loss since all the half-completed projects would be junked. Moreover, if this then led to the collapse of city planning that had been predicated upon the completion of those public works, this would mean dramatic losses in the future as well.

HOW EXCESS DEMAND COULD BE CREATED BY HALVING COMPLETION TIMES

One way to put the economy into a virtuous cycle while overcoming the above-mentioned public allergy is to follow the example of Emperor Ying Zheng and drastically shorten the delivery times for the most meaningful public works projects. If the entire budget were retained, but the required delivery time were halved, for example, this would probably make contractors desperate. They would also become far more intensely focused on the work, since if they do not meet their deadlines, they would not be considered for public works again.

If completion times were halved, that might lead to a sudden shortage in capacity, workers, cement, and steel. Even though there would be excess capacity and supply if the job were done over a period of four years, there would be a shortage of capacity if contractors were told to complete the same task in two years. If that were to happen, there would be a shortage throughout Japan, and, like government spending in a time of war, this might push the economy into a virtuous cycle.

For instance, there are more than 2,000 kilometers of expressway still scheduled for construction. It seems there are some wasteful elements to the expressway plan, so the first thing to do would be to follow Prime Minister Koizumi and Naoki Inose, an outspoken advocate of privatization, and eliminate the 20% of proposed expressway work that is likely to be used least frequently. Of course, routes that are constantly jammed due to excessive demand would not be eliminated.

Meanwhile, for the remaining 80% of works, the government could request that construction be completed in half the time, but with all of the budget initially set aside for this 80%. Those contractors that are unable to meet the request would not be considered again as recipients of public works orders. The same request would be put forward to local government. Of course, shortcuts in the work itself would be penalized. Since Japanese people are probably stricter than other nationalities in observing completion dates, they would probably respond to the challenge.

If the above attempt puts the economy into a virtuous cycle, the next phase of public projects would be offered the same way — that is, with full funding — but would be required to be finished in half the time. This momentum must be maintained for at least three to four years.

If this continued for several rounds, and project after project were completed, then people would change their image of public works as a bottomless pit steadily swallowing money and never reaching completion. They might even feel pride in the succession of projects being finished.

Of course, the fact that construction cannot move forward because the government cannot acquire the necessary land (see Chapter 11) is not going to be solved by halving completion times. In that instance, it might be worth applying special treatment, such as exempting proceeds from land sales to the government from both capital gains tax as well as inheritance tax.

If this were to lead the entire economy into a virtuous cycle, asset prices should stop declining and would probably start rising again. If that were to happen, the goal of balance sheet adjustment would steadily become more achievable. What was initially expected to take five years would probably be achieved in three or even two years. The case would be closed if this then led to recovery of private sector investments sufficient to cause crowding out, because that would mean the balance sheet recession is finally over.

Just the idea that asset prices have stopped falling will ease the anxiety of people in no small way. For without asset prices stabilizing, people cannot plan ahead at all. Once asset prices have stabilized, people will know exactly how long it will take them to repair their balance sheets. That, in turn, will allow them to make forward-looking plans that are consistent with their balance sheet repair schedules.

Even if the bond markets were to suffer a selloff as the fiscal deficit swelled over the near term, in time the balance sheet recession would come to an end, and fiscal retrenchment would once more become a possibility. This improved long-term prospect would probably lead to a more positive reaction in the bond markets. Moreover, if the economy improves, then asset prices should rise.

By contrast, in the current rather half-hearted stop-and-go application of fiscal stimulus, the economy may fail to enter a virtuous cycle for a long time, while the government deficit continues to pile up over the longer term, which leaves open the possibility that people will move to sell bonds at some point.

Rather than continue to spend ¥30 trillion per annum in a stop-and-go fashion and racking up fiscal deficits, if the government moved to create a "war-like" economic situation by placing large orders with strict delivery times so that the mood in the economy changes from that of excess supply to excess demand, it may be possible to end the balance sheet recession much faster than is forecasted here.

MOST DANGEROUS AND YET MOST PROMISING ECONOMY

If Japan were to make it clear to the world that fiscal stimulus is needed because its corporate sector is intent on paying down debt for balance sheet reasons while the household sector continues to save, people would appreciate fiscal stimulus instead of opposing it. Moreover, once this point was understood, international investors would look at Japan in a totally different light.

Of the three major global economic regions — the U.S., Europe, and Japan — Japan is clearly in the greatest peril if the respective governments fail to take any action. After all, Japan has been in a decade-long recession and the sharp decline in asset values means that both individuals and corporations (including banks) have been weakened considerably. Since Japan needs the government's deficit spending to the tune of 6–7% of GDP just to maintain 0% growth, if the government were to pull the plug, the economy would collapse into depression in no time. In contrast, both the U.S. and Europe are still enjoying relatively high levels of economic activity even though some slowdown has been observed recently. Thus, in the absence of government actions, the most dangerous region among the three is Japan.

On the other hand, of the three regions, Japan is likely to react most positively if the respective governments adopt the correct policies. This is because both the U.S. and Europe experienced a big bubble in their stock markets only two years ago, with share prices reaching record highs. But the bubble then collapsed, causing many people to lose not only their wealth, but also their investment bearings. People who thought they were going to make a lot of money then realized that they had become trapped in a bubble.

Having lost their frame of reference as to what are good and bad investments, these people tend to become easily swayed by news of all kinds, since they are no longer sure of what to trust. This adds huge volatility to the markets that cannot be tamed until a new frame of reference is found, a process that takes a long time. In the meantime, instability in the market will persist no matter what action the government takes.

Indeed, optimism and pessimism have alternated on the European and U.S. equities markets every few days or weeks in a roller-coaster fashion ever since the bubble burst. With people losing their bearings, the markets have fluctuated wildly depending on whatever index or announcement happened to be released at the time. Thus, one day it could be the disappointing earnings forecast from a major IT company, while the next day it could be an upbeat announcement from Alan Greenspan.

This being the case, even if the levels of economic activity in the U.S. and Europe are much higher than in Japan today, there are still major uncertainties in terms of stability. In other words, the economy and share prices could rise further, but on the other hand there is also a good chance that they could move sharply in the opposite direction.

This kind of pattern was also observed in Japan after the bubble collapsed. In the 1992–93 period, for example, it was common for people to think that "the sun will rise again" and things would return to where they were before, only to succumb a few weeks later to a kind of universal pessimism. In this kind of situation, the instability will continue no matter what monetary and fiscal policies the authorities adopt. Indeed, the instability will not go away until people start to have renewed confidence in their ability to judge asset prices.

Furthermore, in the case of Europe, the Maastricht Treaty prevents European governments from actively using fiscal stimulus to stabilize the economy. This limitation can cause deadly results if and when Europe falls into a balance sheet recession. In view of the fact that the fall in share prices in Germany and other parts of Europe is far from insignificant, policymakers there should prepare for a balance sheet recession before a full-blown recession hits the region.

INVESTORS HAVE STARTED TO REALIZE THAT DOWNSIDE RISKS IN JAPAN ARE MINIMAL

In Japan, however, the bubble collapsed more than 10 years ago, and asset prices have already fallen very substantially. Commercial real estate has already fallen on average some 85% compared to peak prices, and share prices are also down nearly 70%.

What this means is that (except for the skepticism of Japanese businessmen and overseas investors mentioned above), the Japanese economy and the markets are likely to respond quickly and positively if the government adopts the correct policies (in this case, aggressive fiscal spending) and explains to the world why it is doing so. In other words, if the government were to put in a large enough fiscal stimulus with the proper pledge and justification, as mentioned earlier, Japan would have a tremendous upside potential as an investment destination, without the sort of downside risk that exists in the U.S. and Europe. It could even be argued that Japanese asset prices could go as high as the late 1996 levels if all the policy mistakes made since 1997 were corrected and reversed.

If overseas and Japanese investors realize this, then it stands to reason that if the government were to take the above-mentioned actions, they would bring their money back to Japan. The fact that many international investors are under-weight on Japan could also add to the inflow of funds into the Japanese markets. If that happens, then we could be looking at a "buy Japan" rush — that is, a simultaneous rise in the yen and in Japanese equity prices. This will be a big change from the sort of "dump Japan" selling we have been seeing up to now.

RISING ASSET PRICES WOULD MARK THE START OF A VIRTUOUS CYCLE

If this happens, even though a stronger yen would have a negative impact on the economy, higher share prices would bring major benefits, especially in the context of the balance sheet recession. This is because the rise in equity and other asset prices brings the goal of cleaner balance sheets closer for corporations.

Furthermore, rising share prices make people feel better and brighten up the economy, prompting more people to spend money than otherwise. With both the government (through fiscal stimulus) and people spending more money, corporate earnings improve. That, in turn, adds further upward momentum to share prices. In this way, the economy enters the virtuous cycle. And as long as the fiscal stimulus, which is the key driver of this cycle, is maintained, the cycle can go on for a long time, especially in view of the fact that asset prices have already fallen so low.

Indeed, the aggressive fiscal policies pursued by former prime minister Obuchi caused share prices to spike, boosting equity market capitalization by ¥213 trillion. This period coincided with the global IT bubble, so it would be fair to say that around half this figure, say ¥100 trillion, was due to the IT bubble rather than government policies. Even so, a ¥100 trillion rise in equity market capitalization compared to current levels would still provide a major boost to the economy.

STUCK IN A RUT FOR THE SECOND TIME

At that time, there was no question that a virtuous cycle was starting, as consumer confidence was improving all around. But unfortunately, the

MOF once again put the brakes on fiscal spending. In particular, the then finance minister Kiichi Miyazawa proved unable to stand up to pressure from MOF bureaucrats, and reverted to a complacent stance in which he said that any supplementary budget would only be drawn up after the government had seen the second-quarter GDP statistics that were due for release in September each year. Since this meant no supplementary budget until November at the earliest, such a stance allowed a large deflationary gap to come to the surface during the late spring and summer months of each year. As a result, the virtuous cycle that had started to form lost its forward momentum, and Japan reverted back to the stop-and-go world of the past.

In view of the fact that MOF officials, because of their self-serving fiscal retrenchment mania (explained below), are perfectly capable of making the same mistake over and over again, there is a danger that exactly the same thing might happen again. On the other hand, as long as Japan's political leaders as well as the outside world remain vigilant toward this danger presented by the MOF and take actions to minimize its occurrence, it stands to reason that a virtuous cycle can be both started and maintained.

POTENTIALLY THE ONLY ANCHOR IN WORLD MARKETS

Moreover, from an international perspective, the fact that Japan's economy and stock market will respond to proper government policies has tremendous importance. This is because there is a fear in the global stock market that there is no market that can serve as an anchor anywhere in the world. This is particularly worrisome in the current environment where there is so much uncertainty and instability in the markets. In particular, in an integrated world market where similarly diversified investors participate in all markets at the same time, once one market starts falling, that phenomenon can cause other markets to fall as well. Thus, when the New York market falls, such a fall is often duplicated in Tokyo. And when Tokyo falls, that produces dark clouds over Europe. The poor showing in Europe then comes back to haunt the U.S. market. On so-called Black Monday in October 1987, for example, all the markets fell literally one after another.

With the U.S. and European markets still suffering from post-bubble instability, and both regions suffering from economic slowdown as well, it is still possible that something unpleasant might happen to the global stock markets. But if the Japanese government took the above action and started moving both the economy and the stock markets higher, it would provide an important anchor to the global markets because it would have solid reasons behind its valuations. If the Tokyo market were to stay put in spite of a fall in New York, the European markets may be able to withstand selling pressures as well. If the Tokyo and European markets were to weather the shock, the New York market may get the breathing space it needs to regain stability. In other words, one of the three markets must stand firm if a global crash is to be avoided.

For the Japanese market to operate as an anchor, it will have to attract funds from other regions. That might have some negative impact on other markets. However, having an anchor that can stop the global cycle of stock-market crashes is worth far more to participants in other markets, including those in the U.S. market, than having no anchor at all. At the moment, only the Japanese market has the ingredients necessary to play that role. Although that presupposes correct government actions in Japan, which have not materialized, it is reassuring to know that the possibility exists.

Indeed, there is no time to waste. The sooner the Japanese government takes the appropriate actions, the better it will be for both the Japanese economy and the global markets. The Japanese government showing the way out of balance sheet recession will also be appreciated by all other countries that are now suffering from a similar disease.

THE MOF'S SURVIVAL "DEPENDS" ON A BALANCED BUDGET

Why is it, then, that the Japanese MOF is so insistent on reducing the budget deficit at all times? Indeed, millions of pamphlets which the ministry freely distributes scare people into thinking that a budget deficit today means huge tax increases tomorrow, and thus that the budget deficit has to be reduced as quickly as possible.

The answer to this question lies in a particular position of the MOF. In Japan, the MOF enjoys the kind of power and prestige that few other government agencies anywhere in the world enjoy. Indeed, elected officials, including the prime minister, together with all other ministry officials, to say nothing of business leaders in the private sector, all treat the MOF very, very carefully. In many ways, MOF officials are as close to being considered gods as anyone could get.

This strange position of the MOF in Japan comes from the fact that its officials have the right to say "no" during the budget process. Even though MOF bureaucrats are not elected by the people, they can override the democratic process at will. Since it is they who control the budget, everyone, including the prime minister, has to kowtow to the MOF in order to get anything done.

In many modern societies, the central bank has been made independent of the government in order to shield monetary policy from the whims of politicians. In Japan, a large part of the fiscal policy is also placed outside the democratic process as well. This was done decades ago, probably on the assumption that well-educated and well-disciplined Japanese bureaucrats will do a better job of allocating budget priorities than will elected politicians.

In retrospect, at least until the end of the 1980s, this arrangement did serve some useful purposes because their "no"s kept the government from crowding out strong private-sector demand for investment. At the same time, however, they did immeasurable damage to the democratic process because their power reduced the role of elected officials to that of begging the MOF for more money. Furthermore, politicians cannot be held accountable for not accomplishing their election pledges, because they could always argue that the MOF blocked their efforts.

Although MOF officials did command the respect of the people until the end of the 1980s, their credibility began to suffer following a series of scandals and a poor track record on the economy in the 1990s. The scandals exposed the officials' arrogance and stupidity. Their forecast that 1997 fiscal reform would not hurt the Japanese economy cost them what remained of their credibility. By the second half of the 1990s, for example, few people trusted their economic forecasts or banking statistics.

This situation led to a major breakup of the MOF in 1998, when the Bank of Japan was removed from the MOF's influence and made completely independent, and bank supervisors were grouped into a separate agency, the Financial Services Agency. The MOF's influence and prestige have now fallen to an all-time low.

Naturally, MOF officials had to think about ways to rebuild the ministry's influence, and here, they went back to the basics. In other words, they returned to their right to say "no" during the budget process. After all, without this power, they would have no more influence than the Treasury Department in the U.S. However, with a tarnished image, they needed a legitimacy to justify their "no," and nothing was more ideal for this purpose than the large budget deficit. In effect, the MOF is using the budget deficit as the justification to say "no" in order to regain the influence it has lost over the last decade.

For this strategy to work, the budget deficit must be portrayed as something unquestionably bad. If the budget deficit is viewed positively, as something that is helpful in a balance sheet recession, MOF officials will not be able to use it to legitimatize their "no"s. But if they cannot say "no," no one will pay them any respect.

This requirement makes it difficult for them to admit that Japan is in a balance sheet recession, because doing so will open the door to a positive evaluation of the deficit. Thus, in spite of overwhelming evidence to the contrary, they have continued to insist on the structural argument for Japan's ills. As a result, even though the vast majority of companies are paying down debt even at 0% interest rates, balance sheet problems have never made it to the official explanation for the recession. Furthermore, they have the need to equate the deficit today with dreaded tax increases tomorrow, so that people will not try to override their "no"s.

It must be said that the MOF officials have largely succeeded in their efforts. As a result of their massive propaganda efforts toward a balanced budget for its own sake, it has become very difficult for the media and politicians to think about fiscal stimulus in a positive way, thus depriving Japan of the most potent medicine against the balance sheet recession.

The MOF has succeeded in maintaining power, and many elected officials, including the prime minister, are back kowtowing to the MOF. But they have also succeeded in crushing two virtuous cycles that could have pulled Japan out of its balance sheet recession long ago. Their "no"s have also ended up increasing both the hardship experienced by the Japanese people, as well as the budget deficit, as was painfully clear in the 1997 fiasco.

Put differently, their "no"s probably served a useful purpose from the 1950s up to the 1980s, in the sense that they kept the government from crowding out private-sector investments. However, from the 1990s, when Japan entered its balance sheet recession, the presence of an all-powerful Ministry of Finance hell-bent on reducing the budget deficit has been the single greatest obstacle to Japan's economic recovery.

SPENDING CUTS, RATHER THAN TAX INCREASES

Thanks to MOF's persistent propaganda efforts, the idea that the "budget deficit is nothing but postponement of tax increases" is firmly rooted in the fiscal policy debate in Japan. However, increasing taxes is only one of the many options (for example, spending cuts, debt rollover) for redeeming government bonds. Not only that, increasing taxes is often the worst option.

This is evident from the persistent arguments of former Federal Reserve chairman Paul. A. Volcker and its present chairman, Alan Greenspan, when the budget deficit was a problem in the U.S. in the 1980s, that budget deficits should be reduced through spending cuts and never through tax increases. The structural reforms in the U.S. and the U.K., such as those implemented by President Ronald Reagan and Prime Minister Margaret Thatcher, were all reforms toward a small government based on tax cuts, spending cuts, and deregulation.

More importantly, the choice between tax increases and spending cuts is for the future generation to make; it is not for the present generation to decide. If the balance sheet problem has been overcome and the necessary social infrastructure is in place when the time for government bond redemption comes around, then people in that generation will naturally choose spending cuts over tax increases. In this sense, it is arrogant of the present generation, and disrespectful to the next, to say that "government bonds are a postponement of tax increases."

5

THE MISSING LINK IN MACROECONOMICS

"INVISIBLE HAND" WORKING AGAINST THE ECONOMY

Although many people are opposed to the use of fiscal stimulus, on the grounds that it is against the principle of self-reliance of the private sector, it should be noted that in a balance sheet recession, individual companies are doing the right and responsible thing. The problem is that when that right and responsible action happens to be debt minimization, the fallacy of composition pushes the entire economy into a deflationary cycle.

Since individual companies are doing the right and responsible thing, the government cannot tell them *not* to pay down debt. This means that, in order to maintain economic stability, the government, which is the only entity outside the fallacy of composition, must do the opposite of the private sector in order to neutralize the deflationary pressure from that sector. That is the lesson the human race learned in the 1930s, and it is exactly how Japan managed to stay away from depression in the 1990s. The fiscal stimulus is needed precisely because people are trying to help themselves by taking the right and responsible action.

One of the major premises of Adam Smith's argument that an "invisible hand" will bring prosperity and growth is that businesses seek profit maximization. However, in today's Japan and in many parts of the post-Enron United States, a large number of businesses are actually minimizing debt, instead of maximizing profits. This means the entire economy is failing to meet Smith's fundamental premise.

Not only that, when businesses seek debt minimization, the "invisible hand" works in the opposite direction by plunging the economy into a contractionary equilibrium, as indicated earlier. Even if all the firms in the economy take the right and responsible action at the individual firm's level, they could still plunge the economy into depression through the fallacy of composition if that right and responsible action happens to be debt minimization. This is a world completely alien to the world of conventional economics which is predicated on the assumption that firms are maximizing profits, but unfortunately some countries today are right in the middle of such a world.

Most economists probably recognize the possibility that a limited number of companies at any one time may be forced to seek financial soundness instead of more forward-looking goals such as profit maximization because of their poor business decisions earlier. But it was always assumed that they are a small minority and that the vast majority of companies are forward looking. What they have overlooked, however, is that occasionally, and especially after the collapse of a nationwide asset-price bubble, the ratios of companies looking forward and backward are reversed.

Indeed, the reason we study macroeconomics as a separate discipline from microeconomics is that occasionally, the sum of micro actions does not add up to the macro results. And this is most obvious during a balance sheet recession, where there is an economy-wide fallacy of composition. One may even argue that the only reason there is macroeconomics is that there is a fallacy of composition possibility in economics. If it were not for this possibility, the sum of the micro actions should be sufficient to understand the aggregate economy, and there should be no need to study macroeconomics as a separate discipline.

BALANCE SHEET PROBLEMS: THE BLIND SPOT OF BOTH KEYNESIAN AND MONETARIST ECONOMICS

Economists around the world have been much intrigued by the prolonged and seemingly intractable recession in Japan and have made various analyses and recommendations over the past 10 years. In fact, Japan's experiences during the 1990s have provided the economics profession with a large number of important lessons. For one thing, the Japanese experience has demonstrated both the limitations of monetarism, as well as what was missing all along in Keynesian economics.

Economists who were on the scene from the end of World War II to the early 1970s were mostly Keynesians. It was natural for them to incline toward the Keynesian theory, as they had experienced the Great Depression of the 1930s and witnessed the impotence of monetary policy as well as the desperate need for fiscal policy to support the troubled economy.

After World War II, however, there were no major balance sheet problems in any of the major industrialized economies right up until the end of the 1980s. With the possible exception of some Latin American countries after 1982, balance sheets were clean in most countries, and most companies were forward looking. Although there was a period characterized by corporate and individual aversion to borrowings, as one of the after-effects of the Great Depression, that aversion also subsided over time. As a result, the need for fiscal policy to provide the underpinnings to the economy was declining rapidly. In the United States in 1959, interest rates had returned to the levels of the 1920s.

At the global level, there was strong reconstruction demand in the regions that had been totally destroyed during World War II. The victor nations that had demand–supply gaps were able to close them by increasing exports to the war-torn nations.

This means that there was almost no need for Keynesian policies in the 1950s and beyond, since these policies are most effective when the economy is in a balance sheet recession. Moreover, the use of active fiscal policies during normal times when balance sheets are not impaired invariably results in crowding out of private capital investment because of the increase in interest rates. Furthermore, when the private-sector balance sheets are healthy and businesses are not suffering from extreme cases of "anti-borrowing syndrome," it is perfectly possible to control the economy by easing or tightening monetary policy.

In the 1950s and 1960s, however, the Keynesian theory was revered as almighty, and was used to fine-tune the economy at every opportunity. At that time, no one noticed that Keynesian policies are really only meant for balance sheet recessions. Even though there were well-known non-Keynesians, including Milton Friedman, during this period, they were few in number, and most mainstream economists were Keynesians.

As a result, and in spite of the enormous efforts expended to make the Keynesian policy work, there was little success; the budget deficits kept increasing while inflation and interest rates continued to creep upward. That, in turn, discouraged private-sector investments.

The creeping price increases of the late 1960s and the first oil crisis of 1973 brought on the problem of inflation and lackluster growth — or stagflation, as it was called at the time. Since inflation is largely a monetary phenomenon and monetarist ideas were better suited to deal with it, the whole economics profession began to shift their attention from Keynesian to monetarist ideas. The disillusionment with Keynesian ideas in the 1960s and 1970s also added to the new-found popularity of monetarists.

Although monetarists and Keynesians were more or less equal in strength in the mid-1970s, the double-digit inflation rate of the late 1970s in the U.S. completely tipped the scale in favor of the monetarists. In October 1979, the Fed chairman, Paul Volcker, adopted many of the ideas of the monetarists when he proposed the *Monetary Control Act* as a way to contain the double-digit inflation. For example, the Act specifically called for money supply targeting, something that monetarists had been demanding for a long time. Although the money supply targeting did not work as smoothly as originally expected, the academic world of macroeconomics has since been completely dominated by monetarists.

By the 1990s, most macroeconomists were monetarists; the only Keynesians left were professors aged in their seventies and eighties. This means that most professors of economics today are monetarists.

FAILURE OF "EXPERIMENT" IN JAPAN

Although monetarist ideas were thoroughly discredited in the 1930s, the burgeoning monetarists of the 1980s and 1990s began to comment on the Great Depression as well. They began to claim that the Depression in the United States that began in 1929 could have been avoided had the Federal Reserve Bank of New York not raised interest rates in 1931. They were indeed trying to rewrite history.

They wanted to rewrite history because the accepted notion that monetary policy was ineffective during the Great Depression ran completely counter to their belief that monetary policy, if applied correctly, is *always* effective. Thus, the Great Depression was one piece of historical evidence they could not swallow.

It was at around this time that a perfect "Keynesian World" presented itself in the form of post-bubble Japan where monetary policy was again said to be ineffective. To monetarists around the world, this was a God-given opportunity to test their idea that, even in a depression, monetary policy could be made to work if it was applied correctly. If their policy recommendations succeeded in turning the Japanese economy around, that would also imply that even the Great Depression could have been avoided had the monetary policy been more expansionary. This is why so many noted monetarists have flocked to Japan during the last 10 years.

Advocating "quantitative easing and inflation targeting," they advised the Bank of Japan (BOJ) to take further steps in monetary easing. They claimed that if the BOJ took one additional step, it would turn the economy around for the better. Since each succeeding dose of monetary easing failed to produce results, they kept asking for more. They even suggested that if the banks refused the liquidity supplied by the BOJ, the central bank itself should make outright purchases of or directly underwrite Japanese government bonds in order to supply liquidity to the market. Paul Krugman's suggestion is a typical example, but well-known economic newspapers, including *The Financial Times* and *The Wall Street Journal*, also made similar suggestions. However, if a doctor keeps recommending additional doses of the same medicine when no positive responses are observed, the patient should suspect that the disease the doctor is trying to cure is not the disease the patient has contracted.

In fact, if the monetarists' world actually existed in Japan, each monetary easing should have produced some response, however small, because at margin someone should be responding to the additional liquidity or lower interest rates provided by the BOJ. The fact that nothing is happening in spite of short-term interest rates having been brought down from 8% to 0% should have awakened them to the possibility that something is awfully wrong here.

In advocating the BOJ's direct underwriting of the JGBs, the monetarists actually demonstrated a lack of understanding of a critical point: that what Japan lacks most at present are the borrowers, not the lenders, of funds. In other words, they should have noticed that both the households and businesses in the private sector are either saving money or repaying debt; that there are plenty of lenders, but no borrowers. Indeed, the most precious commodity in Japan today is not liquidity; it is people who are willing to borrow money.

Adding the BOJ as an additional lender by forcing it to underwrite government bonds directly will simply worsen the already serious overcrowding of the lenders. Having more lenders of funds, however, will not improve the situation at all, since that is not where the bottleneck is.

On the contrary, it may further depress long-term interest rates. Although lower long-term rates are generally welcome for the economy, when they are as low as they are in Japan today (1.0% for 10-year JGBs), other problems begin to arise. In particular, at the current ultra-low levels of interest rates, virtually all life insurers are stuck with negative spreads, and all corporate pension schemes are hopelessly underwater. Their plight, in turn, makes everyone nervous. The BOJ's aggressive purchases of JGBs also deprived the bankers of the positive yield course which is necessary for them to rebuild their financial strength. Indeed, the already excessive competition among financial institutions is made much worse by the entry of the BOJ. This excessive competition is weakening all financial institutions. Even though low interest rates are supposed to help the economy, when the rates are this low and still no positive response is observed from interest-sensitive sectors of the economy, the net effect on the economy and the banking sector could actually be negative.

Those monetarists who realized that there is no demand for funds in the private sector began saying that if the BOJ cannot buy JGBs, it should buy non-financial assets. However, no central bank in the world has the power to purchase non-financial assets beyond what it consumes by itself. That power is given to the government as the representative of the people. And that power is called fiscal policy. Thus, the more one examines the claims of monetarists, the more one finds the evidence that monetary policy is ineffective in a balance sheet recession and that fiscal policy should be the appropriate response.

In other words, the Japanese experience has proven that monetary policy does not work when balance sheets are impaired and people are minimizing debt instead of maximizing profits. This fact sends a very important message to the economics profession, which at present is dominated by monetarists.

KEYNESIAN THEORY FAILS TO DISCUSS BALANCE SHEET PROBLEMS

On the other hand, the Japanese experience also exposed serious flaws in the analytical framework of Keynes and his followers. In particular, they failed to make any mention of balance sheets in the formulation of their theory. Thus, they too, just like monetarists, missed the possibility that companies may be minimizing debt instead of maximizing profits. For example, Keynes had to argue that the marginal efficiency of capital must have fallen for corporations to stop investing. But he never offered a convincing argument as to why the marginal efficiency of capital should fall.[1]

More importantly, even though Keynesians recognized the possibility of a "liquidity trap" in which monetary policy becomes totally ineffective, they failed to offer any explanation as to why an economy, which until a short while before had been responding so well to monetary policy, suddenly ceases to do so. Perhaps this is because Keynes himself was a wealthy man and did not have to worry about debts. His post-war followers, the Keynesians, had even less reason to worry about balance sheet problems because there was no balance sheet recession anywhere in the world until Japan fell into one in 1990. Perhaps, as a result, there is a conspicuous absence of the viewpoint of repairing balance sheets in their analysis.

Keynes discussed the possibility of the economy falling into a "liquidity trap," but his explanation as to why it did so was very forced. For example, he argued that when interest rates sink so low that holding (interest-bearing) bonds or cash does not make any difference, a large number of people would keep cash, waiting for the next higher-yielding investment opportunity to present itself. Keynes called this the "speculative demand for money." However, Keynes, just like the monetarists, failed to explore why nothing happened to the economy as interest rates fell.

They both failed to see the cause of the decline in interest rates, which was the loss of private-sector fund demand as a large number of businesses and households placed top priority on paying down debts in order to repair their balance sheets. In that sense, the Keynesian theory so far has been critically incomplete, since it failed to see the fundamental driving force behind the economic problem they wanted to explain.

Even though Keynes got the solution to balance sheet recession correct — that is, deficit spending by the government — the logic he put forward was in terms of multiplier and marginal disutility of labor for those who are unemployed for a long time.[2] He was not arguing for deficit spending as a solution to a balance sheet recession, where companies are no longer operating to maximize profits. It even appears that Keynes came up with the "speculative demand for money" in order to produce a recession and liquidity trap in his model, when in fact the real cause of that phenomenon was the balance sheet problem.

LIQUIDITY TRAP AS A BALANCE SHEET PHENOMENON

Put differently, the balance sheet view presented here suggests that the liquidity trap itself has little to do with the interest rate. This is because, when businesses shift their priorities from profit maximization to restoring sound financial conditions (that is, debt minimization), it not only weakens the aggregate demand, but also makes the economy extremely unresponsive to the central bank's monetary policy due to the disappearance of private-sector fund demand.

The sudden weakness of the aggregate demand scares the central bank and prompts it to lower the interest rate. But because businesses are already in balance sheet repair mode, nothing happens to the economy in spite of lower interest rates. This shocks the central bank, and as if it was in panic, it lowers interest rates even further. But still no positive response is obtained and the economy continues to weaken because the behavior of businesses has already become unresponsive to interest rates. Since the central bank cannot appear idle when the economy is deteriorating, it keeps on lowering interest rates until the rates cannot go any lower, or until everyone realizes that since nothing is responding, there is no point in lowering rates any further.

This end result is what is commonly called the "liquidity trap." It is a result of both the balance sheet recession and the central bank's panic response to that recession. Since conventional economics did not take up the problem of corporate balance sheets, the mechanism through which the liquidity trap is reached has never been analyzed.

More importantly, Japan's recent experiences (and those of the post-IT, post-Enron United States) have demonstrated that the liquidity trap itself has nothing to do with the levels of interest rates. The trap actually emerges the instant businesses shift their top priority from profit maximization to debt minimization. This is because it is at this moment that the economy ceases to respond to interest rates. The level of interest rates at that moment is not relevant.

But when corporations shift to debt minimization, this results in the contraction of both private-sector fund demand as well as aggregate demand.

That, in turn, prompts panic reactions from the central bank, as mentioned above, until it creates a world of ultra-low interest rates. By including the balance sheet problem in the discussion, therefore, the economics profession finally has the answer to the question of why nothing happens while interest rates are falling to such low levels.

In the case of Japan, the economy was vigorous through to the end of the 1980s and was responding well to monetary policy, as shown by the fact that an interest rate of 2.5% had brought on a nationwide asset-price bubble. As the 1990s began, however, the Japanese economy ceased to respond to monetary policy altogether.

The key difference between the 1980s and the 1990s was the health of the balance sheets of banks and businesses. Before the end of the 1980s, virtually all Japanese banks enjoyed a rating of triple As, while the balance sheets of business corporations were also very healthy. They had ample assets as compared with debts.

However, the crash of asset prices from the start of the 1990s brought havoc to corporations' balance sheets. As a result, they all tried to repair their balance sheets. This was a highly commendable and responsible behavior, yet it has resulted in the fallacy of composition when everyone acted the same way at the same time. It is this fallacy of composition that has rendered monetary policy ineffective. This is a very important point that was missing from both the Keynesian and monetarist analyses.

If we incorporate the balance sheet problem in Keynesian analysis, it can fully explain why a robust economy suddenly stalls following the crash in asset prices, as well as the mechanism of the emergence of a liquidity trap. Thus, the Keynesian revolution becomes theoretically complete by incorporating Japan's experiences during the 1990s.

At the same time, the balance sheet analysis also explains why the seemingly effective Keynesian measures failed to produce satisfactory results in the period from the 1950s to the 1970s. During that period, there were no balance sheet problems, and active fiscal policies only resulted in crowding out of private-sector investments. If Keynes realized the importance of balance sheet concerns and included them in his analysis as the key condition for his prescriptions, the Keynesians in the 1950s and 1960s could have avoided the loss of credibility by avoiding the indiscriminate use of fiscal policy.

DEFLATION IS A SYMPTOM OF BALANCE SHEET RECESSION, NOT A CAUSE OF IT

Those economists trained in the monetarist mindset continued to claim that since deflation was the major enemy in Japan, it could be beaten by bringing on inflation. They have never referred to the causes of deflation; Paul Krugman has even written that it was not necessary to explain why the economy was in deflation.[3] Their argument was that whatever the cause, everything would be all right if inflation was brought on.

It is impossible, however, to analyze and bring the Japanese economy toward recovery without understanding the cause of deflation — the damaged balance sheets. In Japan, it was in around 1993 that people suddenly stopped borrowing money because of their concerns regarding their balance sheets, but at that time consumer prices were recording an increase of 1.3% year-on-year and the economy was in inflation. Japanese companies curbed their spending and investment, and rushed to pay down debts despite the fact that the economy was in inflation.

This means that even if inflation is brought back, there is no guarantee that these companies would change their behavior and stop paying down debt. The argument for "inflation targeting" completely misses these realities. To put it differently, unless the actual inflation rate becomes truly outrageous, most businesses will continue to make their most urgent priority the repair of their balance sheets. And as long as they continue to do so, inflation or inflation-based economic recovery is not likely to materialize.

The root of the problem lies not in whether the economy is in deflation or inflation, but in whether or not the economy has a balance sheet problem. If there are no major balance sheet problems, the economy will respond to monetary policy changes; but when there are problems, it will not. In this sense, the present balance sheet recession in Japan has revealed the limitations of monetarism as well.

FISHER'S DEBT DEFLATION VERSES BALANCE SHEET RECESSION

It has been argued that Keynes got the remedy for balance sheet recession correct, but not the cause of the recession. And because he did not correctly specify under what circumstances such a remedy should be used, Keynesian remedy was indiscriminately applied during the 1950s and 1960s, which resulted in its loss of credibility. At the opposite extreme stands Irving Fisher who came up with the concept of debt deflation in 1933.[4] He got some of the reasoning for recession right, but not the remedy. Since many readers of economic literature might be wondering how the present balance sheet recession argument differs from Fisher's debt deflation argument, a short comparison is offered here.

Fisher's debt deflation, just like balance sheet recession, starts with a state of over-indebtedness that leads people to liquidate debt. From there, there are nine steps that, according to Fisher, will lead to debt deflation:

(1) *Debt liquidation* leads to *distress selling* and to (2) *Contraction of deposit currency*, as bank loans are paid off, and to a slowing down of velocity of circulation. This contraction of deposits and of their velocity, precipitated by distress selling, causes (3) A *fall in the level of prices, in other words*, a swelling of the dollar. Assuming, as above stated, that this fall of prices is not interfered with by reflation or otherwise, there must be (4) *A still greater fall in the net worths of business*, precipitating bankruptcies and (5) *A like fall in profits*, which in a "capitalistic," that is, a private-profit society, leads the concerns which are running at a loss to make (6) *A reduction in output, in trade and in employment* of labor. These losses, bankruptcies, and unemployment, lead to (7) *Pessimism and loss of confidence*, which in turn lead to (8) *Hoarding and slowing down still more the velocity of circulation.*

The above eight changes cause (9) *Complicated disturbances in the rates of interest*, in particular, a fall in the nominal, or money, rates and a rise in the real, or commodity, rates of interest.[5]

Although this idea contains many items that are also found in a balance sheet recession, the causality is entirely different. First, as Fisher states on numerous occasions, deflation is the key driver of his concept without which the economy will only suffer a mild cyclical downturn. His items (1) to (5) above are all about price level and monetary changes; there is no change in the real economy. As a result, in Fisher's model, the output declines come toward the end (item 6) of the process.

In balance sheet recession, however, deflation is very much a result, not the cause, of recession. In this type of recession, the output declines come first because the corporate sector has stopped borrowing and spending the household savings. The resultant weakness in the economy causes prices, especially asset prices, to decline. The key driver of balance sheet recession, therefore, is the corporate sector moving away from profit maximization to debt minimization which not only weakens the aggregate demand, but also makes the economy impervious to interest rate changes.

Although both concepts start with debt liquidation, Fisher's argument is very much driven by a fall in prices, whereas balance sheet recession is driven by a fall in corporate borrowings relative to household savings.

For Fisher's process to work, however, prices must fall faster than the pace of debt repayment so that the real debt outstanding will continue to grow. Since money supply is a function of debt levels, this means that prices must fall faster than the contraction in money supply. For that to happen, the velocity of money (item 2) has to fall. (Velocity of money means the number of times money changes hands in a given time period.)

Although prices can fall quickly in commodity markets, such as those for agricultural products, for the overall velocity of money to fall in an industrialized economy, a fall in real factors such as income and output seems absolutely essential. In other words, a fall in the velocity of money without any contraction in real factors such as aggregate demand seems totally unrealistic.

More importantly, because Fisher placed almost exclusive emphasis on monetary contraction and fall in prices as the key drivers of depression, his remedy for depression is also entirely monetary: that the central bank can and should reflate. However, this is where his arguments ran into massive contradictions. This is because he has already argued that people are liquidating debt in his item (1) and that liquidation is causing money supply to shrink in item (2). If that is the case, no amount of liquidity injection by the central bank will increase the money supply and reflate the economy. As indicated in Chapter 3, there has to be private- or public-sector borrowers in order to increase money supply. Since Fisher is openly against government increasing borrowings,[6] in the absence of both private- and public-sector borrowers, the central bank will not be able to reflate the economy at all. And that is exactly what we learned in the 1930s.

There is, of course, a possibility that a deflation is caused by monetary factors. For example, an exchange rate policy that kept the currency too strong or monetary policy that is excessively tight can both bring about deflation. However, these deflations can be dealt with by simply reversing the exchange rate or monetary policy.

When the deflation is caused by a nationwide move by the companies to repair their balance sheets, however, the problem will not be solved until the majority of those balance sheets are actually repaired. For that to happen, the government must maintain fiscal stimulus to keep the economy going so that the companies will have the revenue to pay down debt.

What the above means is that there is more than one cause for deflation. As such, policymakers must first determine which type of deflation they are faced with and design the remedies accordingly.

Even though Fisher's debt-deflation argument is interesting, his exclusive emphasis on price and monetary factors as the driver for economic slowdown makes his theory unrealistic, and even if it is true, his conclusion that the central bank can save the economy through reflation is totally at odds with both the real world and his own theory. The central bank cannot reflate the economy when everybody is paying down debt. Unfortunately, the recent Japanese Ministry of Finance argument that the deflation is a monetary phenomenon and that the Bank of Japan should be held responsible for it[7] shows that they have not learned anything beyond what Fisher was thinking back in 1933.

BALANCE SHEET RECESSION IN THE *IS–LM* FRAMEWORK

What does the above mean in terms of the standard *IS–LM* analysis in economics? First, when corporations enter debt-minimizing mode and cease to respond to interest rate signals, the *IS* curve goes largely vertical with its position determined mostly by the size of government spending. In a case like Japan, where the corporate sector as a whole is paying down debt to the tune of ¥20 trillion a year even at a 0% interest rate, the private-sector *IS* curve ceases to exist in a reasonable range because savings and investment schedules within the private sector never match at any interest rate. The possibility that private-sector savings and investment will never match at any interest rate is usually mentioned in economics classes as an unrealistic theoretical possibility. Following the bursting of a nationwide asset-price bubble, however, it is a highly likely reality. In this situation, the role of government spending in "producing" an *IS* curve becomes critically important. Since government spending is not usually a function of the interest rate, the *IS* curve so produced is likely to have a vertical slope.

The *LM* curve is also problematic, because in the absence of private-sector demand for funds, the size of the money multiplier depends on the size of government borrowings. Thus, the more money the government borrows, the greater the money supply will be. Therefore, the location of the *LM* curve in a balance sheet recession depends on both the stance of the central bank as well as the size of government borrowings.

The shape of the *LM* curve is not particularly relevant in this case, for three reasons. First, one can get a liquidity trap without the "speculative demand for money," for the reasons mentioned earlier. Second, the level of income is largely determined by the location of the vertical *IS* curve which, in turn, is largely determined by the size of government spending. Third, in the absence of private-sector demand for funds, the increase in the government's deficit financing will increase the money supply and move the *LM* curve to the right. In other words, in a balance sheet recession, an increase in the government's deficit spending moves both the *IS* and *LM* curves to the right. The net effect of this is similar to having a horizontal or near-horizontal *LM* curve in the conventional *IS–LM* analysis. These curves are shown in Exhibit 5.1.

A BUDGET DEFICIT IS NOT A TRANSFER OF INCOME FROM FUTURE GENERATIONS

A grave concern that is often voiced is that the budget deficit may be a big burden for future generations. Some commentators have argued that running a budget deficit is like using our grandchildren's credit cards. Even though it is understandable on moral grounds that people become upset about massive borrowings, when that borrower happens to be the government, a somewhat different perspective is needed.

Even though the "grandchildren's credit cards" argument seems correct on the surface, it can be argued that the actual burden of the budget deficit is borne by the same generation that generated the deficit. This is because the government can generate a budget deficit only if the people of that generation do not spend all of their income themselves and instead use the balance to purchase government bonds. The fact that purchases of government bonds reduce the funds that people can use at their discretion means that the burden of the budget deficit is borne by that generation.

Exhibit 5.1   *IS–LM* curves in a balance sheet recession

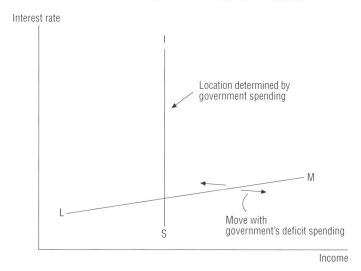

On the other hand, people in future generations, even if their taxes are increased for the purpose of bond redemption, can use all of their income themselves because the redemption will be paid to them. In this sense, it is difficult to say that they are shouldering the burden of the budget deficit of an earlier generation.

Expressed in numbers, let us suppose that the government and the private sector each has an income or tax revenue of ¥100 and that the government issues ¥20 in bonds, which are purchased by the private sector. This means that, in the present generation, the private sector can spend ¥80 and the government sector ¥120, with total spending standing at ¥200. In the future generation, when the government bonds are redeemed, the private sector can spend ¥120, including ¥20 in the redemption of government bonds, while the government can spend ¥80. The total spending here is also ¥200. Since the total amount of money each generation can spend remains the same at ¥200, there is no transfer of income between the generations. The income transfer that took place in this example is from the private sector to the public sector in the present generation, and from the public sector to the private sector in the future generation.

Some economists counter this argument by saying that the present generation may still be able to spend a total of ¥100 if it sells ¥20 in government bonds to the future generation or if it receives the redemption of government bonds after retirement when its tax burden is smaller. In this case, the future generation can spend only ¥80 because it has to pay taxes for the government to redeem bonds. Thus, they claim, there is a transfer of income between the generations.

However, if the present generation can sell government bonds to the next generation at any time (say, tomorrow), there is no reason for the present generation to hold government bonds. Therefore, in order to justify their above-mentioned argument theoretically, they must demonstrate why the present generation, which can sell government bonds to the next generation at any time, should hold the bonds in the first place.

More importantly, the argument that bonds will be redeemed after the present generation retires, and therefore the future generation can spend only ¥80, means that the present generation spends all of the proceeds from the sale of government bonds or funds from bond redemption during its lifetime. It assumes that the present generation leaves no inheritance (both public and privately held properties) to the future generation. But this assumption is totally unrealistic.

In practice, government bonds and other financial assets, as well as social infrastructure, housing, and a great deal of private and public assets, are left by one generation to the next. Such assets may also include the proceeds of bond redemption received by the earlier generation after it retired. But when all these assets are inherited, the transfer of income problem between the generations becomes less important or even negative. Since most people who talk about "grandchildren's credit cards" assume that the government bonds issued by this generation will be fully *inherited* by our grandchildren, they are in fact worrying about a problem that does not exist.

The government budget deficit results in the transfer of income across generations only under a special circumstance in which the government bonds are either redeemed by the present generation after they retire from their jobs or are sold to the future generation, and the present generation spends all the money received from bond redemption or sales during its lifetime. Since these are unrealistic conditions, it is safe to assume that inter-generation income transfer as a result of the budget deficit is not a significant problem.

PASSING ON A HEALTHY ECONOMY TO THE NEXT GENERATION IS MORE IMPORTANT

Some people argue that if public works are to be carried out by deficit financing, what is built must be usable by future generations. Although such arguments sound plausible in regards to private debt, for public debt a different criterion is needed. This is because what one generation passes on to the next includes not only financial and physical assets, but also the health of the economy as a whole. Sometimes it is more desirable for the next generation to inherit an economy that has received sufficient care and is on its way to recovery even if it is saddled with budget deficits, than it is for it to inherit an economy that is deficit-free but is in a critical condition with untreated open wounds and is about to bleed to death.

To understand this point more clearly, let us assume that there were pre-1933 (present) generation A and post-1933 (future) generation B in the United States. Generation A is the generation that, under President Hoover, refused to support the economy through fiscal stimulus although the economy was in serious balance sheet recession. Because it had refused to increase fiscal spending, Generation A did not leave the burden of government bonds to the next generation. (In reality, it did, but assume here for the moment that it did not leave any deficit.) Instead, it left an economy that was in the midst of the Great Depression in which the jobless rate was well in excess of 20% and GDP was only half of what it had been at its peak in 1929.

As a result, Generation B was forced to make enormous public spending in order to cure the wide-open wounds. By 1944, the U.S. budget deficit had expanded to more than 30% of GDP before the nation was finally able to get out of the Great Depression.

If Generation A, like Japan at present, had sustained the level of economic activities of 1929 or 1930 through fiscal expenditures and prevented the wound from opening wide, the burden and pains of Generation B would have been much smaller. Even if Generation B had to purchase all of the government bonds issued by Generation A, it would have been better for it if Generation A had kept the bottom from falling out of the economy through fiscal spending.

The same holds true in Japan. If we call the pre-June 1998 generation Generation A and the post-June 1998 generation Generation B, the former is the generation that plunged the economy into a near-meltdown by launching fiscal rehabilitation through tax increases and spending cuts. Those policy actions also prompted both domestic and foreign investors to get the hell out of Japan, resulting in the "dump Japan" market phenomenon. As a result, the simultaneous drops in the values of the yen and equities torpedoed not only the Japanese financial system, but also the entire Asian economies.

In June 1998, the then prime minister Hashimoto admitted that he had made a mistake and turned fiscal policy 180 degrees by putting in place a massive ¥16 trillion supplementary budget. In other words, the government moved toward regaining the stability of the economy. Unfortunately, the damage was already done and the wound was so big and deep that more fiscal stimulus, plus packages to repair the banking system, were needed. As a result, the subsequent cost of the cure (the budget deficit) sharply expanded from ¥22 trillion in 1996, the year before fiscal rehabilitation was launched, to ¥37 trillion in 1999. At present, the budget deficit is around ¥30–35 trillion.

If Generation A had not taken the wrong policy of fiscal rehabilitation in 1997, the cumulative budget deficit would have been at least ¥30 trillion below the present level and the economy would have been much better than it is now. After all, in 1996, before the fiscal reform policies were put in place, Japan recorded a growth rate of 4.4%, which was higher than any other G7 country. If the fiscal stimulus was not cut in 1997, therefore, the growth momentum from the previous year could have been maintained, instead of the economy collapsing into five quarters of negative growth. In other words, Generation B would have been much better off had Generation A refrained from embarking on the fiscal rehabilitation agenda in 1997.

Viewed in this light, when we say that what we build with budget deficits should be something that can be used by the next generation, we mean not only physical capital but also the health of the economy as a whole. It is often much more desirable to inherit a healthy economy with some budget deficits than a deficit-free but half-paralyzed economy.

During the Great Depression brought on by President Hoover's misguided "sound government finance" policy, millions of youths were too poor to attend school and had to look for jobs. Their life plans were as good as being destroyed by the government. If it were not for the war, which ended the Great Depression, a whole generation could have lost its educational and vocational opportunities.

Japan already has 3.7 million people out of work and many of them are having a very hard time making ends meet. It is likely that a large number of students have been forced to give up their studies, while many families have had to cut back on spending on their children's education. The plight of this generation is the real cost of ill-advised fiscal rehabilitation.

Although the advocates of fiscal rehabilitation always admonish that we must not leave debts to our children, the two examples cited above show that even if a generation tries to reduce its budget deficits (because of worries about the burden to be shouldered by its offspring), if the economy is in balance sheet recession, both the budget deficit and the economy could become much worse.

Debates on government budget deficits among economists have seldom included the issues of the health of the economy to be passed on and of inherited assets other than government bonds when discussing the inter-generation income transfer. By not including these matters, the conclusions they reached were frequently biased against the government running a budget deficit. This omission, together with their lack of understanding of the dynamics of balance sheet recession, made them excessively cautious toward the only medicine that can treat a balance sheet recession.

A "BAD BUDGET DEFICIT" CROWDS OUT PRIVATE-SECTOR INVESTMENT

The above discussion appears to suggest that there is really no cause for alarm with a budget deficit, which is of course not true. The discussion appeared to suggest this, because the budget deficit was viewed strictly from the accounting point of view. The conclusion that there is a transfer of income between the generations only when there is no inheritance between them assumed that the budget deficit itself has no adverse impact on the path of economic growth. Once the issue of the growth path is included, however, a somewhat different conclusion is obtained.

If the budget deficit expands while the private sector has a strong appetite for capital investment, interest rates will rise due to the competition for funds between public- and private-sector borrowers. This is likely to result in crowding out of private-sector capital investment.

If we assume that the soundest economic growth in the medium term will be based on the accumulation of capital stock by the private sector rather than by the public sector (because the private sector can usually allocate resources more efficiently than the public sector), the rise in interest rates and the resultant crowding out of the private-sector investment will depress the economy's medium-term growth rate. In other words, if the government crowds out the accumulation of capital stock by the private sector, the potential growth rate of the economy would be lower than in the case where the government did not engage in such activities.

For example, if the economy, which could have grown at an average annual rate of 3% for 10 years, realizes only a 2% average annual growth because of the crowding out of private-sector investments by the government, the level of GDP 10 years later would be much lower than it would be otherwise. In other words, the budget deficit, which crowds out private-sector investment, also decreases the income of future generations. This is different from the income transfer assumed in a statement such as "using future generations' credit cards," but it still affects the level of income of future generations.

The budget deficit that causes crowding out of private-sector investment is clearly harmful. Deficit financing should not be used when there is strong private-sector investment demand except in extreme cases of emergency, such as wars and natural disasters. A budget deficit that crowds out private-sector investment is a "bad budget deficit."

A "GOOD BUDGET DEFICIT" DURING BALANCE SHEET RECESSION

At the other extreme is a balance sheet recession like the one Japan is currently experiencing, where private-sector demand for investment is clearly insufficient relative to the savings available. In this type of recession, a large number of firms are giving top priority to repairing their balance sheets by paying down debts. As a result, financial institutions are awash with funds, resulting in record low interest rates. In sum, this is not a condition in which the public and private sectors vie for funds.

Furthermore, with the household sector still saving while the corporate sector is no longer borrowing, a huge deflationary gap is created which could plunge the economy into a vicious cycle toward depression. In such a case, unless the government borrows and spends the surplus funds in order to fill the deflationary gap, the economy runs the risk of falling into a vicious cycle, as we witnessed in 1997–98. As described in Chapter 1, if such a condition is left alone, the economy will head toward a contractionary equilibrium, which will be reached when people are so impoverished that they cannot save at all.

At that point, the income of a large number of people will likely have dropped to a fraction of what it was, as we witnessed during the Great Depression of the 1930s. Moreover, once an economy is damaged to this extent, it takes an enormous amount of time and massive fiscal spending to repair it.

Thus, in a balance sheet recession, if the government does not make enough fiscal spending and allows the level of economic activity to fall sharply, it not only depresses the living standards of the next generation but also increases their budget deficit. If the people's income, which could have been maintained at ¥1,000 had the government taken proactive fiscal measures, falls to ¥500 due to the government's failure to act, the government has depressed the living standards of the next generation by not embarking on deficit spending in a timely fashion. Therefore, a proactive budget deficit in a balance sheet recession can be called a "good budget deficit."

This shows that the budget deficit can raise or lower the rate of growth, as well as the levels of income, in the medium and long term (compared with the case in which no fiscal spending is made). A budget deficit that crowds out private-sector investment reduces the rate of economic growth in the medium and long term, but a proactive budget deficit in a balance sheet recession raises the rate of economic growth in the medium and long term.

In sum, it can be said that in a normal world, in which most businesses behave in pursuit of profit maximization, private-sector demand for funds would respond to changes in interest rates. In such a world, the monetarist claim that business conditions should be controlled by monetary policy applies. In this world, fiscal spending should be restrained because it causes crowding out. In other words, the smaller the government, the better it is for the economy. All the major economies, following the end of World War II, were in this world until Japan fell into a balance sheet recession starting in the early 1990s.

However, when a nationwide asset-price bubble emerges and bursts perhaps once in scores of years, corporate demand for funds sharply diminishes because most firms have shifted their number one priority to debt minimization. Then, the economy fails to respond to levels of interest rates, giving rise to a balance sheet recession in which both the money supply and GDP depend on the fiscal policy of the government, the sole remaining borrower. In this world, money supplied through monetary easing is unable to leave the financial institutions and enter the real economy if the government abandons its role as the sole borrower. When the economy is in this state, the bigger and more proactive the government, the better it is for the economy.

The signals that tell the policymakers which world the economy is in are the levels of private-sector fund demand and interest rates. If the economy is in a normal world, robust fund demand would be accompanied by a normal level of interest rates, with the former responding quickly to the changes in the latter. If the economy is in a balance sheet recession, very weak fund demand would be accompanied by exceptionally low interest rates, with the former hardly responding to the changes in the latter.

What is important is to clearly distinguish balance sheet recession and other types of recession. In a situation which is not a balance sheet recession, or in which businesses are not showing its after-effects (that is, the anti-borrowing syndrome), monetary policy should be used to fine-tune the economy. This is because if fiscal policy is used to control the fluctuation of the economy, crowding out may result and the risk of depressing the medium- and long-term economic growth will increase. The post-war Keynesians who assumed that fiscal policy can fine-tune the business cycles in any phase of the economy were clearly wrong.

Keynes was right during the Great Depression, when there were massive balance sheet problems. But applying the Keynesian policy during the 30 years following World War II, a period in which no balance sheet problems were encountered, was misguided.

It is now clear that the mistake of applying Keynesian policies was made in those 30 years because Keynes himself did not have balance sheet considerations in his theory. With the key defining characteristic missing from the Keynesian theory, it was applied indiscriminately in those years, resulting in its loss of credibility.

Unfortunately, a large number of economists in Japan and abroad are still unaware that Japan is in a balance sheet recession. As a result, they are still saying, "Japan may be postponing the necessary structural reforms with fiscal spending," or "The Bank of Japan has a lot more to do." Ten years from now, and after the experiences of other countries are added, the same economists will probably be saying, "Keynesian theory should be applied when the economy is in balance sheet recession."

ENDNOTES

1 John Maynard Keynes, *The General Theory of Employment, Interest, and Money* (New York: Harcourt, Brace & World, 1964), pp. 110–15.

2 *Ibid.*, pp. 128–29.

3 Paul Krugman, "It's Baaack: Japan's Slump and the Return of the Liquidity Trap," *Brookings Papers on Economic Activities*, No. 2, 1998, p. 172.

4 Irving Fisher, "The Debt-Deflation Theory of Great Depressions," *Econometrica*, October 1933, pp. 337–57.

5 *Ibid.*, p. 342.

6 *Ibid.*, p. 347.

7 Hiroshi Watanabe, Director General, Ministry of Finance, quoted in *Reuters*, January 22, 2003. http://www.briefing.reuters.com/cgi-bin/tlogin.exe.

6

HASTE ILL-ADVISED IN DISPOSING OF NON-PERFORMING LOANS

SOLVING THE BAD LOAN PROBLEM WILL NOT IMPROVE THE ECONOMY

The present condition in which monetary policy has become powerless has great implications for the problem of disposing of banks' non-performing loans. The problem of NPLs has been touted as a pillar of the Koizumi Cabinet's reforms, and many commentators both within and outside Japan have been calling for a quick solution to this problem.

However, given the fact that the balance sheet problem is ubiquitous in Japan, the present move to dispose of the NPLs as quickly as possible is not only wrong but also very dangerous. A large number of people are influenced by terms such as "non-performing" or "bad," and feel that the Japanese economy would improve if only this problem were solved. However, this proposition needs to be examined more carefully.

Based on the monetary condition described in the previous chapter, there is actually little reason to believe that the economy will improve even if the whole problem is solved. This is because the delay in the disposal of NPLs is not a constraint on economic recovery.

It is not a constraint because, if it were, Japanese interest rates should be much higher, as mentioned at the very beginning of this book. More precisely, if the NPL problem were really a constraint on the economy, one has to assume that the banks are unable to extend credit because they are saddled with massive amounts of NPLs, a fact that has worsened their capital ratio. Thus, in spite of the existence of creditworthy borrowers with interesting investment projects, the bankers' inability to lend is keeping those investment activities from materializing, or so the argument goes.

But as mentioned at the beginning of this book, if this was the case, bank lending rates in Japan must be increasing rapidly. This is because if there is a large number of creditworthy and willing borrowers, while banks have only limited amounts of funds which they can lend, there would be a race to get that money. Would-be borrowers would be engaged in a bidding war among themselves to get the limited funds available from the banks, thus sharply bidding up bank lending rates.

Indeed, when the U.S. had the same problem back in 1991–93, the lending rate of U.S. banks stayed very high at over 6%, even though the Federal Reserve had brought money market rates down to 3%. At that time, there was a nationwide credit crunch brought about by the collapse of the leveraged buyout (LBO) and commercial real estate markets, both of which hurt the capital ratios of U.S. commercial banks. Because of their capital problems, the banks could not lend even though the central bank was providing ample liquidity. The fact that banks could not lend while borrowers fought for the limited funds resulted in very high lending rates from the banks. (Although some of this rate structure was engineered by the Fed, as explained on pages 165–68, such high rates could not have been maintained in the absence of a strong demand for funds.)

If bank lending rates were really rising, one could say that the banks' limited capacity to supply funds is the bottleneck and that the economy is stagnant because of the NPL problem at the banks. If this were the case, the banks' NPL problem should be solved as soon as possible, even if it takes a large injection of public funds to do so.

However, nothing like that is happening in Japan today. Quite the contrary, interest rates in Japan keep falling and are now infinitely close to zero, which is the lowest level in history. Furthermore, the spread between the short-term money market rates and banks' lending rates remains minimal. This is because, as seen in Chapter 3, the corporate sector is now a supplier of funds to the banking system to the tune of ¥20 trillion a year. In other words, the demand for funds collapsed faster than supply, which resulted in fierce competition among lenders for the few remaining borrowers.

What this means is that even if God were to present Himself today and dispose of all the NPLs of Japanese banks, there would still be no reason for the Japanese economy to improve, since the bottleneck is on the fund demand side and not on the fund supply side. However, if God *were* to remove all the debt overhang of Japanese corporations, there is a good chance that the Japanese economy would in fact improve, because those companies would no longer have to worry about paying down debt. At the minimum, the ¥20 trillion a year debt repayment by the companies would stop, which should eliminate deflationary gap equivalent to 4% of GDP. However, the amount involved may be a tad too large even for Him to take it back. When the bottleneck is on the fund demand side, therefore, there is really no reason to rush through the cleaning up of the NPL problem within the Japanese banking system.

HAVING REAL BANKS IS STILL NO SOLUTION

This view is often countered by the argument that many potential borrowers have gone to the banks but were refused loans, and that therefore the banks must be reluctant to lend. And an opinion like this seems to reach politicians and journalists faster than others. One should, however, exercise caution in giving credibility to such views.

Without doubt, the banks are more cautious than they were 10 years ago. Unfortunately, most borrowers still remember how generous bankers were 10 years ago, and many feel that the banks' lending attitudes will have "normalized" only when they return to what they once were. Indeed, many people still recall that in those wonderful days, just one telephone call was enough to have the banks falling over themselves to hand over money. It is on the basis of this comparison that they feel that banks' attitudes have toughened and they are now reluctant to lend.

However, it was the banks' behavior during the bubble that was abnormal. Even though the pendulum might have shifted too far in the opposite direction, the situation today is much closer to "normal" than that which existed during the bubble days. As Exhibit 3.1 in Chapter 3 indicated, except for the nationwide credit crunch of 1997–98, the Bank of Japan's *Tankan* survey of over 5,000 borrowing companies in Japan indicated that Japanese banks were quite willing lenders for most of the last 10 years. Therefore, one should exercise caution in labeling the banks as being reluctant to lend, as they are simply using appropriate credit screening.

This is not to suggest that Japanese banks' lending ability is satisfactory. Quite the contrary, their risk assessment capabilities are far from perfect. Some businessmen will even argue that there are really no banks in Japan today, only over-sized pawn shops. And the better the businessman, the more critical he tends to be of Japanese banks. Indeed, Japanese banks need to significantly improve their credit assessment capabilities before they will be ready once more to compete in the global marketplace.

However, the point that is often missed is that even if all the banks in Japan acquired the latest risk assessment capabilities and tried to lend aggressively with their newly acquired skills, the amount of lending increase would still be a drop in the bucket compared to the deflationary gap that exists in the Japanese economy today. After all, this is an economy where the corporate sector as a whole is paying down debt to the tune of ¥20 trillion a year while the household sector is saving nearly ¥30 trillion a year, all in spite of zero interest rates. To think that additional risk-taking by the banks can fill this ¥50 trillion gap is unrealistic. Thus, even though an improvement in the Japanese banks' ability to extend credit is needed for the survival of individual banks, that is not where the greatest challenge lies for the Japanese economy.

AMERICA'S FORMULA FOR SOLVING THE SAVINGS AND LOAN PROBLEM SHOULD NOT BE USED IN JAPAN

Why, then, is it dangerous to make haste in disposing of NPLs? It is because the quick resolution of NPLs makes sense only when the banking problem is small compared to the size of the economy.

First of all, it is worth noting that those who argue for a quick resolution of the NPL problem either have no actual bank supervision experience, or have experience only of dealing with the Savings and Loan (S&L) crisis of 1989. In other words, they base their argument solely on the successful resolution of the S&L crisis. Those with more experience than just the S&L crisis are much less enthusiastic about using the formula in Japan. Indeed, there have been more serious banking crises than the S&L crisis in the U.S. banking industry during the last 20 years, and the approaches that U.S. authorities took to resolve them were also very different.

As for the S&L crisis, faced with the failure of a large number of those institutions, in 1989 the U.S. authorities created the Resolution Trust Corporation (RTC), a public financial institution, to liquidate the assets of failed S&Ls. The federal government had had a deposit insurance system, the Federal Savings and Loan Insurance Corporation (FSLIC), for these institutions, but since the number of failed S&Ls was so large, the FSLIC itself went bankrupt in 1989, forcing the federal government to create the RTC.

The RTC sold off the assets of failed S&Ls very quickly, resulting in some short-term decline in asset prices, but their subsequent recovery turned the U.S. economy around. Large profits made by the people who had purchased these assets at low prices had the effect of reassuring investors, which in turn set the floor for asset prices. Thus, the RTC's bold moves solved the problem in one stroke and turned the U.S. economy around.

Based on this U.S. success, the Koizumi Cabinet's "bold policy for structural reform," which was probably written by Heizo Takenaka, the state minister in charge of both the Financial Services Agency and economic and fiscal policy, recommends that Japan should use this RTC (it is called the RCC, or Resolution and Correction Corporation, in Japan) formula to dispose of NPLs promptly.[1] Indeed, it states that quick disposal of NPLs is the number one priority of the Koizumi government.

The problem, however, is that the S&L example is no model for Japan. This is because the S&Ls as a whole made up only a tiny proportion of the U.S. economy. In fact, even though there were thousands of S&Ls, they held only 5% of the total assets in the United States.[2] Only part of that 5% had gone sour, while the remaining 95% was in good hands.

In addition, the problem had occurred only within the S&L industry. In 1989, all other types of financial services providers, including insurance companies, commercial banks, and investment trusts, were healthy and free of the problems that had beset the S&Ls. This important point was also noted by Stefan Ingves, vice governor of the Swedish central bank at the time of the Nordic banking crisis, who said in a recent speech, "The widely studied U.S. Savings and Loan (S&L) crisis ... was not really a systemic one. Rather, the S&L crisis affected a subsector within an otherwise functioning large financial market."[3] If 95% is in good hands and only 5% is affected, the patient can withstand the surgical operation to remove that 5%.

However, this surgery still cost U.S. taxpayers US$160 billion.[4] Even though 95% was in sound health and only a portion of the 5% was liquidated, the cost to the taxpayer was nearly 3% of the GDP of the United States. This is how the problem was solved in the U.S.

In Japan, on the other hand, the nationwide decline in asset prices has resulted in the loss of 85% of the value of commercial real estate and 93% of the value of golf club memberships. It is said that ¥1,200 trillion in wealth, or two-and-a-half years worth of Japan's GDP, has been lost as a result of the decline in asset prices. In addition, a large part of the losses was suffered directly by the financial institutions, which means that probably 95% of financial institutions in Japan have some kind of problem. Five percent of Japanese financial institutions may be in sound health, but 95% have such problems as NPLs, credit rating problems, and/or problems with their capital ratios.

RAPID SALE OF NPLs WILL ONLY DESTROY VALUE

What, then, will happen if a treatment used when 5% of the assets were rotten while 95% were sound is used in a situation where 95% of the assets have problems and only 5% are healthy? Needless to say, it would destroy the economy. There would be turmoil if 95% of assets were put up for sale while only 5% were willing to buy. Foreign investors might enter the market if the assets put up for sale were located in central Tokyo, but there would be no possibility of that happening in the provinces. Trying to dispose of NPLs quickly in such an environment would only depress asset prices drastically and make the balance sheet problems many times worse for everyone, including the banks.

In fact, there was a case of a borrower in a prime location in a regional city who defaulted, and the bank tried to liquidate his assets. Although the bank put the property up for sale, there was no buyer, which is to be expected in an environment where so many businesses have balance sheet problems. As there was no buyer, the property price kept falling until it was low enough to find a buyer. The problem is that if other borrowers in the same area were revalued using the price obtained in this deal, all of their loans would be classified as problem loans as the value of the collateral has fallen to a fraction of its original value.

This shows how precarious Japan's situation is. To advocate the rapid liquidation of NPLs when there are so few buyers left is not only unrealistic but also extremely reckless.

In the Nordic banking crisis of the early 1990s, the authorities took pains to ensure that the asset values of banks were protected "through careful management," rather than destroyed "through [a] rapid fire sale," according to Stefan Ingves. This was because the Nordic crisis was a systemic banking crisis where "no private investors were available — as they seldom are in a systemic crisis."[5]

Unfortunately, none of the senior officials in the United States, including the former Treasury secretary Paul O'Neal, have ever had to deal with a systemic situation like the one Japan finds itself in today. All they know about is the S&L fiasco, and so they urge Japan to follow their example. But the S&L formula, which was used when 5% of the assets were in trouble, is no model for Japan, where 95% have problems. The use of the RTC formula in present-day Japan is nonsense.

JAPANESE CASE HAS SIMILARITIES TO THE LATIN AMERICAN DEBT CRISIS IN 1982

Has the United States ever experienced a situation like Japan's? In recent history, the closest the U.S. has come to a situation like the one we have in Japan today is the Latin American debt crisis of 1982. Between the second half of the 1970s and 1982, hundreds of American banks, including all of the big banks, formed syndicates to lend massive amounts of money to Latin American countries, including Mexico, Brazil, Argentina, Chile, and Venezuela. Just like the Asian boom prior to the currency crisis of 1997, there was a Latin American boom among bankers, lasting from the late 1970s until August 1982. There were 15,000 banks in the United States at that time, and in addition to all of the big banks, an enormous number of small and medium-sized banks were involved in the Latin American lending boom. Big banks in Japan, Canada, the Arab nations, and Europe also got on the bandwagon to lend to Latin America.

The Falklands War between the United Kingdom and Argentina, which broke out in 1982, forced these banks to re-examine the risks of lending to Latin America. And problems arose all at once. In August 1982, Mexico realized that it had no dollars with which to make debt payments. Then, Brazil, Argentina, Venezuela, and Chile got into trouble one after another, creating a massive banking crisis.

In that year, the outstanding balance of loans to less developed countries (LDCs), primarily the Latin American countries, by the eight largest banks in the United States alone amounted to US$38 billion, which was equivalent to 147% of their own capital. This means that as of that moment, these big U.S. banks were all virtually bankrupt. And a total of US$176 billion, including the US$38 billion extended by the above-mentioned U.S. banks, was in de facto default.[6]

This was the same systemic risk as the one Japan is facing today, because not just a few banks but the entire banking system had fallen into the Latin American quagmire. The then Federal Reserve chairman, Paul Volcker, made a phone call to the Bank of Japan governor, Haruo Maekawa, on that critical Friday night (Saturday in Japan) in August of that year to ask for his help. According to a BOJ secretary to Governor Maekawa, Volcker's first words to Maekawa were that the American banking system might not last until the Monday. The crisis was that serious.

One of the agencies of the U.S. government that was monitoring the international syndicated loan market was the International Financial Market Section of the Research Department of the Federal Reserve Bank of New York, the central bank of the United States. The person in charge of syndicated loans was none other than myself. I vividly remember those days. I recall that when the crisis hit, I felt as if my desk had exploded in my face.

In fact, every week from 1979 until immediately before the Mexican debt crisis surfaced, the Federal Reserve Bank of New York, which was the only agency of the U.S. government that had the capability to assess country risk, had been summoning the key executives of major American banks to warn them. We would ask them why they were lending so much money to Latin American countries, which were mostly under dictatorships, where inflation was going through the roof, and where both economic management and the current account performance were very poor. We advised them that lending to such countries was bound to cause them trouble and that they should reduce their exposure to Latin America.

Although the Federal Reserve Bank of New York had been issuing these warnings for four years before the crisis, the American banks in those days failed to heed them. Not only that, their exposure to Latin America doubled between 1979 and 1982.[7]

The background to this reckless behavior on the part of U.S. banks was that they were losing their traditional business (lending operating capital to U.S. companies) due to the development of the commercial paper market. At the same time, Walter Wriston, the then chairman of Citibank who was said to be the Don of the U.S. banking industry, called upon banks to lend to overseas public agencies, saying that private businesses might fail, but not the government's. This created an explosive boom in lending to overseas public agencies among the U.S. banks. Among the world's nations, the Latin American countries attracted the most attention because U.S. banks thought they knew the borrowers, and those borrowers also paid high interest rates.

Because of these conditions, when the boom was over and a true debt crisis erupted, we at the Federal Reserve Bank of New York told ourselves, "It serves them right. We've told them so. Let's get them. We'll bring them back to New York and force them to restructure their businesses."

"DON'T GIVE THE BANKS EXCUSES TO FLEE"

On the day the crisis erupted, however, we received a personal instruction from Paul Volcker, who was then in Washington, D.C. His instruction stunned us. It basically said, "Whatever it takes, make sure that U.S. banks stay on in Latin America and keep lending. Don't give the banks excuses to flee Latin America."

While we had thought "It serves them right! Let's get them," our orders were just the opposite. They said that even if we had to bow our heads low, we should ask the banks to keep lending money to Latin America. This order struck us like a bolt from the blue. However, it did not take us long to understand why.

If one bank tried to flee from Mexico by taking whatever dollars were left in the country, that bank might save itself. However, as no more dollars would be left in Mexico, all the other banks would face a massive Mexican default which, in turn, could propagate throughout Latin America and result in the failures of most of the U.S. money center banks. In other words, if one bank tried to flee, every bank would try to flee. If such a situation was allowed to develop, the borrower would have to announce default officially. That, in turn, would mean bankruptcies for almost all major U.S. banks. If all the big U.S. banks went bankrupt on the same Monday, it would have caused a panic that would plunge not only the U.S. economy but the world economy into a depression. The problem was so grave that it was not an ordinary banking crisis; it was a massive systemic crisis.

In view of this reality, we had to call on each of the hundreds of banks in the United States, asking them not only not to recover funds from Latin America, but also to continue lending to the region. Indeed, my job during that time was to produce a list of all the U.S. banks with an exposure of more than US$1 million to Mexico. That list was then given to the district Federal Reserve banks so that the officers in charge could contact those banks and try to persuade them to keep lending to Latin America. The officers in charge also emphasized that we were all in it together and shared a common destiny. Although those of us at the New York Fed were privately outraged, we had to ignore our personal feelings and ask the banks to continue to extend credit to Brazil and Argentina.

Soon after August 1982, all of the loans to Latin American countries were, in effect, NPLs. However, Volcker had ordered the three bank supervising authorities in the United States *not* to treat those loans as NPLs. If they had declared them to be NPLs, the banks would have had an excuse to flee, saying that they could be sued by their shareholders if they continued to show NPLs in their books. As the banks had the right to flee, if one bank fled, every other bank would also have tried to flee, destroying the entire banking and economic system in the process. If that had happened, not only Latin America would have become what Indonesia was in 1997, but the whole U.S. financial system would have collapsed with it.

The U.S. monetary authorities also had to ensure that foreign banks did not leave Latin America or cut their credit lines to U.S. banks that were highly exposed to Latin America. Even though foreign bank exposure to Latin America was much less than that of the major U.S. banks, they agreed to stay on in the interests of global stability. Their cooperation, in turn, kept the U.S. banking system afloat.

JAPAN SHOULD LEARN FROM THE HANDLING OF THE LATIN AMERICAN DEBT CRISIS

Although it was through an almost ultra-legal means, the financial authorities in the United States at that time steamrollered through, declaring that loans to Latin America were not NPLs and forcing the banks to continue to lend to those nations. While this was going on, they also worked diligently to help both the borrowers and lenders recover their health, while minimizing any moral hazard problems on the part of the banks. In fact, the Federal Reserve Bank of New York at that time had a monitoring system that could detect the movement of every dollar between Mexico and U.S. banks.

Furthermore, the U.S. authorities did not seek to place responsibility for the crisis on any one bank in particular. Although the authorities were aware of all the problem loans the American banks had extended, they did not make an issue of it or criticize the management of U.S. banks. Microeconomic orthodoxy was put aside in favor of macroeconomic survival. Such a high-level judgment was needed when there was a systemic risk and the cooperation and solidarity of all the banks was essential.

Furthermore, if a single U.S. bank had walked into a U.S. District Court and asked it to declare Mexico formally to be in default, the court would have had no choice but to do so. But such a formal declaration would have killed the U.S. banking system instantly. The risk of such a situation was contained through the adoption of what we now call the "convoy" formula. The Federal Reserve Bank of New York put together a convoy of hundreds of banks and managed to keep each and every bank from acting against the common good so as not to let the damage spread. In those days, the term "convoy" formula did not have the kind of undesirable connotation it has today.

The U.S. authorities took three to four years to improve the financial conditions of both the borrowers in Latin America and the lenders. A large tax break was also given to the banks in 1987. And it was only after both parties had regained stability that the banks began using Brady bonds to write off their exposure to Latin America, while the World Bank and the IMF helped the economic management of the borrower countries. Through this process, the banks gradually abandoned their claims.

When the crisis hit, the U.S. authorities never called for prompt disposal of NPLs, because the problem was so enormous that it was quite clear that trying to do so would break down the U.S. economy and, hence, the world economy. In fact, when Citibank, which had recovered its strength by May 1987, tried to dispose of its loans to Latin America as NPLs, Paul Volcker publicly voiced his objection. His concern was that if one bank that had recovered strength behaved in such a way as to make it look good, it would create a climate in which every other bank would feel obliged to follow suit, and thus could risk the collapse of the overall agreement between the borrowers and the lenders that had been struck with so much effort.

Thus, the resolution of the crisis that started in 1982 took more than a dozen years. Although it had been very time-consuming, the problem was solved in its entirety, demonstrating that, despite the enormity of the problem, it was possible to solve it if it were handled correctly.

More importantly, except for the tax break given to the banks in 1987 and some funds that went into Latin America indirectly through the IMF, it cost the American taxpayers nothing. When the Latin American debt crisis erupted in 1982, it was nearly 10 times more serious than the S&L problem. However, as it was handled correctly, the burden to the taxpayers was zero, while the S&L problem cost them US$160 billion.

The Latin American debt crisis offers a valuable lesson to today's Japan. With all the large U.S. banks and hundreds of others in trouble, the situation was just like the present situation in Japan. Volcker was quick to see that the problem was a systemic crisis and placed top priority on the stability of the financial system as a whole, rather than on seeking microeconomic orthodoxy. Although it took more than a dozen years, and ultra-legal means were sometimes used, ultimately the problem was solved without any cost to the taxpayer. On the other hand, the RTC formula adopted to deal with the S&L problem solved the problem quickly and appeared to be efficient, but it cost taxpayers US$160 billion.

On examining various recent debates on the disposal of NPLs in Japan, it is shocking to note the near total absence of reference to the Latin American debt crisis. That crisis has been forgotten by the general public in the U.S., including academics and people in the mass media, probably because it occurred 20 years ago and cost taxpayers nothing.

It may have been forgotten because the entire problem was resolved within the Federal Reserve and the commercial banks, and neither side had much reason to publicize what they were doing, given the sorry state of U.S. banks at that time. As a result, the U.S. Congress did not have to amend the budget in order to resolve the problem. This made it difficult for outsiders, including academics today, to obtain information on this crisis, unlike the S&L problem. Perhaps because Volcker's solution worked too well, the lessons of those days are beginning to fade.

VOLCKER'S CONCERN ABOUT THE U.S.–JAPAN PERCEPTION GAP

In June 2001, Paul Volcker was interviewed by *Shukan Toyo Keizai*, an economics weekly, and the views he expressed were clearly different from the general opinion in the United States. He was quoted as saying:

> My colleagues in the United States argue that the conditions in Japan would improve only if the problem of non-performing loans is solved. I do not share their view.... If [the disposal of non-performing loans] is carried out immediately, the financial burden [to the taxpayers] would be too large and the shock on the economy would be too great. However, as it needs to be implemented as soon as possible, we need to understand the level of *speed limits* to see how fast we can proceed [emphasis added].[8]

As I wanted to know the English expressions he had used, I called the editorial department of the magazine. They did not have an English transcript, but told me that the interview had been arranged at Volcker's request. This indicates that Paul Volcker has a very strong sense of crisis about the fact that the views held by high officials in the present U.S. government are so wide of the mark.

But the point is that there are still some people in the United States who remember what actually happened at the time of the Latin American debt crisis in 1982. Since systemic financial crises do not occur very frequently, there are few people who have had experience in dealing with them. Thus, Japan should be listening more carefully to people like Volcker who *have* had experience and get them on its side in rebuffing those who try to force unreasonable solutions on Japan.

If the price of commercial property in all the major U.S. cities, ranging from Manhattan to San Francisco, plunged as much as 85%, no one in the United States would ever suggest solving the problem promptly by using the RTC formula. There would be no one left in the country with a strong enough balance sheet to buy. The Fed chairman or the Treasury secretary would likely say that the only way to solve the problem would be by taking things slowly, as Japan is doing now.

I had a chance to test this hypothesis. In April 2001, Nomura Securities Company Ltd., the parent company of my employer, invited a former top Treasury official to make a speech in Tokyo. During his presentation, the official cited how the United States had handled the S&L crisis and stressed that if Japan moved as quickly as the United States did at that time, then asset prices would soon reach a trough and Japan would then be able to put the problem of NPLs behind it. Then, someone in the audience raised his hand and said, "Richard Koo, who is sitting right next to you, has a different opinion. Please listen to what he has to say and then respond to him."

As I was seated with the sponsor of the meeting, I was not prepared to comment, but since I had been asked by our client to speak, I pointed out the difference in the scale of the present bank problem in Japan and the S&L problem in the U.S. I said that not only did the S&Ls have only 5% of total U.S. assets at the time of the crisis, but it was only the S&Ls that had problems; the other financial institutions were healthy. In Japan, however, 95% of financial institutions have some kind of problem and perhaps only 5% are trouble-free. I added that if 5% of the assets were put up for sale while 95% were in good health, there would be buyers, but that if the situation were reversed it would create turmoil.

Visibly surprised by my comments, the former official, who is usually full of confidence, instantly backed down, saying: "I didn't realize that there was such a big difference between the situations in Japan and the United States. Perhaps I have been rather cavalier in my comments on this matter." It was the first time I had heard him use the term "cavalier" in regard to his own comments. He then turned to me and asked, "If that is the case, what would you do?"

I pointed out that in a situation like this, one should use the formula the U.S. adopted at the time of the Latin American debt crisis in 1982, and I explained what happened at that time from my own first-hand experience. He said, "You may be right. It is important to dispose of non-performing loans promptly, but securing the stability of asset prices and the economy as a whole is even more important." This episode indicates that some of the key officials in the U.S. government have not been sufficiently briefed about the full extent of Japan's banking problems.

FOREIGN VIEWS TOWARD JAPAN WILL CHANGE

Indeed, the majority of people who urge Japan to use the RTC formula are implicitly assuming that the fall in asset prices in Japan was in the same range as that in the United States in 1989. They are usually astounded by the severity of the problem when they see in the data that the fall was as large as 85%. These people do not know the true picture in Japan.

In fact, in July 2001 I had a chance to discuss the Japanese banks' NPL problem with U.S. officials in Washington, D.C. I told them, "You are advising Japan to dispose of non-performing loans using the RTC formula the United States used in 1989. But have you calculated how much of a burden it will impose on the Japanese taxpayers in the event that Japan accepts your advice?" As I described earlier, the disposal of its NPLs using the RTC formula has cost U.S. taxpayers as much as US$160 billion.

As I had expected, they answered "No." This was totally irresponsible. They were demanding that Japan apply the same formula they had used when 5% of the financial institutions were in trouble to a situation in which 95% of the institutions are damaged, and yet they had not calculated its costs. Had they done so, they would have realized immediately that the cost of using the RTC formula in Japan would be astronomical and that their demand was totally unrealistic. It was a prescription written by people who had never diagnosed the patient, namely the Japanese economy.

If Japan explains its situation clearly, the outside world will understand. Unfortunately, the situation becomes more confusing, as even Heizo Takenaka, who has no bank supervision experience and is no expert on banking crises, is insisting on using the RTC formula. Prime Minister Koizumi should exercise the utmost caution in this matter.

The view that it might be dangerous for Japan to dispose hastily of its NPLs is gradually gaining ground. For example, the paper I wrote on this matter in March 2001 and which I presented in New York was awarded the Abramson Prize of the National Association for Business Economics (NABE) in the United States. This association, for which Alan Greenspan served as chairman at one time, has recognized my paper, which presented the same argument that I am making in this book, as the best thesis of 2001. Incidentally, the ceremony was held at the World Trade Center in New York on the evening of September 10, 2001. I went to New York to attend the ceremony and was in the building the following morning, together with other members of NABE, when the terrorist attacks occurred.

Although some officials in the United States are still unaware of the severe lack of demand for funds in Japan and are urging Japan to dispose of its NPLs promptly, on the assumption that this is where the bottleneck is for the economy, the stance of the United States toward Japan will change in the not too distant future once the facts are made better known.

Paul Krugman, for example, has finally recognized that there is no demand for funds in Japan and has commented that the prompt disposal of NPLs was not the appropriate measure to bring about the recovery of the Japanese economy.[9] As I mentioned earlier, if NPLs were the constraint, interest rates would be rising. But actually they are continuing to fall. Furthermore, the Japanese money and bond markets, through ultra-low interest rates, are appealing to the world every second that fund demand in Japan is extremely weak. Therefore, it is only a matter of time before the outside world becomes aware of this fact.

When that happens, the U.S. stance toward Japan regarding the disposal of NPLs will change. However, Japan is not communicating enough. In this sense, unless Japan sends the right message more often, it could be forced into taking the wrong medication. When that wrong medicine causes a catastrophe, the United States has only to say, "Sorry, we didn't know," but those of us who live in Japan will face not only an economic collapse but also an enormous repair cost arising from having taken a misguided step.

ECONOMY TO BENEFIT FROM DEBT–EQUITY SWAPS OR ABANDONING OF CLAIMS

The economic consequences of the disposal of NPLs will depend very much on the form it takes. If the disposal means liquidating failed borrowers and putting them out of business, the chain of bankruptcies and unemployment resulting from this would damage the economy enormously in a balance sheet recession. Moreover, the rapid-fire sale of assets and the deterioration of the economy would further depress asset prices and create more NPLs.

The fact that the Koizumi government has been stressing the "pain" of reforms, while Takenaka admits that they would increase the number of jobless by hundreds of thousands, indicates that they are thinking of this method. Given the size of the problem, such a route could put the Japanese economy into an extremely dangerous vicious cycle.

On the other hand, there are such methods as debt–equity swaps (exchanging the finance receivables for the borrower's shares) and debt forgiveness. These approaches will have minimal negative effect on the economy and, although the banks would suffer losses, the unburdened borrowers would be able to take forward-looking actions. Adopting these approaches could have a positive effect on the economy.

Under the present circumstances in Japan, where the liquidation of failed borrowers brings little value, both the private sector and the government should actively promote debt-equity swaps and debt forgiveness, so that as many businesses as possible can start looking forward as soon as possible. In other words, if the losses to the banks are the same, they should be made in a form that will bring the economy toward an expansionary equilibrium. At the time of the 1982 Latin American debt crisis, when the United States faced a large systemic risk, as Japan does now, the problem was solved by debt forgiveness, which took the form of Brady bonds.

Of course, measures against the moral hazard problem associated with debt forgiveness must be put in place. But in a balance sheet recession, the main thrust of the policy should be to protect the economy from the fallacy of composition as much as possible. Except for extreme cases, shakeout and liquidation should be kept to a minimum so as not to further accelerate the contraction of the economy.

However, there are those who argue strongly against the idea that the disposal of NPLs should be made through debt–equity swaps or the abandonment of claims, rather than through liquidation of the borrowers. They argue that it would keep alive the companies that should have been liquidated a long time ago, and that excessive competition with these "bad" firms depresses the earnings of "good" companies and makes the entire economy fragile. This argument is shared by a large number of Japanese business executives, as well as by overseas commentators.

I heard a similar argument from a senior officer of the Federal Reserve Board a few years ago. He said that the shrinking of the interest rate spread resulting from excessive competition among financial institutions would weaken the financial system as a whole, and that the banks with sharply reduced capital that could trigger such excessive competition should therefore be removed from the market.

He was absolutely right when viewed from a micro perspective. Excessive competition weakens everyone.[10] Furthermore, nothing disciplines a corporation more than the fear that it could go bankrupt. Moreover, nothing rewards well-managed companies more than the disappearance of poorly managed competitors.

WHEN THERE IS AN AGGREGATE DEMAND SHORTAGE, BUSINESS SHAKEOUTS WILL ONLY SHRINK THE ECONOMY

However, this is a view from the micro perspective of a corporate executive. For a policymaker, a totally different perspective might be required at the macro level. This is because most corporate executives assume that even if a troubled company, A, is removed from the marketplace, there would be no change in the aggregate demand and the surviving businesses could share the business of the now defunct company. But in a nationwide balance sheet recession when everyone is paying down debt, there is probably a 20–30% over-supply in every industry. Therefore, an aggressive industry shakeout will shrink the economy as a whole by 20–30% before it does anything else.

The troubled company, A, may be regarded in its industry as a factor in excessive competition, but the total demand created by the existence of company A is probably many times larger than in the case when company A is closed and its employees are let go. In other words, when all industries have their company As, liquidating them all at the same time will result in a massive shrinkage of aggregate demand in the economy.

Corporate executives operating at the micro level, however, do not see this danger. On the contrary, they are all saying to themselves, "If only company A would withdraw from the market, the rest of us would be able to make decent profits. That fellow is making the rest of us awfully miserable." They want everyone except themselves to be put out of business.

The danger of liquidating companies too quickly was proven by Andrew Mellon, President Hoover's Treasury secretary. When he "liquidated everything that was rotten," the GNP of the United States was halved, which means the demand for the surviving businesses was also halved. In addition, the people who had been working at the failed companies became a public burden, taxing society further. Law and order, as well as the morals in society, also deteriorated.

If excessive competition stems from the behavior of a handful of businesses in an industry, while most other industries are healthy, removing such businesses through a shakeout and liquidation would be the right thing to do. But when the shortage of demand and excessive competition are caused by the nationwide fallacy of composition in all industries, the only solution is to increase aggregate demand. If a rapid shakeout of companies and banks is still desired, the government must prepare a truly massive fiscal stimulus in order to neutralize the deflationary impact of such a move. The efficiency loss from such a large fiscal stimulus may actually negate any efficiency gain from the rapid shakeout of companies.

If only 5% of the whole is affected, as in the case of the S&L problem in the United States, the liquidation of the weakest businesses would solve the problem, as the official at the Federal Reserve Board has suggested. However, a totally different perspective is required when 95% of the economy is in trouble.

NO VENTURE CAPITAL IN JAPAN

Another unfortunate fact is that Japan lacks venture capital in the true meaning of this term. This is why people expect too much from the banks and ask why banks do not lend to people who undertake new things, such as venture businesses.

These people are forgetting what the term "venture" means. It is the same as "adventure," in the sense that frequently, only one company out of eight really succeeds. Put another way, this means that seven out of eight firms fail or are absorbed by others somewhere down the line. They are called venture businesses precisely because, on average, only one out of eight companies will succeed.

The so-called venture capitalists in the United States are bold people, with substantial assets who are also extremely well informed about the industry in which they invest. They invest at their own risk and stake their own money in the types of businesses among which only one in eight may succeed. Needless to say, they examine the businesses very carefully and, especially regarding new product development, demand that the management follow the originally promised timetable at any cost. They build their investment strategy in such a way that the success of one venture will amply offset the losses at many others and still bring them large profits.

On the other hand, as Japan has become a mass middle-class society, it has failed to nurture such bold, wealthy venture capitalists. Not only that, its tax system, which is called the most communistic tax system in the world, has prevented the emergence of such people.

Japan's ruling party realized the seriousness of this problem several years ago and revised the law so as to treat gains from stock options as one-time income with a lower tax rate. The party hoped to produce a number of successful venture capitalists, so that those people who have made a great deal of money will make further investments, thus expanding the circle of venture capital investments. Recently, however, the National Tax Administration Agency, which is always hungry for more tax revenues, has caused great confusion by saying that it would retroactively treat gains made from stock options as ordinary income, thus slapping massive tax bills on those who have made money on stock options in the past. As long as such betrayals and contradictions are allowed in the tax policies, sound venture capital will never develop in Japan.

On the other hand, as bank employees are salaried employees, they are not in any position to take large risks where seven out of eight borrowers might fail. From the standpoint of bank employees, one success out of eight means that, on average, at least three or four businesses will fail before there is one success. In the world of salaried employees, the loans officer would be sacked if so many of his borrowers were to go bankrupt. Or he would be transferred to some remote province where his job would be to make the rounds of the villagers on a bicycle to collect their savings deposits. The government's bank examiners will not condone such risk-taking, either. Providing venture capital is not the job for salaried bank employees.

In other words, it is unreasonable to expect Japanese banks to behave like a venture capitalist. Venture capital investing is for venture capitalists and not for the banks. However, as Japan has failed to nurture venture capitalists, expectations are pinned on the banks and they are blamed for not lending money to everyone. But such expectations can only result in disappointment, if not in disaster. What Japan needs to do is to nurture venture capitalists, not criticize the banks for not lending to venture businesses.

SOUTH KOREAN SUCCESS NOT DUE TO BANKING SYSTEM REFORMS

It is said that the economy of the Republic of Korea has been faring very well as a result of bold consolidations and the mergers of banks. Based on this spectacular success record, many have argued that Japan can do the same and return to the path of self-sustaining growth through structural and banking reform.

Without doubt, the Republic of Korea has executed major surgery on its banking system, and its economy has been faring very well. However, one should be very cautious in gauging the extent of the link between the present good health of the Korean economy and the banking system reforms.

Since the Asian currency crisis, the value of the Korean won has declined by 40%. As South Korea, like Japan, is an exporting nation, the depreciation of its currency by as much as 40% has naturally brought a dramatic increase in external demand. In fact, at one time the Korean currency had lost as much as 73% of its value, which prompted a Korean automaker to run an advertisement in the United States which showed two Korean cars and a Japanese car and asked American consumers, "For the same price, which would you buy?" Similarly, if the yen's exchange rate were ¥200 to the dollar today, Japan would be booming without any trace of a balance sheet recession.

The point is that the prime engine of the recovery of the Korean economy has been the recovery in the competitiveness of its products in the export market brought about by the weak won. The Korean recovery is attributed primarily to the exchange rate adjustment, without which no amount of banking system reforms would have buoyed the economy.

The Republic of Korea was able (or forced by the Asian crisis) to adjust the exchange rate because the nation was basically a deficit nation in terms of its current account balance. No trading partner can complain if a nation with large trade deficits reduces the value of its currency, because it is a perfectly justifiable policy response aimed at restoring equilibrium in the trade balance.

POLICY SHOULD MATCH INITIAL CONDITION

In contrast, Japan is a surplus nation with one of the world's largest trade surpluses. And this has been the case for decades. If a nation with such a huge trade surplus tries to devalue its currency because it does not have enough demand at home, the world trading community would not remain silent. Japan would have been roundly criticized if it had attempted to do so.

In fact, Japan has tried to push the yen weaker many times over the last three decades. But each time, their efforts were cut short by an uproar in Washington and elsewhere about the size of Japan's trade surplus. And in all cases, once the trade problem hit the front pages of newspapers, the foreign exchange market pushed the yen higher, not lower. Most recently, as mentioned in Chapter 3, when Eisuke Sakakibara, then vice minister of finance in charge of international affairs, tried to intervene in the foreign exchange market to push the yen down in June 1999, he met with fierce opposition from U.S. Treasury Secretary Summers. Contrary to his intentions, Sakakibara's attempt ended up sharply increasing the value of the yen.

This to say that the initial condition, as it is called in economics, is entirely different for South Korea and Japan. The initial condition for South Korea is that it is a deficit country. A deficit country means it does not have enough savings at home. The appropriate policy response of a country with a trade deficit would be reliance on external demand through a weak exchange rate.

The initial condition for Japan is that it is a surplus country with excess savings at home. The appropriate policy response for a country with a trade surplus would be stimulation of domestic demand through fiscal stimulus. In other words, the government should be borrowing and utilizing the excess savings at home.

This may give the impression that Japan is placed at a major disadvantage because of its trade surplus. However, a weak currency means that domestic labor and assets are sold cheaply to foreigners and, without doubt, this has a negative impact on the welfare of the people through the deterioration of terms of trade. In other words, South Korea is making a new start after making itself very poor.

This is amply shown by the fact that, in spite of the current fine performance of the Korean economy, Korean nominal GDP in 2001 in dollar terms was only 81% of its level in 1996, a year before the bursting of the Asian bubble, as shown in Exhibit 6.1. In contrast, the Japanese nominal GDP today in dollar terms is 37% greater than in 1989, a year before the bursting of the asset bubble in Japan.

Thus, it is not possible to make a general comment about which is better: dependence on external demand through a weak currency, or stimulation of domestic demand through the mobilization of fiscal policy. Each has its pros and cons. The important thing is for each nation to fully understand its initial condition and adopt a policy that matches it. At present, both Japan and the Republic of Korea appear to have met this requirement, even though Japan can and should apply a little more fiscal stimulus.

In terms of initial condition, one country that started with a very poor initial condition in terms of NPLs is China. It is said that Chinese banks' NPLs amount to as much as 40% of GDP. This is not surprising in view of the fact that most state-owned enterprises in China are experiencing great difficulty in surviving and prospering in the increasingly open and competitive economy.

China was also visited by foreign investment bankers and asset strippers who urged Chinese officials to move quickly on their NPL problem. Even though the Chinese were initially persuaded by such arguments, they eventually decided to go at their own pace. And in spite of this slow pace of NPL disposal and even deflation, the Chinese economy is growing at

Exhibit 6.1 Korean GDP in dollars is still below its 1996 level

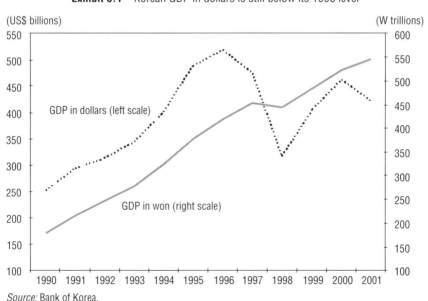

Source: Bank of Korea.

7–8% a year, proving to the world that the disposal of NPLs is not a prerequisite for economic growth.

The Chinese decided to go at their own pace probably because the problem is so big that its quick resolution would have dislodged both the economy and the society into total disarray. They probably also realized that the NPL problem is no constraint on economic growth, that other countries faced with similar systemic problems, such as the U.S. during the Latin American debt crisis in 1982 and the Nordic countries in the 1990s, all went very slowly with their NPL disposals.

ENDNOTES

1 Council on Economic and Fiscal Policy (CEFP), "Basic Policies for Macroeconomic Management and Structural Reform of the Japanese Economy," June 21, 2001. http://www5.cao.go.jp/shimon/index-e.html.

2 FDIC, *History of the Eighties: Lessons for the Future* (December 1997), *Volume I: An Examination of the Banking Crises of the 1980s and Early 1990s*, Chapter 4, "The Savings and Loan Crisis and Its Relationship to Banking," p. 168. http://www.fdic.gov/bank/historical/history/167_188.pdf; Department of Commerce, "Economic Report of the President 1996."

3 "The Nordic Banking Crisis from an International Perspective," Speech by Stefan Ingves, IMF Director, Monetary and Exchange Affairs Department, Seminar on Financial Crises, Kredittilsynet, the Banking, Insurance and Securities Commission of Norway, Oslo, September 11, 2002. http://www.imf.org/external/np/speeches/2002/091102.htm.

4 FDIC, *op. cit.*, p. 169.

5 Speech by Stefan Ingves, *op. cit.*

6 FDIC, *op. cit.*, Chapter 5, "The LDC Debt Crisis," p. 192. http://www.fdic.gov/bank/historical/history/191_210.pdf.

7 *Ibid.*, p. 210.

8 Paul A. Volcker, "Prompt Disposal of NPLs is Needed, but Setting a Speed Limit on the Pace of Disposal is also Important (*Jinsoku na Furyo-saiken Shori ga Hitsuyo daga Shori no Seigensokudo wa Daiji*)," *Shukan Toyo Keizai*, June 23, 2001, p. 58.

9 Paul Krugman, "A Leap in the Dark," *The New York Times*, July 8, 2001.

10 The excessive competition here should include the BOJ purchases of JGBs that are flattening the yield curve and weakening all financial institutions.

7

UNDERSTANDING THE MISUNDERSTANDINGS: THE REAL STORY

The discussion so far has shown that the disposal of non-performing loans should not be forced through. However, there are those who argue that what Japan has done so far has either postponed or delayed the solution. They claim that the government did not attempt to reduce the number of banks, of which there were too many, until a few years ago; that it did not actively enforce disclosure; and that it injected capital into all the banks without investigating management responsibilities. They claim that these policies made the banks complacent and resulted in the slow disposal of NPLs, which could have occurred more quickly.

Since these criticisms were reported widely in the English-language media, many of the readers of this book may think they are correct. However, they contain a serious misunderstanding resulting from both the poor reporting in English, and the lack of understanding of the Japanese economy and its institutional framework.

THE NUMBER OF BANKS IS *NOT* THE KEY ISSUE

First, the banking problem in Japan is not a matter of the number of banks. The root cause of the problem is the severe shortage of creditworthy and willing borrowers relative to the volume of savings Japanese banks and capital markets must place. As noted earlier, while the household sector has been saving as usual, the corporate sector, which had been the borrower, is now paying down debts to the tune of ¥20 trillion a year. As a result, there is an excessive competition to lend among the lenders because of a serious shortage of borrowers. This is why the yields on bonds in the capital market and bank lending rates are both at their lowest levels ever recorded. This is a problem for the entire financial sector, including the banks and the capital markets.

Because the problem is the shortage of fund demand relative to the amount of funds available, it cannot be solved no matter how much the number of banks is slashed. Under the present circumstances, as long as there is more than one bank and the principle of competition is at work, the interest rate spread will continue to remain very thin regardless of the number of banks in the economy. Conversely, if the amount of available funds is limited while there is a large number of borrowers, all the banks will be able to get a large interest rate spread regardless of the number of banks. Indeed, that is what happened in the United States between 1991 and 1993.

The problem that Japanese banks face today is a macro problem, which cannot be solved through management efforts at the level of individual banks. In this sense, as long as the corporate sectors remain in balance sheet repair mode, banking will remain a structurally depressed industry. There is little hope for the repair of Japan's banking system, including its low profitability problem, until the companies are finished with their balance sheet repairs and are willing again to borrow. Unfortunately, most people, including Masajuro Shiokawa, the finance minister, fail to understand this.

Until a decade ago, there were 15,000 banks in the United States, but no one made an issue of this large number, because it is the market that decides the number of banks as long as there are no entry restrictions. In contrast, Japan had very strict entry barriers until a few years ago. As a result, the number of banks is likely to have been smaller than what the market principle would have dictated. Today, however, entry barriers to banking in Japan are in some ways lower than in the United States, since the latter still discourages entries from other industries. Under these circumstances, it is inappropriate for anyone to discuss whether there are "too many" or "too few" banks. Only communist central planners have the right to discuss the "appropriate number" of banks in an economy.

NO SAFETY NET, NO DISCLOSURE

The reason why disclosure was delayed for so long in Japan is that its deposit insurance was empty. The deposit insurance for American S&Ls, the FSLIC, also became empty by 1989, forcing the federal government to put together the RTC. But the Japanese deposit insurance had been virtually empty for years before it was finally replenished in February 1998.

Before February 1998, therefore, if officials with the Bank of Japan or the Ministry of Finance had called on banks and urged them to disclose their true financial health, they would have been asked, "Are you sure we can implement disclosure? If we release these bad figures and cause a run on the bank, how are you going to deal with it with an empty deposit insurance system?" Given the size of the problem, this response would have silenced any responsible bank regulator in any country.

If disclosures had shown that a large number of banks were in trouble, it would have caused runs on the banks. If the public realized that the deposit insurance system was also empty, the ensuing panic could have destroyed the financial system in no time. Having a reasonable-size safety net is the precondition for disclosure, especially when the problem is already so big. When systemic risk is everywhere, therefore, it is extremely irresponsible and dangerous to force disclosure without first providing a safety net.

If disclosures are made as a result of the urging of analysts and the media, and they cause a panic across the nation, the analysts and journalists would not be held responsible. They would simply walk away from the problem by saying, "I was right. The problem was bigger than previously reported." The media urge disclosures because it is their job to disclose things, which is understandable. But responsible monetary authorities should never force disclosures when there is no safety net, since the consequences of the collapse would have to be borne by the public as a whole.

Unfortunately, most commentators who were calling for more disclosure never understood the point that the provision of a safety net must come before the disclosure. Furthermore, those commentators, particularly those in the Japanese media, were openly opposed to any use of public funds to solve the banking crisis, thus making the provision of a safety net almost impossible. Many commentators subsequently softened their position by saying that they would consider using public funds to repair the banking system *after* the facts had all been disclosed. They did not realize that in a banking crisis, one cannot proceed in that order.

Indeed, the resistance demonstrated by the Japanese people to the use of public funds to solve the banking problem before October 1997 was beyond anyone's imagination. For example, in 1992, when the then prime minister Kiichi Miyazawa hinted at the use of public funds, he met with such a strong reaction that he had to withdraw his comments immediately. At that time, I was the only person to publicly support the use of public funds to solve the banking problem. Everyone else was against the idea, arguing that if there is a problem, banks should help themselves first.

PEOPLE FELT NO PAIN BEFORE OCTOBER 1997

The Japanese public felt this way because, unlike the U.S. banking crises, which often caused a credit crunch, Japanese banks at that time were still offering excellent services to the general public, including the borrowers. The services to the borrowers were particularly good because, as mentioned earlier, the private-sector demand for funds declined faster than the banks' ability to supply funds. As a result, bankers were becoming desperate for borrowers. Indeed, many corporate executives were wined and dined by the bankers for the first time in their lives in a complete reversal of roles. In the world before October 1997, therefore, banks were very willing lenders, as indicated by the *Tankan* survey of borrowers by the Bank of Japan (Exhibit 3.1 in Chapter 3).

This means that before that time, the banking problem had scarcely impacted on people's lives. As a result, the general public could not understand why public funds should be used to rehabilitate the banks. And because of this resistance, the deposit insurance system remained empty, making it impossible to implement bank disclosures. This is the key reason why the disclosure in Japan was delayed for so long.

Put differently, had the credit crunch which adversely impacted on people's lives happened sooner than October 1997, the entire bank rescue effort by the government could have started sooner as well. Thus, the same problem that torpedoed the effectiveness of monetary policy — that is, the demand for funds falling faster than supply — also created the huge delay in the government's effort to deal with the banking crisis.

The credit crunch finally started in October 1997. It started because the ill-advised attempt in 1997 by the then prime minister Hashimoto to reduce the budget deficit prompted a large number of domestic and foreign investors to flee Japan in the phenomenon known as "*Nihon Uri*," or "dump Japan." This produced a simultaneous fall of the Japanese stock market and the yen, both of which hit Japanese bank capital directly. Additional clarification of capital regulations announced by the government in October 1997, together with the weak yen and the stock market, precipitated a massive nationwide credit crunch.

Suddenly, the major banks realized they would have to cut ¥15 trillion,[1] or the equivalent of 3% of Japan's GDP, from their assets if they were to meet the Bank for International Settlements' (BIS) capital adequacy ratios in March 1998, which was only six months away. When other banks were added, the amount of assets that had to be cut was even larger. The mad rush to cut lending by all banks followed, resulting in a massive nationwide credit crunch, as can be seen in Exhibit 3.1.

After the credit crunch had started, however, the public felt the pain for the first time, and the government's response was anything but slow. Starting from complete scratch, the government put together the ¥30 trillion, or US$230 billion, package and enacted it by mid-February 1998. Given the extreme resistance the Japanese people had shown toward any use of public funds to bail out the banks up to that point, this was nothing short of lightening speed. This speed also showed how devastating the credit crunch was. And it was through this package that the safety net was finally provided in February 1998, when ¥17 trillion was put into the deposit insurance.

This was an enormous amount of money; at an exchange rate of ¥106 to the dollar, it would have equaled the entire cost of the S&L clean-up in the U.S. As soon as this ¥17 trillion was made available, officials of the Banking Bureau of the Ministry of Finance rushed to the Federation of Bankers Associations of Japan and told them to make disclosures at once based on the standards of the U.S. Securities and Exchange Commission (SEC). The officials at the MOF thought they could now handle any situation because ¥17 trillion would be enough to handle five or six bank failures the size of Hokkaido Takushoku Bank, the first city bank that failed in Japan in November 1997.[2]

With the money in the deposit insurance, the banks, which had been hiding behind the empty deposit insurance, had no further excuses not to make disclosures. The financial statements for the year ended March 1998, prepared in accordance with the SEC standards, were released in May of that year, finally paving the way for disclosures. More and more disclosures have followed since then, also because of this ¥17 trillion in the deposit insurance. The Financial Services Agency has also become much more aggressive since February 1998 in telling banks to get their act together. In that sense, it can be said that this ¥17 trillion finally normalized Japan's bank supervision.

The reason the Japanese banking industry had long depended on the convoy arrangement, or the procedure in which the speed of the entire convoy is determined by that of its slowest vessel, was that there was no money in the deposit insurance system. Under the convoy arrangement, well-performing banks were frequently asked to support poorly performing banks. Since no funds, including public funds, were available from outside of the banking industry, MOF had no choice but to form a convoy.

Contrary to popular belief, particularly in the English-speaking world, no one in Japan liked the convoy system: the MOF did not like it, neither did the industry. Indeed, it was said in banking circles in the mid-1990s that no one should accept a dinner invitation from the MOF. This is because such an invitation invariably meant that that bank would be asked to chip in on a rescue mission for some other poorly managed bank. However, since no funds were coming from outside of the industry, there was no other choice for the MOF or the banking industry.

The injection of ¥17 trillion into deposit insurance thoroughly removed the need for the convoy arrangement. Indeed, except in the foreign press, one heard a lot less about the convoy arrangement in Japan after February 1998.

CAPITAL INJECTION MEETS FIERCE OPPOSITION FROM OVERSEAS

In addition to the ¥17 trillion injected into the deposit insurance system, the government put aside ¥13 trillion to shore up the banks' own capital. The objective of the scheme was to inject capital in order to end the nationwide credit crunch, which started in October 1997. However, when the scheme was announced, it was severely criticized not only in Japan but also around the world.

Lawrence Summers, then the deputy secretary of the U.S. Treasury, criticized Japan loudly, saying that the "bad" banks should be allowed to fail first before the government put money into "good" banks, and that strict conditionality for restructuring should be imposed on the banks before any public funds were injected. He was visibly annoyed when, in mid-March 1998, the Japanese government announced that all major banks would get the money with almost no conditions attached.

Summers was not alone in opposing the Japanese government's move. Practically every one of the Western press, including *The New York Times*, *The Washington Post*, *The Wall Street Journal*, and *The Financial Times*, fiercely opposed it. It was also reported that foreign monetary authorities, who were getting information from these media, sent all sorts of protests to the MOF. Their argument was that Japan should separate the "good" banks from the "bad" banks, let the "bad" banks fail, and put the money into the "good" banks. Some argued that if a bank did not have enough capital, it should be required to raise the capital itself, and that it did not make any sense for the government to put up the money. They argued that if the banks were forced to make the effort to raise capital themselves, it would make them stronger and more responsible banks.

The overseas mass media, in particular, said that the true intention of the Japanese government was to maintain the convoy arrangement and that the whole scheme was designed to preserve the collusion between the Liberal Democratic Party and the banking industry. The *Financial Times*' Lex column of February 9, 1998, for example, states that "... if they have more capital, banks will lend more so averting the painful credit crunch which is hitting many of the government's small business supporters — raw pork-barrel politics.... As a result, the plans look more a recipe for bolstering the status quo rather than a basis for the sort of deep seated restructuring Japanese banking so badly needs."

However, nothing was further from the truth. In fact, the reality was just the opposite of what was reported in the Western press, both in the political and financial spheres. Politically, the LDP was angry with the banks and was hell-bent on letting them fail. The LDP hated the banks because the bankers had given them such a chilly treatment when the LDP was in opposition during the administration of Morihiro Hosokawa between August 1993 and April 1994. Therefore, the LDP really wanted to show the banks who was boss by slapping very harsh conditionality on capital injection.

When the bill to inject public funds passed the Diet in February 1998, the injection program actually required that the banks be classified into three groups: those in the lowest group must be allowed to fail, while the money went only to the two highest groups. Moreover, the banks that wished to receive the public funds were required to produce management restructuring plans and to come before the seven-person committee headed by an outspoken professor at Keio University, Yoko Sazanami, who would be working with the Prosecutor's Office so that judgment could be passed on the merits of the plan as well as on the past inadequacies of the bank's management. These examinations were to be made public, which meant that the LDP was about to conduct a people's court to prosecute bank executives.

TWO CONTRADICTORY GOALS WITH ONLY ONE TOOL

I was the person who stopped the government and the LDP from doing this. On television and through other media, I argued that the first order of business should be to end the credit crunch, which had started in October 1997. This is because, as can be seen in Exhibit 3.1, the credit crunch was so severe that it was literally killing the economy. Indeed, bank branch managers in those days were under orders to cut 10% of lending every six months so as to meet the BIS capital adequacy ratios. Although the banks were doing the right thing by trying to meet the BIS ratios, no economy could survive if all the banks start cutting lending by 10% every six months.

I argued that demanding harsh conditionality from the banks in exchange for a capital injection in this environment was counterproductive. This was because, for the nationwide credit crunch to end, bankers must relax their lending standards, while the conditionality that people were talking about would have forced bankers to become even more selective with their borrowers in order to improve their return on equity (ROE) and return on assets (ROA). In other words, the two goals of ending the credit crunch and strengthening bank management were contradictory.

More importantly, I knew that no banker in his right mind would come up to the people's court and beg for a capital injection. This is because they had a far more reasonable choice of meeting the capital requirement by reducing lending. Indeed, most bank analysts were telling the banks *not* to take the government's money, which could only worsen their already dismal return on capital. The above-mentioned Lex column in *The Financial Times*, for example, argued that "The real concern is why a top Japanese bank should be raising capital when the industry suffers not from a shortage of capital, but a surfeit. Of course, Japanese banks are undercapitalized in relation to their assets. But the problem is not so much a shortage of capital as too many low-yielding assets... ."

Indeed, all the bank analysts and rating companies were telling bank managements *not* to accept government funds in order to increase capital. Moreover, they were urging them to assume more stringent lending attitudes. They claimed that the banks should cut off all borrowers who did not contribute to better bank profits.

Similar views were held in Japanese academic circles as well. For example, Professor Heizo Takenaka of Keio University, in a one-to-one debate with me on January 13, 1998,[3] opposed the injection of capital on the grounds that the Japanese banks' capital was too large, so that they should either increase their earnings 10-fold or reduce their capital to one-tenth. He even claimed that, "to increase capital at this time is against the direction which Japanese financial institutions should follow in the long term."

The Financial Times and Professor Takenaka were right at the micro level. From the perspective of improving bank management, instead of increasing capital, they should reduce lending to those borrowers who did not pay a high enough interest and only deal with those who were willing to give banks high risk-adjusted returns. It should be a case of scaling down business and pressing ahead with restructuring even if it meant the death of many borrowers, both at home and abroad. Assuming that everything else remained constant, such a strategy would increase the ROE and ROA of that particular bank, which would reduce its cost of funds and improve its credit rating.

However, if all the banks followed such a strategy at the same time, the Japanese economy would collapse overnight. Even if an action is right at the micro level, it can result in macro failure if everyone were to take the same action at the same time. In other words, even in the banking area, there was a serious case of fallacy of composition.

Furthermore, the problem the Japanese government was trying to resolve was the credit crunch. Indeed, the only reason the Japanese people accepted the use of public funds was because the credit crunch turned out to be so painful. With the crunch already having a devastating impact on the economy, if the problem was not resolved, the whole economy, together with its banking system, could have collapsed altogether.

ZERO APPLICATION FOR CAPITAL INJECTION

The fact that the LDP and many others, including the U.S. Treasury, wanted to impose strict conditions for capital injection made bankers' decisions extremely easy. When the program was announced in the middle of February

1998, not a single Japanese bank applied for capital injection.[4] With everyone from analysts to rating agencies telling the bank management not to take the money, the banks had no reason to apply for capital injection. And none of them did.

Unfortunately, no one outside Japanese banking circles understood this point — that bankers actually had a choice of reducing assets and were very much inclined to go in that direction. That is why there was a nationwide credit crunch in the first place.

More importantly, the fact that not a single bank stepped forward and asked for a capital injection *was not reported in the foreign press*. Many of them also failed to report the extreme severity of the credit crunch in Japan. This inept reporting, together with the fact that most people outside Japan were not told of the chilly relationship between the banks and the LDP, led most foreigners to simply *assume* that Japanese politicians wanted to help their banker friends and that bankers were rushing to take the money being offered. This is most amply demonstrated in the above-mentioned Lex column of *The Financial Times*. Thus, a massive misunderstanding developed between the policymakers in Japan and the outside world.

Within Japan, political leaders were in a panic, not knowing what to do when not a single bank applied for the capital injection. Outside Japan, monetary authorities and other observers were in a panic as well, thinking that a massive moral hazard problem was in the making on the assumption that the bankers were rushing to accept capital from their political buddies in the government. A key observer in the Federal Reserve even thought that the credit crunch was a conspiracy by the bankers to get a capital injection!

ORDINARY VERSUS SYSTEMIC BANKING CRISES

Against those voices who demanded the liquidation of rotten banks and strict conditionality, I argued that this was not the time to shut down banks, for the following reason. My training at the Federal Reserve Bank of New York had taught me that there are actually two types of banking crisis: an ordinary one and a systemic one. And one can make a grave mistake unless one knows exactly which type of crisis one is dealing with.

Ordinary banking crises, which Deputy Secretary Summers and many others apparently had in mind, are those situations where there are a few poorly performing banks, while a large number of banks are in good health. Most ordinary crises, including the S&L crisis in 1989, fall into this category. In these cases, ordinary solutions, like the ones Summers suggested, should be pursued.

In other words, the authorities should let the rotten banks fail and protect their depositors with deposit insurance, while protecting the good borrowers of the failed banks by selling the claims on them to other healthier banks. As there is already ¥17 trillion in the deposit insurance, it can deal with the depositors of the failed banks. By selling the good assets of the failed banks to other banks, the authorities will protect the good borrowers of the failed banks from any sudden disruption in financing.

HOKKAIDO CASE ALMOST CRUSHED BORROWERS

However, in February 1998 the major premise for using this formula was not in place in Japan. This is because it was no longer the case of a few poorly performing banks in the midst of many healthy banks: it was a case of *all* banks having serious capital problems, stemming mostly from the simultaneous fall of the yen and the stock market. This was why banks across the nation were reluctant to lend. They were cutting off funds even to businesses which had been their clients for decades, on the grounds that they did not have enough capital to continue lending.

This created a problem for the good borrowers of the failing banks. This is because even if finance receivables against them were placed on the market, there would be no buyers because all the other banks were having capital problems and were cutting off even their own borrowers. This means that the good borrowers from the failed banks could not be moved to other banks and therefore would be asked by the collection agencies to repay their loans immediately.

Of course, if there were many other banks that were willing to lend to these borrowers on their own, they could borrow from these banks to repay the loans to the collection agency. However, this option does not exist when there is a nationwide credit crunch. Thus, allowing the banks to fail under such circumstances would crush not only the rotten borrowers but the good borrowers as well.

Indeed, many good businesses failed in the U.S. during the nationwide credit crunch of 1991–93 for the same reason. They just happened to be borrowing from the wrong bank. When that bank failed in the midst of a nationwide credit crunch, those borrowers had no place to turn to. In fact, at a seminar held in Tokyo a few years ago, a U.S. businesswoman who had lost a lot of money during the 1991–93 credit crunch in the U.S. told the Japanese audience to be very careful when choosing a bank from which to borrow money. This is because in a nationwide credit crunch, the bank's fate could well be the borrower's fate. Shutting down banks in this environment, therefore, could lead to an economic collapse of unimaginable magnitude.

In Japan, such a situation actually developed with a vengeance in Hokkaido after the failure of Hokkaido Takushoku Bank in November 1997. Although this bank could have been saved — if the government and the central bank had been willing — the LDP allowed it to fail because it wanted to send a message to the world. In those days, Japan was being roundly criticized for not allowing its rotten banks to fail. Other countries looked down on Japan, saying, "The Japanese government is talking about a financial Big Bang and self-responsibility, but it cannot even let a rotten bank fail." Others were urging Japan to liquidate its troubled financial institutions and enterprises and sell their assets to entrepreneurs who could make better use of them.

Without doubt, assets would be used more effectively and the economic recovery would come sooner if these assets were shifted from managers who are hell-bent on paying down debts and are unable to think in a forward-looking manner, to those who are free from such burdens. By abandoning Hokkaido Takushoku Bank, the reform-minded Hashimoto government wanted to show the world that it was able to let rotten banks fail and that it was serious about the structural reform.

The major premise for such actions to be taken, however, is the existence of private-sector investors who are willing to take over the good assets of failed banks. Unfortunately, there were no such investors in Japan in early 1998, exactly as feared by Stefan Ingves during the Nordic banking crisis. This is because the problem in Japan at that time affected not just a few financial institutions, as in the case of the S&Ls in the United States in 1989, but all financial institutions, as in Sweden in 1991.

In November 1997, when the Hokkaido Takushoku Bank failed, the nationwide credit crunch was already well under way. The banks were not lending because they had to meet the capital adequacy requirements of the BIS, and this was a problem not only for a few banks but for all the banks. As a result, when Hokkaido Takushoku Bank failed, there was absolutely no financial institution willing to take over its good assets.

The fact that there were no takers for the assets of Hokkaido Takushoku Bank in the midst of a nationwide credit crunch meant that all of its assets would be taken over by the collection agency. This prospect created a massive crisis among the bank's borrowers, and the entire economy of Hokkaido began to crumble.

As it was felt that the economy of Hokkaido would collapse if no action were taken, local business leaders and public financial institutions such as Hokuto Koko worked desperately around the clock to find institutions to take the good assets of the failed bank. In the end, public financial institutions, together with a small private bank called Hokuyo Bank, managed to bring back stability to the economy of Hokkaido.

Although such measures had kept the Hokkaido economy from collapsing altogether, it was still shaken very badly at that time. It was said, for example, that when a company with its headquarters in Hokkaido applied for a loan in, say, Tokyo, as soon as the address was written on the loan application the request was rejected because the loan officer assumed that the Hokkaido economy was collapsing and that any company with headquarters there could not be a good risk. Given the fact that the failure of only one bank had caused such turmoil, one can imagine what might have happened to the entire economy if more banks had been allowed to fail across the nation all at once.

HOW RELIABLE ARE THE FOREIGN BUYERS?

It may be said that if there were no buyers in Japan, how about selling the assets to foreigners? Indeed, a large number of foreign companies are in Japan today buying assets left and right, often at bargain prices.

The image of foreign buyers in the Japanese market held by those abroad, however, is somewhat inconsistent with the true picture. This is because since many foreign journalists in Tokyo do not speak Japanese, their sources are very frequently the foreign financial institutions operating in Japan. For foreign financial houses in Japan, brokering or selling Japanese assets to investors abroad has been a big business. In order to advance their business, they typically tell journalists that the Japanese are slow in disposing of their assets and that if they were to sell more and sell faster, the reform would move forward and the economy should recover faster as well.

Representatives of these financial institutions have told Japanese political leaders and the mass media that propping up the economy through fiscal policy would only prolong the psychology of dependence in the Japanese economy and delay the structural reform, which in turn would keep assets from being put on the market. Even though the real intention of these financial institutions was just to buy the assets more cheaply, they argued that fiscal support should be withdrawn so that Japanese assets would be transferred to forward-looking entrepreneurs sooner who can use them more effectively. As a result of such "talking the book" by foreign financial institutions which are widely disseminated by the foreign media, there is an impression outside Japan that foreign buyers are everywhere, and that the only thing missing is the Japanese sellers.

What actually happened was quite different. First, it is true that during the latter half of 1996, a huge number of so-called asset strippers came to Japan from the United States looking for attractive investment opportunities. Asset strippers are people who make a living out of buying distressed assets and repackaging them for resale later. Many of them actually worked with the RTC during the S&L crisis in the U.S. in 1989. Many of these asset strippers asked to see me in my capacity as the chief economist of Nomura.

They seemed to think that if they worked with Nomura, the largest of the Japanese securities houses, they would be able to get good deals on Japanese assets. And they were all pushing strongly for the above-mentioned agenda, which included a scaling down of the fiscal stimulus and more rapid liquidation of troubled financial institutions.

Following the advice of these Western reformists and asset strippers, Prime Minister Hashimoto adopted an austere fiscal policy and allowed the shakeout of financial institutions, actually allowing a number of them, including the Hokkaido Takushoku Bank, to fail. The result, however, was exactly the opposite of that predicted by the reformists and asset strippers, in that the entire economy collapsed and plunged into a meltdown situation, with five consecutive quarters of negative growth. The asset strippers did not realize that, unlike the S&L crisis in the U.S., Japan was in a nationwide balance sheet recession.

What the Western media did not report, however, is the fact that when things did not turn out as expected, the foreign asset strippers all went back home. Seeing the total collapse of the Japanese economy, those asset strippers who had been saying that they would buy Japanese assets only if they were put on the market all took flight. This is amply shown in Exhibit 7.1, which shows the dramatic fall in inward foreign investment in 1997. As a result, no foreign buyers showed up when Japan needed them most — that is, when the Hokkaido Takushoku Bank failed.

Exhibit 7.1   Fiscal reform prompted foreign investors to stay away from Japan

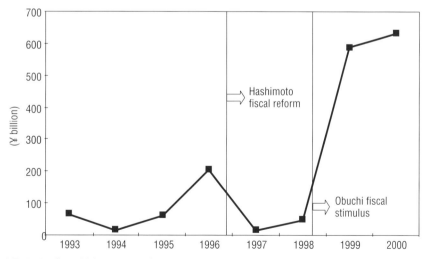

First-time foreign direct investment in Japan

* Excluding financial, insurance, and real estate sectors.

Source: Ministry of Economy, Trade and Industry, "Survey of Trends in Business Activities of Foreign Affiliates."

In those days, when the Japanese economy and financial system were in tatters with the failure of the Hokkaido Takushoku Bank (and, later, the Long-Term Credit Bank of Japan), no foreign entity stepped forward as a buyer. And the economy was in tatters because the Hashimoto government decided to cut the fiscal stimulus and instead push for the structural reform as advocated by so many foreign commentators, including asset strippers.

This response of foreign buyers is actually quite natural and should have been expected. This is because when the bottom has fallen out of the economy, no one can calculate the future income stream of assets with any degree of accuracy. When foreign companies, especially those in the United States, plan a purchase of large assets, they put them through a rigorous examination so that later they can withstand the scrutiny of shareholders and investors back home. This process is called due diligence and is a major undertaking involving accountants, economists, and lawyers. But such due diligence is absolutely impossible to conduct when the bottom has fallen out of the economy and there is no knowing how far it will fall. Thus, when the economy began collapsing in the second half of 1997, no foreign investors could conduct their due diligence, and as a result, they all left Japan.

MACROECONOMIC STABILITY MUST NEVER BE SACRIFICED

The point here is that foreign buyers are interested in Japanese assets only when the Japanese economy itself is stable. If the economy collapses as a result of the removal of the fiscal stimulus, there will be no foreign buyers either. Even though foreign commentators assume that foreign buyers of Japanese assets are always there, in the real world, that is not the case at all. And this was amply shown during the 1997–98 crisis starting with the collapse of the Hokkaido Takushoku Bank.

The lesson from this incident is that no matter whether reformists from abroad demand that the government presses ahead with structural reform, the macroeconomic measures to assure the stability of the economy must never be removed. This is because once the economy itself becomes unstable, the foreigners forget what they have been preaching only a few weeks earlier and take flight. The people who bear the cost of repairing the subsequent damage are the local residents of the country, and not the foreign asset strippers who run away.

Japan is not the only country that is visited by foreign asset strippers. They visit any country with NPL problems and preach that, rather than adopt macro-stability packages which only add to the sense of complacency and increase the psychology of dependence, the problem assets should be put on the market to speed up structural reform. They say this because they feel they can buy assets more cheaply and quickly if their advice is followed.

The policymakers of a nation, however, should never heed the entire advice of asset strippers without thinking about its implications. If macro stabilization measures are neglected, resulting in the instability of the economy, every one of these foreign investors will just flee the country. Indeed, it is interesting to note that, once the Japanese government realized that it had made a mistake and reversed its fiscal policy by putting in a massive fiscal stimulus and bank rescue packages totaling ¥100 trillion, or nearly US$900 billion, to stabilize the economy, foreign buyers came back. And they did buy a substantial amount of assets, including the Long-Term Credit Bank, *after* the stability of the economy was regained. The return of foreign investors is also shown in Exhibit 7.1.

From the Hokkaido experience, therefore, it was clear that the Japanese economy would have collapsed completely if the government had allowed a large number of banks to fail and tried to put their assets on sale. Under such circumstances, the only alternative for it was to save all the banks, including the bad banks, so as to maintain the banking functions of the financial system and bring stability back to the economy. In other words, structural reform is impossible without economic stability.

However, this incident in Hokkaido has created a large perception gap between Japan and other countries. Because of the poor reporting of Japanese regional developments in the foreign press, most foreigners were totally unaware of what actually happened in Hokkaido. In those days, I went around the world to explain what had happened. No one knew anything about it; not only that, most people did not even know where Hokkaido was. I explained that it was from Hokkaido that Jody Foster was launched into space in the movie *Contact*. They then realized that Hokkaido is one of the four major Japanese islands.

The Japan-bashing regarding capital injections can be attributed to foreigners' ignorance of what had happened in Hokkaido and of the fact that when the injection was offered, not a single bank applied for it. Their ignorance of these two facts caused a massive misunderstanding that is still very much apparent today.

In any event, since the case of the Hokkaido Takushoku Bank, a consensus has been formed among Japan's political leaders that, in the absence of any buyers, banks should not be allowed to fail. This prompted them to add nationalization as a policy option to ensure that banks continue to operate even if their capital is wiped out. Allowing the banks to fail was not an option, because if it were allowed, what had happened in Hokkaido would have spread to all of Japan.

Seven months after the failure of Hokkaido Takushoku Bank, the Long-Term Credit Bank of Japan also went bankrupt. The Japanese MOF again tried to engineer its merger with the Sumitomo Trust & Banking or other banks, but every one of them fled because they did not have enough capital. No foreign banks raised their hands either, because no one could make any move in the unstable situation that existed in mid-1998. In the end, the government had to nationalize it using the powers it gained in legislation passed in February 1998.

THE GOVERNMENT MAKES A U-TURN

For political leaders in Japan to realize that the country is in the midst of a systemic banking crisis is one thing. For them to appreciate that individual banks had no appetite for the government's capital injection was quite another. Even though the leaders of the LDP were aware that the only way to correct the credit crunch was to enhance bank capital, there were also those in the Party who were hell-bent on criticizing the banks. Many in the mass media were also still clamoring to hold bank management responsible for the crisis.

In this conflicting situation, I argued that if the ship is sinking, the first order of business should be to stop the water from coming in so that it won't sink any further. The question of who poked the hole in the hull can be resolved after the hole is repaired and the ship is no longer sinking. Furthermore, the only reason the Japanese public accepted the capital injection was because they wanted the government to end the credit crunch.

I argued that imposing strict conditionality on capital injection was a case of one tool trying to achieve too many objectives. The only tool was capital injection, but the objectives included everything from ending the credit crunch to the quick disposal of NPLs. No one, not even God, could have achieved all these goals at the same time with just one tool. In particular, the aims of ending the credit crunch and cleaning up the banking system were totally contradictory. The former needed the banks to lend more, while the latter required that banks become a lot more strict with their lending.

As though that were not bad enough, the time was extremely limited. The market and the press were full of talks about the end-of-fiscal-year crisis in March. That was only four weeks away.

I was particularly afraid of the zero-application possibility because there had been a case exactly like that in the United States in the 1930s. To begin with, the Japanese scheme to purchase preferred shares of banks was modeled after a scheme used by the newly elected President Roosevelt in 1933. At that time, the Great Depression was at its worst, with the jobless rate hitting 22%. Roosevelt realized that the root of the financial problem was the shortage of capital on the part of the banks and he decided to inject capital into U.S. banks through the Reconstruction Finance Corporation (RFC). His scheme had been to reinforce the capital of the banks and end the credit crunch by making them issue preferred shares for purchase by the government.

When the scheme was put in place, however, not a single U.S. bank applied; they were afraid of being labeled as "dangerous" banks. Bankers were also alarmed by the prospect of being put under the government's scrutiny and control.

Being fearful of the scheme ending in failure, Roosevelt asked heads of major banks, including what became of Morgan Bank, to apply for the scheme. The Morgan Bank in those days enjoyed the highest rating among the U.S. banks and by no means suffered from a capital shortage. Nevertheless, at the personal request of the president, it agreed to issue preferred shares for purchase by the government. After this agreement was made public, other banks began to apply for the scheme, thus making it possible for the government to take the first step toward getting the nation out of the Great Depression.

As this case illustrates, bankers everywhere are very conscious of their prestige and reputation. Unless this is taken into account in implementing a policy, the policy itself could end in failure. Since I had first proposed the entire capital injection scheme in public in December 1997, on a popular Sunday TV program hosted by Kenichi Takemura, I did not want it to end in failure. From the beginning, therefore, I warned TV audiences as well as key politicians in Japan about the risk of zero applications and pointed to the example of President Roosevelt and the Morgan Bank. Unfortunately, the LDP at that time hated the banks so much that it ignored my repeated warnings and decided on the people's court approach, with a seven-person committee working with the Prosecutor's Office.

However, when not a single bank came forward, as I had feared, the politicians panicked, because zero applications meant that there would be no improvement in the banks' lending attitude and the Japanese economy would continue to deteriorate. Therefore, taking a leaf out of Roosevelt's book, they forced the Bank of Tokyo Mitsubishi, which at that time boasted the highest rating among the major Japanese banks, to apply for the injection of capital.

After the bank, which needed no capital from the government, reluctantly applied for ¥100 billion, other banks followed suit. With the exception of a few banks that applied for more, all the others applied for ¥100 billion each. This finally made it possible for the government to inject ¥1.8 trillion into the banking system. In the process, the people's court became a court in name only.

Unfortunately, the fact that the government had to change its policy because no bank applied for a capital injection *was not reported in the foreign press*. As a result, most foreigners still believed that bankers rushed in and got their money without any conditions attached, and that they were able to do so because of the cozy relationship between the politicians and the bankers. This monstrous misunderstanding abroad is continuing to haunt Japan's effort to deal with its banking problems to this very day.

In a balance sheet recession, which is caused by the fallacy of composition, micro and macro will send conflicting signals in almost every area, and banking is no exception. From the macro perspective, the banks should have immediately accepted the entire ¥13 trillion. In order to end the nationwide credit crunch, the government should have made the bankers accept the money, even if it had to beg them to take it. From the micro perspective, however, the banks should not have accepted the money, which lowered their already low return on capital.

I had hoped that, at a time like this, Japan's political leaders would have shown their leadership qualities. I had hoped that the prime minister would step forward and say that he understood that the banks did not want the money, but he hoped that they would accept it in order to end the nationwide credit crunch. Since there were many opponents of the scheme, I believe that it was necessary for the government to explain to the people why the scheme was necessary and to ask the banks to come forward. However, such leadership was not forthcoming and only ¥1.8 trillion was injected into the banking system even though the government had allocated ¥13 trillion.

The amount of ¥1.8 trillion was not enough when the scale of the problem was said to be ¥50 or ¥100 trillion. If the whole of ¥13 trillion, equivalent to US$100 billion, had been injected at that time, the tide could have been turned. However, finding themselves on the horns of a dilemma between macro and micro, and being criticized by the U.S. Treasury and uninformed mass media both at home and abroad, both the banks and politicians wavered, which has resulted in a sorry outcome.

Even so, the injection of capital to all banks had the effect of ending the panic withdrawals of deposits, which had started at the end of 1997. The "Japan premium" the Japanese banks had to pay in raising funds overseas also declined sharply by April 1998. In that sense, it was better than nothing, but ¥1.8 trillion was still not enough to turn the tide. With the macroeconomy still collapsing as a result of the removal of the fiscal stimulus, share prices and the yen continued to fall, and by the summer of 1998 banks had again to assume stringent lending attitudes in order to defend themselves. That, in turn, depressed the economy further, and the situation became even worse.

BANKS NEED TO ENHANCE CAPITAL

Even though the Hashimoto administration finally admitted that the fiscal reform was a mistake and reversed its fiscal policy in June 1998 by enacting a ¥16 trillion supplementary budget, it was too late to save the LDP in the upper house elections in July. With the LDP losing the upper house, the policy initiative moved to the opposition, who understood nothing about the banking crisis and were totally against capital injection. As a result, there was a complete policy vacuum in Japan during the summer months when the economy was collapsing left and right.

Alarmed by the total lack of policy initiative when the stock market was falling to its post-bubble low, the media star Soichiro Tawara (a Japanese Larry King?) asked me during his very popular Sunday TV program to educate the four policy heads of the opposition parties live on camera. Thus, I had to confront the four in front of millions of TV viewers and explain to them, step by step, why the current banking crisis was different from many other crises at home and abroad, and why, without a capital injection, both the economy and the banking system would go down the drain.

Then, in October 1998, the opposition made a 180-degree turn. Naoto Kan, head of Minshuto (the Democratic Party of Japan), who had been advocating bank-bashing and was openly critical of the capital injection scheme, made an about-face and called for the enhancement of the banking system. The plan he suggested, which included an enlarged capital injection scheme, totaled ¥50 trillion. By this time, the majority of those polled in opinion surveys were responding that an additional capital injection was unavoidable, while two of the four major dailies (*Nihon Keizai Shimbun* and *Yomiuri Shimbun*) also began to call for the enhancement of banks' capital. As a result, the Diet passed a package of ¥60 trillion to deal with the problem in the financial system. The earlier allocation of ¥13 trillion for capital injection was increased to ¥20 trillion.

By the early autumn of 1998, people in other countries also realized the importance of capital injection. For example, the IMF, which had been severely criticizing Japan, wrote in its *IMF Survey* dated August 17, 1998, that the restructuring of the Japanese banks based on the market principle should be a medium-term task and that it was urgent to enhance the capital of weak banks.

Deputy Secretary Lawrence Summers and other high-ranking government officials in the United States also shifted their position in the autumn of 1998 and began to question whether ¥13 trillion was enough. Even though they still maintained that a strict conditionality was needed, they eventually said that, according to their calculation, an injection of ¥15–25 trillion was needed.

At about the same time in September 1998, I had a chance to talk one-to-one with a top official of the Deutsche Bundesbank for about half an hour in Vienna. I explained the background to the need for ¥13 trillion, citing the example of what had happened in Hokkaido. He was rather skeptical at the beginning but eventually said, "If that is the case, Japan should make the capital injection as soon as possible." He even added, "Each day of delay will increase the burden to the people further. Take action promptly."

Finally, in March 1999, with the ¥60 trillion package and both foreign and domestic opinion much more in favor of capital injection than a year ago, nearly ¥10 trillion was injected into the banks. However, the Bank of Tokyo Mitsubishi, which was forced into taking the capital the last time around in order to lead the way for the rest, was so sick of the experience that it refused this time to take any money from the government. Even though some conditionality was attached to the injection, the understanding was that it would not be enforced too strongly.

The injection finally turned the tide and the nationwide credit crunch was eased dramatically, as shown in Exhibit 3.1. If the conditionality had not been imposed, the recovery in bank lending and the economy might have been even more dramatic. In any case, this ¥60 trillion package, together with the total of ¥40 trillion in supplementary budgets to stimulate the aggregate demand,[5] finally stabilized the Japanese economy and the banking system. In other words, it cost Japanese taxpayers ¥100 trillion to repair the damage caused by the overzealous attempt by the Hashimoto government to push through both fiscal and banking reforms in the middle of a balance sheet recession. And as mentioned earlier, it was *after* this ¥100 trillion repair bill that foreign investors returned to Japan to buy assets.

STRINGENT INJECTION CRITERIA COUNTERPRODUCTIVE

The Japanese people agreed to the ¥60 trillion package only because they wanted the credit crunch to end so that the economy could move forward again. However, when it came to the stage of actually injecting capital, the authorities did attach conditions, although the understanding was that those conditions should not get in the way of easing the credit crunch.

Unfortunately, once the credit crunch problem was largely resolved and the economy began moving forward, those critics who had nothing better to do started arguing that bankers were not meeting the management reform deadlines and that the NPLs of those banks were actually increasing. Some even argued that the whole capital injection exercise was a failure because Japan is still stuck with a sick banking system characterized by a low return on capital and huge NPLs.

These critics never realized that the original capital injection scheme was devised to end the crippling credit crunch. And in order to achieve that goal, it had to put aside other issues such as the disposal of NPLs. If the injected funds had been used to dispose of NPLs, there would not have been any reason for the credit crunch to end, and the Japanese economy would have been thrown into an abyss. And if the economy really collapsed, the NPLs of the banks would have grown several times the original amount.

In this sense, the authorities' attaching conditionality to capital injection was not only self-contradictory but also dangerously misleading as to the original purpose of the injection. From the beginning, there was no hope of attaining both the end to the credit crunch and reduced NPLs at the same time with just ¥10 trillion of capital injection. To give an impression that both can be achieved at the same time with just one tool is both greedy and irresponsible.

Indeed, in a hearing conducted by the Financial Services Agency in 1998, several persons, including myself, warned that it is a contradiction to demand an end to the credit crunch and management reforms, including the disposal of NPLs, at the same time. We argued that neither objective would be attained if the authorities chased after two hares at the same time, so to speak.

Although the laws stipulated that the precondition for the injection of capital was the restoration of banks' financial health, the total of ¥10 trillion injected by March 1999 should be regarded as being aimed only at ending the credit crunch and not at writing off banks' NPLs. It is meaningless, therefore, for the authorities or the media to make an issue out of the fact that the banks' management reform plans have not been met. It should let bygones be bygones and move on to the next task.

It is anybody's guess as to how those foreign monetary authorities who criticized Japan might have reconciled the conditionality requirements and ending of the credit crunch themselves. In other words, if the bankers, on the grounds that their ROE needed to be raised, refused to take the money the government thought was necessary to end the credit crunch, what was there for the government to do? Furthermore, if the prolonged confrontation over the conditionality made the nationwide credit crunch worse, who would be held accountable for the situation? If the actions the U.S. authorities took in the 1982 Latin American debt crisis or the 1991 credit crunch are any guide, it is likely that even the U.S. government would have relaxed the conditionality in order to get the economy moving again.

ENDNOTES

1 *Nihon Keizai Shimbun*, October 27, 1997.

2 *Nihon Keizai Shimbun*, May 14, 1998.

3 *Nihon Keizai Shimbun*, January 13, 1998.

4 *Nihon Keizai Shimbun*, February 23, 1998.

5 Prime Minister Obuchi implemented a supplemental budget totaling ¥24 trillion in November 1998 on top of Prime Minister Hashimoto's supplemental budget of ¥16 trillion enacted in June 1998.

8

FOUR KINDS OF BANKING CRISES AND THE ROLE OF THE BLANKET GUARANTEE

U.S. ALSO SAVED ALL ITS BANKS

Although many people both within and outside Japan criticized the scheme of helping all the banks, when the United States itself had faced the problem of capital adequacy of banks across the nation between 1991 and 1993, it also saved them all without asking difficult questions. At that time, the banks across the United States were in a crisis because of the crash of the leveraged buyout market after the boom years of the 1980s and the collapse of the mini-bubble in the commercial real estate market, which was suffering from over-supply. In fact, the over-supply problem was so serious that it was said that the market would not recover before 2000. As a result, a large number of banks were saddled with capital adequacy problems and were unable to lend.

This, combined with much stricter examination by the bank regulators who were responding belatedly to the S&L fiasco two years earlier, created a nationwide credit crunch. As this took place during the Gulf War, it did not draw much attention at first. By the time policymakers realized what was happening, however, the economic situation was so bad that President George Bush, Sr., the hero of the Gulf War, lost his re-election campaign to the newcomer from Arkansas, Bill Clinton.

The seriousness of the U.S. credit crunch can be seen in Exhibit 8.1, which shows that from the end of 1990 to around 1993, banks were withdrawing credit every quarter for three years. With tens of thousands of businesses failing as a result, it was said to be the worst recession since World War II. Unfortunately, this crisis came right after the S&L crisis of 1989. Since the U.S. taxpayers and politicians were exhausted by the clean-up of the S&L fiasco, which cost them US$160 billion, they were in no mood to cough up billions more to rescue the commercial banks.

Exhibit 8.1   U.S. experience with nationwide credit crunch in 1991–93

Funds raised by non-financial corporate sector in the U.S.

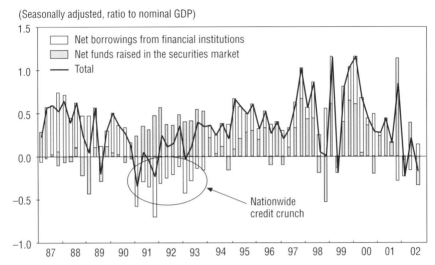

(Seasonally adjusted, ratio to nominal GDP)

Source: Federal Reserve Board, "Flow of Funds in the United States."

Faced with this situation, the Federal Reserve moved to provide relief to all banks. That is, while acquiescing to the banks maintaining the prime lending rate at 6%, it reduced the federal funds rate, which is the cost of funds to the banks, to 3%. In other words, the Federal Reserve created a situation in which the deposit rate was 3%, but the lending rate was 6% plus the spread. This means that all banks were able to earn more than a 3% interest rate spread, which was twice the normal spread (Exhibit 8.2).

This was a very unfair policy. Depositors were able to get only 3% when they lent to the banks, but had to pay over 6% when they borrowed from the same banks. It was the same as raiding depositors to recapitalize the banks. Moreover, all banks, both good and bad, were able to earn the 3% spread. In other words, the government had provided relief to all banks.

The huge interest rate spread of 3% made it possible for the banks to write off non-performing loans and increase capital. Given the fact that the interest rate spread prior to the adoption of this scheme was 1.5%, the three years of the larger interest rate spread was equivalent to boosting the capital asset ratio of U.S. banks by 4.5 percentage points (1.5% multiplied by three). Other things being equal, a bank with a capital ratio of 6% when the scheme went into effect was able to increase it to 10.5% after three years.

The scheme helped the banks to regain good health and to resume lending in 1994, which put the U.S. economy back on to a recovery course. Put another way, short of a capital injection by the government, this was the only alternative available to the U.S. authorities at that time.

Exhibit 8.2 "Fat spread" to all banks saved the U.S. banking system

Interest rate spread between funding and lending rates of banks

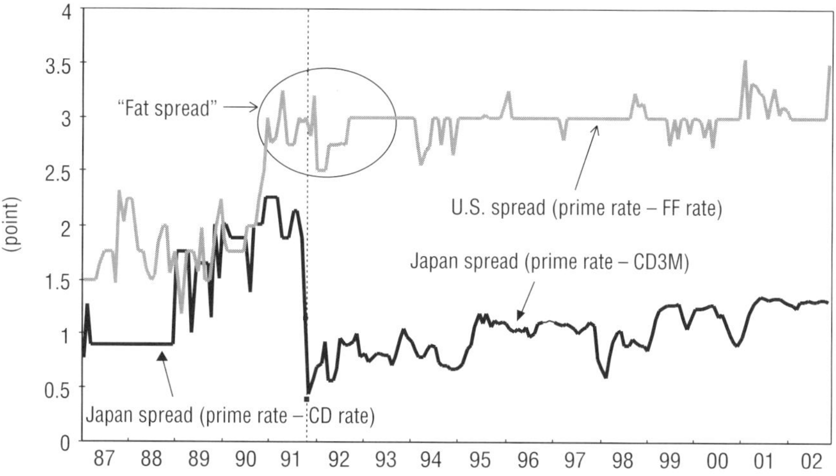

Source: Nomura Research Institute (NRI).

The same scheme was adopted by Australia at around the same time. The Finance Ministry of Australia called it the "fat spread" scheme. The country managed to save its banking system during the first half of the 1990s, when asset prices plummeted, by adopting this scheme. Luckily for both the U.S. and Australia, there was still a demand for funds when their banking problems arose. This means there were plenty of borrowers who were willing to pay the fat spread. That, in turn, helped the banks recapitalize themselves. Furthermore, once the banking problems were resolved, the two economies could move strongly forward because the key bottleneck, the banks' inability to lend, was removed. These examples show that in both the United States and Australia, the authorities provided relief to all the banks, including the good banks and the bad, to solve the problem of the nationwide credit crunch.

If Japan had been able to use this fat spread scheme, it could have solved the problem without using politically expensive "public funds." However, since there was no demand for funds in Japan for so many years, interest rates had already fallen to the lowest levels ever recorded when the problem of the credit crunch arose. If it had occurred in, say, the 1991–92 period, when interest rates were still high and there was a demand for funds, rather than in October 1997, the authorities could have reduced the official discount rate while leaving the short-term prime lending rate unchanged to create a fat spread.

However, since the credit crunch started when the short-term prime rate stood at 1.625% and the official discount rate at 0.5%, it was impossible to create the fat spread unless a large negative official discount rate was adopted. This is why the Japanese government was forced to come up with the scheme that President Roosevelt had used in 1933, when the United States was experiencing what Japan is experiencing today.

THE DIFFERENCE BETWEEN THE U.S. AND JAPANESE BANKING CRISES

The banking crises in the U.S. over the last two decades all took place in an environment where there was always a healthy demand for funds from the corporate and household sectors. And because there was a demand for funds, a fat spread could be charged to repair the banking system. Since the bottleneck in the U.S. economy was the troubled banking sector, once the banking sector was repaired, the whole economy could move forward on the back of a healthy corporate demand for funds.

In Japan, however, the economy lost forward momentum precisely because of the disappearance of corporate demand for funds. In such a situation, the first order of business should be to repair the corporate sector before the banking sector, because the corporate sector is where the bottleneck is in the economy. Otherwise, there will be no revenue stream for the banks to use to repair themselves.

The fact that there was no demand for funds also meant that Japanese banks were being asked to dispose of NPLs and to enhance their capital with a spread only one-third the size of that in the United States in 1991–93. Moreover, the magnitude of the decline in asset prices and the size of the NPLs in Japan are far greater than those experienced in the United States during the last 20 years. In other words, even under the best of circumstances, it would take far longer than it did in the United States to solve the banking problem in Japan.

Unfortunately, most observers in the U.S. assumed that the banking problem in Japan was similar in nature to what they had encountered themselves, and recommended the treatment that had worked for them. This is why they demanded a quick resolution to the banking problem above all else, not realizing that the banking problem was *not* the bottleneck in the Japanese economy.

Furthermore, many Americans had forgotten about the Latin American debt crisis of 1982 and the nationwide credit crunch between 1991 and 1993. People only remembered the well-publicized S&L crisis in 1989 and the RTC. This is because both the Latin American debt crisis and the 1991–93 crisis had been handled very quietly by the Federal Reserve and the banking industry, and therefore did not remain in people's memories. Naturally, there was no reason for the Federal Reserve or the banking industry to advertise the fat spread.

When I talk to commercial bankers in the U.S. about the similarities between the present situation in Japan and the 1991–93 crisis in the U.S., they understand instantly what I mean, because they remember the hardship the U.S. banking industry went through during those years. They also recognize the similarity with the Latin American debt crisis of 1982. And in both cases, they show great appreciation for the leadership of the Federal Reserve. However, even these American bankers have never experienced a situation where the vast majority of companies are paying down debt at 0% interest rates.

The Wall Street types and academics, however, need to be told what happened to the U.S. in those years, because they were not the key participants in the 1982 or 1991 crises. The only banking crisis they remember is the S&L crisis. As a result, they are asking the Japanese to repair their banking system before anything else. They do not realize that the problem Japan is facing is totally different from their S&L crisis.

FOUR TYPES OF BANKING CRISES

The above indicated that the major difference between the Japanese and the U.S. banking problems is that, in the U.S., all three recent banking crises — in 1982, 1989, and 1991 — happened at a time when there was abundant demand for funds in the domestic economy. In other words, the U.S. problem during the last 20 years was that the banks were trimming their sails even though there were large numbers of willing and creditworthy borrowers. However, post-bubble Japan and now Taiwan, and possibly even the post-Enron U.S., are faced with the problem that borrowing companies are so concerned about their balance sheets that they have basically stopped borrowing. As a result, the demand for funds is failing to recover even though lending rates have been brought down to historically low levels.[1]

Under these circumstances, it would be fair to say that problems at the banks do not constitute the main impediment to economic recovery. To that extent, there is no reason to rush to dispose of NPLs either. After all, the whole point of pushing the banks to dispose of their NPLs is to enable them to take risks and lend money again. However, when there is no demand for funds from businesses even at 0% interest rates, there is no reason for the economy to improve, no matter how many NPLs the banks dispose of.

Quite the contrary, rushing to dispose of NPLs in a "fire sale" fashion under the current conditions could be extremely dangerous, because such moves could cause the economy and asset prices to slide even further, thereby generating still more NPLs. Paul Volcker was trying to warn that the problems could snowball in this way when he said that Japan should establish a speed limit on how fast banks can dispose of NPLs.

Putting this all together, it appears that there are four types of banking crises and four different ways of dealing with them, depending on whether there is any demand for funds, and whether the problem affects the whole of the banking system or only part of it. They are:

- Type (I): A localized crisis where there is demand for funds.
- Type (II): A systemic crisis where there is demand for funds.
- Type (III): A localized crisis where there is no demand for funds.
- Type (IV): A systemic crisis where there is no demand for funds.

These are shown in Exhibit 8.3.

Exhibit 8.3 Four types of banking crises and four ways of dealing with them

		Demand for funds	
		Normal	Weak or Non-existent
Banking crisis	Localized	(I) Rapid disposal of NPLs Pursue accountability	(III) Normal disposal of NPLs Pursue accountability
	Systemic	(II) Cautious disposal of NPLs Recapitalize banks by giving them fat spread	(IV) Cautious disposal of NPLs Capital injection with public funds if necessary

Source: Nomura Research Institute (NRI).

On this basis:

- The 1989 S&L crisis falls into Type (I).
- The Latin American debt crisis of 1982, the nationwide credit crunch in the U.S. between 1991 and 1993, and the Nordic banking crisis in the early 1990s fall into Type (II).
- Japan prior to 1995 (for example, problems at two credit cooperatives) falls into Type (III).
- Japan since 1996, Taiwan since 2000, and the U.S. Great Depression of the 1930s fall into Type (IV).

Viewed in this way, the only category in which rushing to dispose of NPLs would be the best approach is Type (I). In all other categories, a cautious approach would produce better results. In Type (II) and (IV) systemic crises, attempting to sell NPLs when there are hardly any buyers runs the risk of pushing down asset prices even further, which could lead to a much weaker economy and the emergence of even more NPLs. In other words, rushing to dispose of NPLs only "destroys value," to use Stefan Ingves's term, and makes the situation much worse. Indeed, the U.S. dealt with its Type (II) NPL problems at a slow and cautious pace.

There is no such danger of snowballing problems in Type (III), but there is still no real point in rushing to dispose of NPLs, because they do not constitute the main impediment to economic growth. There is certainly no reason to use taxpayers' money to speed up the disposal process in a Type (III) crisis.

Meanwhile, in Type (II) systemic crises, where there is still demand for funds, the authorities can strengthen the banks by providing a fat spread — in other words, lowering the rate at which the central bank supplies liquidity to the banks while allowing them to keep their lending rates high. Indeed, this is exactly how the U.S. resolved its 1991–93 nationwide credit crunch. Although this is an extremely unfair method, to the extent that it involves a transfer of income from deposit holders to the banks, it is politically expedient in that the government does not need to use public funds.

In Type (IV) cases like Japan's, however, insufficient demand for funds makes it impossible for the central bank to use the fat spread solution. In this type of crisis, the government needs to step in with capital injections in the event that further instability emerges. This is why the U.S. went for this option in 1933, as did Japan in 1998 and 1999.

MOUNTAIN OF "PROBLEM LOANS" IN ADDITION TO "BAD LOANS"

A senior U.S. Treasury official who worked on the S&L crisis told me that the burden on the taxpayers could have been reduced by at least US$50 billion if the S&L assets had been disposed of more slowly. In other words, the cost would have been US$110 billion, rather than the US$160 billion it actually cost the government.

The reason why the RTC formula is still given high marks in spite of the higher cost is that it allowed the government to say with confidence that there were no more NPL problems earlier than otherwise would have been the case. This gave a sense of assurance to the entire U.S. economy that there were no more problem loans that could suddenly disrupt asset prices, and the economy started growing. The government was able to declare an end to the problem sooner, because the crisis was very much limited in scope to the S&L industry and non-S&L financial institutions were more or less in good health. Thus, in a Type (I) banking crisis, it makes sense to push for a quick disposal of NPLs even if the short-term cost is higher.

On the other hand, in present-day Japan, even if the authorities and banks manage to dispose of the ¥40 trillion in NPLs that the banks admit they have, that would still leave around ¥150 trillion in "problem loans."[2] Moreover, in July 2001 the government admitted, based on its own calculations, that the disposal of ¥15 trillion in NPLs of the major banks alone would increase the number of jobless by nearly 200,000.[3] Most private estimates were many times higher. Economic deterioration of such a magnitude would also bring down asset prices from their current levels. The deterioration of the economy and the decline in asset prices are bound to further increase NPLs. If only 10% of problem loans today turn into bad loans tomorrow, that alone would defeat the whole effort of writing off the ¥15 trillion in NPLs of the major banks in the first place. In other words, an over-zealous attempt to dispose of NPLs in the current environment could actually increase the quantity of NPLs.

The point is that even if the authorities and the financial institutions did their best to dispose of the NPLs, they would not be able to announce an end to the problem for many years. Given this situation, worries about the future will not be dispelled even for the most confirmed optimists. The magnitude of the problem in Japan today is just so much greater than the S&L case in the United States.

If one cannot give the all-clear any time soon, no matter how much haste one makes, there is no reason to make haste at an additional cost to the taxpayers. Even in the United States back in 1989, if the situation had been such that there was no prospect of completely solving the problem in two to three years no matter how much haste the authorities made, they would not have rushed to solve the problem at an added cost of US$50 billion to the taxpayers. In fact, at the time of the Latin American debt crisis in 1982, which did not lend itself to a quick solution, the United States opted to go slowly and chose a formula that would first bring stability to the banking system and the economy, rather than rushing pell-mell into a solution. Thus, in Type (II) and (IV) crises, NPL disposal has to go slowly and cautiously.

PLAYING THE BLAME GAME IS NOT PRODUCTIVE IN A SYSTEMIC CRISIS

Moreover, during systemic crises in which all the banks are suffering at the same time, it is difficult to apportion individual blame and to pursue accountability. Furthermore, pushing for accountability in a systemic crisis can easily make a workable policy unworkable. That, in turn, could increase the ultimate cost to taxpayers many times. For example, as indicated earlier, when the Japanese Diet passed the plan to inject capital into the banks in February 1998, the then government attempted to pursue accountability via a seven-person committee. However, when the plan was unveiled, not a single bank applied for funds. But without capital injection, the problem of the credit crunch that the Japanese economy was suffering from would not be resolved. Ultimately, the government had to abandon the attempt to play the blame game.

In the same way, during the 1982 Latin American debt crisis, which was a

Type (II) crisis, the U.S. authorities could not and did not pursue the accountability of the individual bank executives involved, because they needed the agreement of the entire banking sector if they were to avert a catastrophe. By side-stepping the accountability issue, the authorities managed to solve the Latin American debt crisis — which is said to have been 10 times bigger than the S&L crisis — without costing taxpayers any money. Moreover, during the nationwide credit crunch between 1991 and 1993, the Fed provided a fat spread to all banks, both good and bad. In other words, when the U.S. faced a systemic crisis, accountability was not pursued.

In the Swedish banking crisis of the early 1990s, it is true that the managements of two failed banks, Nordbanken and Gota Bank, were replaced. What is often not mentioned, however, is that both of these banks were 70% owned by the government in the first place. Furthermore, the embarrassed Swedish government bought back all the shares of these two banks held by the private sector at the price the private sector had paid for them. Thus, the taxpayers actually bailed out private-sector shareholders of the failed banks, a very interesting case of "accountability" indeed.

Unfortunately, the media and academia are full of people who mistake any kind of crisis for a Type (I) crisis, and recommend solutions to that type of crisis whether or not they are appropriate to the crisis at hand, not just in Japan, but all over the world. Although these people are free to say whatever they want, policymakers of countries with a systemic banking crisis should know better.

At the minimum, policymakers of affected countries should check whether the symptoms of Type (II), (III), and (IV) crises are present in their banking problems. For example, if all banks are suffering from the same problem, the problem is likely to be a Type (II) or (IV) crisis. If historically low interest rates have failed to produce any pick-up in demand for funds, it is highly likely that the crisis is of the Type (III) or (IV) variety. And if these symptoms are present, the authorities should consult those who actually have experience in dealing with these types of banking crisis, and ignore the noise from those who only know about Type (I) crises.

Calls for the rapid disposal of NPLs in today's Type (IV) crisis in Japan — not just from the Koizumi Cabinet, but also from all those who have never had to deal with a Type (II) or (IV) crisis themselves — can only do major damage to the economy. Just as the calls for fiscal reform in 1997 almost destroyed the Japanese economy and ended up increasing the budget deficit, calls for the rapid disposal of NPLs could devastate the economy while increasing the quantity of NPLs.

In this sense, Japan should alert the outside world to the fact that its present situation is not the Type (I) crisis that they perceive it to be. Rather, it is facing a Type (IV) systemic crisis, in which all the banks are facing similar problems. Unless such an effort is made, the perception gap will become even wider and Japan could be forced to swallow the wrong medicine.

REGULATORY INADEQUACIES HAVE MADE MATTERS WORSE

Looking back at those confusing days between October 1997 and March 1999, it must be said that a slightly different scenario could have been written had a different regulatory infrastructure been available to the Japanese authorities. In fact, many suggestions and demands that came from the U.S. banking authorities and elsewhere probably assumed that Japan already had such an infrastructure. In particular, if the bank regulators had a strong enough bank examination mechanism that enabled them to *prove* that certain banks clearly had excess liabilities, they could have forced them either to increase their capital on their own, accept a capital injection with conditionality, or face nationalization.

However, the Japanese examination system was quite inadequate, with only 500 examiners available to examine bank assets. In comparison, the United States had 8,000 professionals engaged in the comparable task. Since the total size of the bank assets of the two countries was virtually the same, the average Japanese examiner had to do the work of nearly 16 U.S. examiners. Besides, of the 500 Japanese examiners, only 200 from the Bank of Japan were said to be capable of conducting real examinations. As a result, the authorities did not have adequate information to tell the banks what to do, and in the case of capital injections, had to wait for applications from individual banks.

It was not just manpower that the Japanese bank supervisors lacked. Until April 1998, they did not have sufficient authority either. I was astounded to learn, on moving to Japan from the Federal Reserve Bank of New York, that the Japanese examiners did not have the same strong authority the U.S. examiners had, and that, at least until February 1998, the best they could do was to give advice.

In addition, they were equally powerless vis-à-vis other ministries and agencies. For example, the National Tax Administration Agency (NTA) was able to levy taxes completely independently of the Ministry of Finance's Banking Bureau's efforts to dispose of banks' NPLs as quickly as possible. In other words, even though the MOF was trying to get the banks to write off their problem loans, the NTA was dead against it for fear that such disposal would result in lower tax receipts.

Furthermore, the NTA has the power to ignore loan classifications by the banking authorities. Indeed, the tax agency has its own definition of NPLs which states that the condition of the borrower must deteriorate to an absolutely hopeless level before a tax-free write-off by the bank is allowed. This provision made it very difficult for bankers to write off NPLs without paying exorbitant taxes. The NTA's desire for tax receipts was such that if a bank foreclosed the borrower and sold off its assets at a very low price, it ran the risk of being charged a "gift tax."

Since no banker in his right mind will pay taxes in order to write off problem loans, this requirement by the NTA was the single most important reason for the slowness of NPL disposal by Japanese banks up until 1998. In fact, not a few banks had found themselves in a dilemma, with the MOF telling them to write off NPLs, and the NTA telling them not to do so.

Some — but not all — of this nonsense was resolved in a conference held by the Banking Bureau of the MOF and the NTA in 1998. First, the Japanese tax code states that, if a bank reserve against a non-performing loan does not meet the NTA's own super-strict definition of NPLs, the bank will have to pay all the taxes up-front. In other words, the write-offs have to come from the bank's after-tax profits. But after 1998, it was agreed that the taxes overpaid can be counted as deferred tax assets in the Tier I capital of the bank for a maximum of five years.

As a result of this arrangement, Japanese banks finally obtained some incentive to write off their problem loans. Between 1992 and 2001, and contrary to the popular belief in the English-speaking world that they have done very little to dispose of their problem loans, Japanese banks wrote off ¥90 trillion,[4] or nearly US$800 billion, of which ¥40 trillion was disposed of after the agreement. The figure of ¥90 trillion is equivalent to almost 20% of Japan's GDP and is by far the largest NPL write-off in the history of mankind. During the same period, the total number of bank employees fell nearly 30%, from the peak of 463,000 in 1993 to 333,000 in 2001,[5] indicating that restructuring is also progressing, albeit at a somewhat slower pace than would be typical in the U.S.

The above arrangement also means that the more Japanese banks write off their problem loans, the greater the accumulation of deferred tax assets in their Tier I capital. As a result, well over 40% of the Tier I capital of Japanese banks is now made up of this tax credit. Although this is a rather unnatural state of affairs, the blame for this goes straight to the NTA, because if the NTA allowed banks to write off NPLs tax-free, there would be no reason for Tier I capital to be filled with deferred tax assets. Instead, it would be filled with cash.

This measure was a second-best solution, undertaken only because the NTA refused to change its tax code to make it easier for banks to write off NPLs tax-free. (Since the NTA has the power to initiate tax audits on anyone, most people in Japan do not want to confront the agency.) But for the first time ever, Japanese banks had an incentive to dispose of their NPLs quickly. The value of the deferred tax assets that could be accumulated as Tier I capital was limited to the value of estimated taxable income over the next five years times the effective corporate tax rate, and the deferred assets were only good for offsetting taxes incurred within the following five-year period.

TAKENAKA'S PROPOSAL: NO GOOD AND MUCH HARM

Perhaps because he was unaware of this historical background, Heizo Takenaka, the Financial Services Agency minister, came up with a plan in October 2002 to limit the amount of deferred tax assets that could be counted toward Tier I capital, from five years worth of taxable income times the corporate tax rate, to one year's worth of taxable income times the corporate tax rate. He argued that since the U.S. has a strict limit on how much deferred tax assets can be counted as Tier I capital, Japan should do the same. In effect, he was (inadvertently) trying to return to the financial landscape that existed before the adoption of tax allocation accounting in 1998. This would have removed any incentive Japanese banks had to dispose of their NPLs quickly. Under the Takenaka plan, therefore, bad loan disposals would be significantly delayed regardless of who was running the banks.

Furthermore, banks that were declared to be undercapitalized as a result of the above change would have to sharply reduce their lending in order to bring their capital adequacy ratios back to the critical 8% line. This would result in a credit squeeze many times worse than the one Japan experienced in 1997–98 and might well have delivered a crushing blow to the economy. Some analysts have predicted that implementation of the Takenaka proposal would have reduced loans outstanding by some ¥100 trillion,[6] or 20% of GDP, the deflationary effect of which would have been unimaginable.

Takenaka's plan, therefore, stood in perfect opposition to the Koizumi administration's avowed goals of defeating deflation and disposing quickly of the nation's bad loans. Moreover, it had absolutely no merits to speak of. It is no wonder, then, that it was abandoned soon after its announcement, when its failings were pointed out by the bankers. Takenaka was forced to change course and is now trying to do something about the real source of the problem, the NTA. In the U.S., this kind of problem with deferred tax assets does not arise because the tax authority, the Internal Revenue Service, does not challenge the rulings of the banking authorities.

The Takenaka shock nonetheless destroyed the sense of trust that existed between the banks and the FSA. Not knowing what to trust anymore, the bankers have become extremely cautious. As a result, a renewed credit crunch has begun since late 2002. This can be seen in the last entries of Exhibit 3.1 in Chapter 3.

Shockingly, many foreign journalists in Tokyo did not bother to find out how the deferred tax assets came about and praised Takenaka while calling those who opposed the plan "reactionary." Many, for example, used the term "watered-down" to suggest that Japan was retreating from its reform agenda.[7] The fact of the matter, however, is that both the LDP and the banks opposed Takenaka's plan because they knew Japan's tax code, while Takenaka apparently did not. This is not the first time that Takenaka has made a fool of himself over financial matters, but it is even more shocking to note that so few foreign journalists bothered to investigate the exact nature of the problem.

Since the early 1990s, I have been advocating that the Japanese system for bank examinations should be enhanced five-fold, if not 10-fold, because it was quite clear to me that the work of examiners would multiply several-fold with the bursting of the asset-price bubble and financial liberalization. Some of this enhancement materialized when, starting in February 1998, the legal powers of Japan's bank examination system were fortified to a level comparable to that in the United States. This was clearly demonstrated when Nippon Credit Bank was nationalized in October 1998. Nevertheless, it is still hardly sufficient in terms of manpower and authority vis-à-vis other ministries, especially the NTA.

I heartily agree with strengthening bank examinations, because there is nothing worse than a situation where outsiders feel that the examining authorities do not have an accurate picture of the full extent of the NPL problems. Nevertheless, I am against directly linking the results of the examinations to management reform orders or pressing the issue of management responsibility. This is because if one acts according to the manual based on microeconomic orthodoxy when there is a systemic risk, it could result in an even greater financial crisis, which ultimately will result in a much bigger burden on taxpayers.

In particular, Japan has been in recession for the last 10 years, and its asset prices are down to one-tenth of their peak values. This means that most corporate borrowers are pushed to the extreme limit of their existence. If the banks then rigorously applied the strict lending standards imposed by the FSA, there would only be a handful of companies left who would qualify for a loan. But shutting down the entire economy is not an option. Thus, a high-level political judgment is needed as to how flexible the banking authorities should be in dealing with a crisis of this magnitude. There is no easy answer to this question. What is certain, however, is that sticking to microeconomic orthodoxy is no solution.

Moreover, even if Japan had the best supervisory capabilities, the government would have still found the goals of ending the devastating credit crunch of 1997–98 and cleaning up the banking system contradictory. In view of the fact that resolving the credit crunch was much more urgent than cleaning up the banking system, it is not at all unreasonable that the Japanese have decided to deal with the former first.

Needless to say, the next task is the disposal of the NPLs. However, since NPLs are not a constraint on economic recovery, this task should not be given top priority at the expense of other policy goals. The actual disposal of NPLs should be implemented according to the financial strength of each bank and at a rate that will not damage the stability of the economy as a whole. If the disposal of NPLs is pushed through faster than what the banks can bear, the taxpayers must be made ready to close the gap created by the additional speed.

THE WORST TIME TO DISCUSS REMOVAL OF THE BLANKET DEPOSIT GUARANTEE

Displaying their complete lack of understanding of financial and banking matters, reformists in the Koizumi Cabinet have weakened the Japanese economy considerably by pushing strongly for the removal of the blanket guarantee on deposits which has been in effect since 1996. Their push to remove the guarantee, which will mean that the deposit insurance will protect deposits only up to a maximum of ¥10 million, has created large and unnecessary instability of bank deposits since late 2001. That, in turn, has made bankers unwilling to lend, as they cannot be sure of the stability of their deposits.

Most structural reformists in Japan argue that since the protection of deposits in full would make bank management irresponsible, it should be ended as soon as possible. They argue that the removal will prevent poorly performing banks from attracting deposits by offering high interest rates and using the money for high-risk, high-return investments in order to make up their losses in one stroke. If these banks succeed with their high-risk, high-return gamble, the benefit will accrue to the bankers. If the gamble fails, the government will have to pick up the losses. Thus, the full protection of deposits would create the moral hazard of poorly performing banks offering high interest rates to attract deposits to bet on high-risk, high-return investments. They argue that the removal of the guarantee will increase the tension between the banks and the depositors and encourage bank management to improve its operations.

Even though the above view is reasonable as a theory in normal times, in a nationwide balance sheet recession, an overzealous attempt to remove the guarantee could cause irreparable damage to the economy. Moreover, even among the major nations with advanced financial systems, the United States is the only nation that has the explicit provision to pay off depositors only up to the insured maximum as a policy option in a bank failure. Other advanced countries have, in practice, almost always protected depositors. Furthermore, even the United States has used the scheme to pay off depositors only up to the insured maximum in very rare cases.

The reason that most countries do not use deposit-payoff as their main policy option is that the cost to the national economy of making depositors worry about their bank deposits is too great. It is also because the moral hazard of the kind mentioned above can be prevented to a great extent by rigorous bank examinations by the authorities.

The reason the U.S. has deposit-payoff as an explicit policy option is because it has a very different banking structure compared to most other countries. Unlike countries where the number of banks is rather limited, the U.S. has nearly 10,000 banks, with very few barriers to entry (and exit). Not too long ago, the number was as high as 15,000. With this many banks, and many of them very small, the authorities need as many policy tools as possible to handle banking problems of all kinds.

In Japan, like in most other countries, the number of banks is limited. As a result, the banks tend to be bigger than in the U.S. This means that if the Hokkaido Takushotu Bank, which failed in November 1997, had to be liquidated using the deposit-payoff scheme, the amount involved (adjusted for the size of the economy) would have equaled the entire 47 years worth of actual deposit-payoff in the U.S. In the case of the Long-Term Credit Bank, which failed in June 1998, it would have equaled 382 years worth of deposit pay-off in the U.S.[8] It is obvious that such a scheme is totally unrealistic in Japan.

Furthermore, in Japan, ¥250 trillion, or approximately half of the total deposits of ¥500 trillion, comprises large deposits of more than ¥10 million. A great majority of such deposits are funds which local governments and private corporations are maintaining to pay wages and salaries to their employees. In other words, they are directly linked to the lives of tens of millions of people.

In spite of this reality, Heizo Takenaka has given the public an impression over the years that deposit-payoff is the global standard and that most countries have never protected depositors beyond the insured maximum. Even though his argument was contrary to the facts, the "reform-minded" Koizumi government, which has claimed that everything is fine with Japan's banks, announced the removal of the blanket guarantee in October 2001 and actually removed the guarantee on all time deposits starting on April 1, 2002. However, this has caused massive instability of deposits since late 2001, as can be seen in Exhibit 8.4. This instability also shows that the Japanese public do not trust the Koizumi Cabinet's argument that everything is fine with the Japanese banking system and that the removal of the blanket guarantee will not result in any negative consequences.

In addition, since time deposits, which account for nearly half of total deposits, have become unstable, banks do not feel safe about extending any credit. After all, they are able to extend credit to businesses because of funds held in time deposits. They do not feel safe enough to extend loans to businesses when most of their funds are in demand deposits, which could be withdrawn at any time.

The deposit instability has resulted in a hardening of lending attitudes by the banks and pressure on borrowers to pay down debts, which has depressed the Japanese economy in no small way. Exhibit 3.1 in Chapter 3 clearly shows that the banks' reluctance to lend has worsened since the end of 2001, when it became increasingly clear that the Koizumi government would go ahead and remove the blanket guarantee on time deposits. Thus, Japan is re-entering the world of the credit crunch simply because the Koizumi government wanted to remove the blanket guarantee prematurely.

THE DEPOSIT-PAYOFF DEBATE HAS ALREADY DAMAGED THE ECONOMY

These worries of depositors, together with the credit crunch induced by the instability of bank deposits, are probably subtracting a substantial amount from the Japanese GDP already. It would be a true miracle if the economy manages to enter a self-sustaining growth path, with so many people

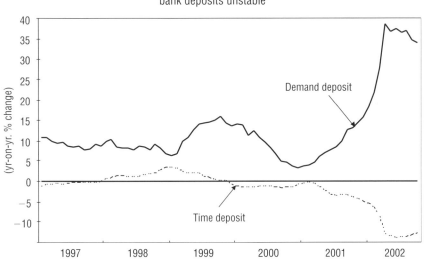

Exhibit 8.4 The removal of the blanket deposit guarantee on time deposits made bank deposits unstable

Source: Bank of Japan.

worrying about where to put their money and bankers unable to perform their function of a financial intermediary because of the instability of deposits. Even so, if the banks are fully creditworthy, then removal of the blanket guarantee should cause no problem. Unfortunately, the actual creditworthiness is nowhere near those levels that are needed for such removal.

One of the measures of the banks' creditworthiness is their rating. Generally speaking, for banks to function properly, they must have at least a "C-plus" to a "B" rating. However, according to Moody's, with the exception of the Bank of Tokyo Mitsubishi and Shinsei Bank, which are rated "D-minus," all major Japanese banks are rated "E," which is the lowest rating (Exhibit 8.5).

Even though rating agencies are not always correct, these ratings of Japanese banks appear reasonable in view of the fact that this is a country

Exhibit 8.5 Credit ratings of Japanese banks are too poor to remove the blanket deposit guarantee

Moody's bank financial strength rating

Rating	Bank of America NA	Citibank NA	JP Morgan Chase Bank	Bank One NA	Mellon Bank NA	Bank of Tokyo-Mitsubishi, Ltd.	UFJ Bank, Ltd.	Sumitomo Mitsui Banking Corp.	Mizuho Bank, Ltd.	Mizuho Corporate Bank, Ltd.	Daiwa Bank, Ltd.	Asahi Bank, Ltd.	Shinsei Bank, Ltd.	Mitsubishi Trust & Banking Corp.	Sumitomo Trust and Banking Corp.	Mizuho Asset Trust & Banking Co.	UFJ Trust Bank, Ltd.	Chuo-Mitsui Trust & Banking Co., Ltd
A																		
−	●	●																
+			●															
B				●	●													
−																		
+																		
C																		
−																		
+																		
D																		
−						●							●					
+														●	●			
E							●	●	●	●	●	●				●	●	●

Note: As of November 1, 2002.
Source: Moody's.

where the price of commercial property has declined by a national average of 85%. Since the decline in asset prices always hits financial institutions hard, the above ratings do not seem totally off the mark. The definition of the "E" rating is that the bank requires "assistance from outside" and is unable to stand alone.

In the history of the major advanced countries since the end of World War II, there has been no case where the entire creditworthiness of the banking system has fallen so low that all its major banks were rated as "D" or "E." Asking depositors to be responsible when choosing a bank under such circumstances is nothing short of madness, for there is really nothing to choose.

With banks' ratings being what they are, if a bank goes under and the authorities go ahead with paying off depositors only up to the insured maximum, many large depositors will lose money. Such an event will prompt all other large depositors with all other banks to ascertain whether or not their deposits are safe. Chief financial officers of companies would be summoned by the presidents of their firms and asked about the ratings of their own banks relative to the one that went under. But, at present, all the major banks in Japan are given the lowest ratings of "D" or "E," which means that there is not much difference between the one that went under and the others.

Businesses and local governments will then feel that their banks are not safe either, and large deposits across the nation will become unstable. Some heads of businesses and local governments may conclude that, since deposits earn hardly any interest, it is better to put them in postal savings or convert them into cash. If this should turn into runs on the banks by large depositors across the nation, Japan's financial system would collapse in an hour.

Already, there are long waiting lists in many banks across the country for customers wishing to rent safe deposit boxes (or bigger safe deposit boxes) so that they can hoard cash. Deposits with the postal savings, which is fully guaranteed by the government (although no interest is paid on amounts above ¥10 million), are also growing rapidly. Some well-known companies are so disgusted with this Koizumi nonsense that they have already asked all their employees and suppliers to open postal savings accounts so that payments to them can be made through the postal system.

Indeed, when a key White House aide on economic policy became aware of the instability of deposits in Japan (shown in Exhibit 8.4), he was shocked. "Doesn't Mr. Koizumi have an advisor who understands economics?" he asked. The problem is that Mr. Koizumi does *not* have an advisor who understands economics. After all, it had been his economics minister, Heizo Takenaka, who had been the strongest and loudest advocate for the quick removal of the blanket guarantee in Japan.

For example, when Shizuka Kamei, then the chairman of the Policy Planning Committee of the LDP, decided to postpone the lifting of the blanket deposit guarantee after consultation with the other parties in the coalition government in December 1999, it was Takenaka who criticized Kamei the loudest. Takenaka was so outraged that, in a nationally televised panel discussion in which we both took part, he gave a mark of "F," or 35 points out of 100, to the economics policy of the Obuchi Cabinet which had made the decision. (I gave the Cabinet 85 points.)

I shudder to think what would have happened if Kamei had *not* made this decision, which he knew would be very unpopular with the reformist-dominated media. The reason that there has not been a major financial panic in Japan, despite the existence of an enormous bad loan problem and the horrendous credit rating of Japanese banks, is because the removal of the blanket guarantee was postponed at that time.

After all, one cannot even talk of a normal economy when the deposits in the banking system are so unstable. It is indeed comical that Takenaka, when he replaced Hakuo Yanagisawa as head of the FSA in September 2002, suddenly changed his stance and agreed to a two-year postponement of the removal of the blanket guarantee on demand deposits. Perhaps the White House advisor mentioned above had something to do with the sudden change in Takenaka's position.

If most banks are rated "B," with only a sprinkling of banks rated "D" or "E," the collapse of a bank rated "D" would not plunge depositors with other banks into a panic, because everyone would feel that it was the depositors' fault for having chosen a bank with such a low rating. However, that is not the situation in Japan.

More importantly, even though Takenaka is popular with the Western press because of his reformist image and current position of favoring capital injections into Japanese banks (unlike in 1997, when he was opposed to strengthening bank capital), the current deposit instability problem cannot be addressed with capital injections. This is because the 1997 credit crunch was brought about by the simultaneous fall in the value of the yen and the stock market hitting both the numerator and denominator of the capital adequacy ratios of Japanese banks. In this situation, an injection of capital into the banks could resolve the credit crunch, and it did.

The current credit crunch, however, is caused entirely by the instability of bank deposits. And this was brought about entirely by the Koizumi government's decision to remove the blanket deposit guarantee on time deposits. Thus, this problem cannot be solved unless bank deposits become stable again and the funds that left time deposits return to those accounts so that the banks can lend again. But that will not happen with the kind of credit ratings Japanese banks now have, unless the blanket deposit guarantee is reintroduced. To solve this problem with capital injections will be both extremely costly and inefficient, since this is not where the problem lies.

More precisely, if the injection is going to be of a huge amount, such as ¥50 trillion or ¥100 trillion, it will probably solve both the deposit instability problem, as well as the NPL problem, by drastically increasing bank capital. If the amount is ¥10 trillion, which is a much more realistic number politically, the 1998–99 experiences indicate that the ratings of banks will not improve by much. But if the ratings remain the same, the deposit instability problem will remain as well. In other words, the credit crunch problem will not be resolved with a capital injection of such a magnitude.

Even in the U.S., the law-makers were completely exhausted when they allocated US$160 billion for the S&L clean-up in 1989, which was 3% of U.S. GDP at that time. Thus, for the commercial banking problem of 1991, the authorities had to use a fat spread for recapitalizing the banks. Japan has already spent over ¥20 trillion on capital injections, nationalization, and other expenditures related to its banking problems, which is over 4% of its GDP. It is not realistic politically to expect it to spend another ¥50 trillion.

Under the circumstances, therefore, the best approach is for the government to put back the blanket deposit guarantee for all deposits until the majority of Japanese banks have regained their normal credit ratings. In the meantime, the FSA should be fully engaged in improving the health of the banks while remaining alert to the risk of the moral hazard problems that come from such a blanket deposit guarantee.

AUTHORITIES WOULD HAVE ONLY A FEW HOURS TO COPE WITH FINANCIAL PANIC

The reformists, who know about financial panic only from books, argue that if a systemic crisis occurs, deposits will be protected in full. At the same time, they say that extensive debates and examinations are necessary to judge whether a situation is really a systemic crisis. This shows how ignorant they are of the workings of financial systems. The fact that all the banks have the worst possible rating, and that the deposits are now so unstable, is ample evidence of the existence of an enormous systemic risk. In other words, the flight of capital could be triggered at any time by the smallest of surprises.

From the viewpoint of the stability of the banking system, the worst that could happen is not a run on the banks by small depositors, but the flight of the large depositors. The former can be calmed quickly if the monetary authorities have ready a large fleet of cash-carrying vans and wave wads of banknotes in front of television cameras. But if large depositors were to draw down their deposits by billions or tens of billions of yen, the authorities could not handle the situation, even if they sent every one of their cash-carrying vans.

Furthermore, when a financial panic actually occurs, the authorities will have only a few hours in which to calm it. When Continental-Illinois Bank went under while I was with the Federal Reserve Bank of New York, the authorities had only a few hours in which to take appropriate measures. The troubled bank was a long-established money-center bank in the U.S. Since the regulations in the state of Illinois had not allowed banks to open branches, it had developed to such a size primarily by dealing with large depositors around the nation. However, the instant a rumor spread that the bank was likely to have made large loans to Pen Square, another troubled bank, its large depositors took flight all at once. The bank collapsed only two days after the problem surfaced and was promptly nationalized. There was simply no time to summon the committee members to hold a meeting.

NO FOREIGN FINANCIAL AUTHORITIES COMPLAINED ABOUT THE POSTPONEMENT OF PAYOFF

In order to remove the blanket deposit guarantee at any cost, there was a time when Takenaka and his allies loudly argued that the removal of the guarantee was an international commitment and that postponing it would cause further deterioration of Japanese bank ratings. However, in his book *Yabuniramino kinyu gyosei* (*Squint-Eyed Bank Supervision*), published in January 2002, Sei Nakai clearly writes that it was not an international commitment.[9] Nakai is a former top official of the Banking Bureau of the MOF who was in charge of the blanket guarantee when it was put in place.

Furthermore, when Kamei postponed the removal of the blanket guarantee in late 2000, no foreign governments complained about the postponement. On the contrary, they indicated in various meetings that they understood the Japanese action. Moreover, there was absolutely no damage to the ratings of the Japanese banks. Moody's released a statement on January 24, 2001,[10] soon after Kamei's decision, saying that it understood the Japanese action and that further support would be needed, even beyond the new March 2002 deadline for removal. The statement said, "Moody's remains confident that *depository obligations will be fully protected* over the long term, *even after March 2002*" (emphasis added).

This was a reasonable reaction, judging from the common sense in the financial world. It also showed that those people who had claimed that the lifting of the guarantee was an international commitment were just lying to the public.

The story does not end there. On March 27, 2002, when it became obvious that the Koizumi government would indeed remove the blanket guarantee on time deposits starting April 1, 2002, Moody's issued a warning that it would re-examine the ratings of the six major Japanese banks in a negative direction. This was five days before the actual removal of the guarantee. When the government removed the guarantee in spite of the warnings, Moody's downgraded the six banks in July.

What Moody's has done here is to indicate that the higher ratings of Japan's banks in the past were granted only because of the existence of the blanket deposit guarantee. Now that the Koizumi government had removed this support to the banking system, Moody's had no choice but to downgrade those banks, exactly as it had warned it would do in its statement of January 24. The reality of international finance was the exact opposite of what Takenaka thought it to be.

The blanket deposit guarantee should have been lifted only after the FSA and the banks had spent years of steady effort winning the trust of the Japanese public and the international financial markets. It will take a long time to regain the trust that has been lost. Indeed, during the past few years, none of the Japanese banks (with the exception of the born-again Shinsei Bank) has been upgraded, while there have been countless banks that have been downgraded, including the six downgraded in July 2002.

Furthermore, the outcome of the special examinations of banks and the financial results of the banks for fiscal 2001, together with the statement from the Bank of Japan released on October 7, 2002, all show that the situation has become increasingly worse. Under these circumstances, it would have been a miracle if the deposits had remained stable following the removal of the blanket guarantee. In this sense, the argument within the ruling parties in favor of maintaining the blanket guarantee on deposits is reasonable enough.

A 10-YEAR PLAN NEEDED TO FULLY REPAIR THE BANKS

How long will it take for a typical Japanese bank to recover its normal rating? Judging from the experiences of the U.S. banks during the second half of the 1980s and the first half of the 1990s, it will take a minimum of five to six years under the best of circumstances and probably well over 10 years under normal circumstances.

For example, Citibank in the U.S. had the same long-term debt rating (Exhibit 8.6) in 1991 as the Tokyo Mitsubishi Bank has today. At that time, Citibank was narrowly saved from oblivion by a capital injection from a Saudi prince. From that point onward, Citibank rebuilt itself with drastic restructuring. It was also helped greatly by the Fed's policy of fat spread,

Exhibit 8.6   Credit ratings of Japanese banks are too poor to remove blanket deposit guarantee

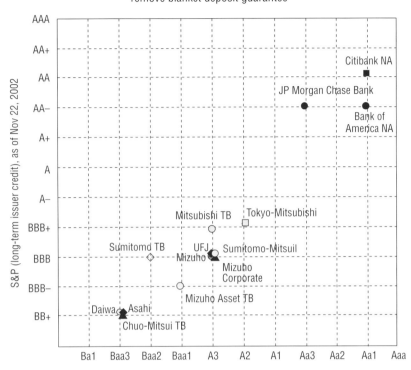

Sources: Standard & Poor's; Moody's.

which gave every bank in the U.S. the risk-free 300 basis points spread mentioned earlier. Furthermore, the U.S. economy began to do much better after the nadir of 1991. Even with all this help, it still took six years, until 1996, for Citibank to recover its credit rating.

For Japanese banks operating in a far more unfavorable environment, it is likely to take many more years than six before their ratings are restored to anywhere near creditworthiness. Indeed, a Citibank official who was involved in the bank's desperate effort to recover in 1991 told the author that the maximum fall in real estate prices which the bank had to deal with was 25%, with most assets falling less than 20% in value. In Japan, the comparable number could go as high as 85%!

Many commentators, including Minister Takenaka, had argued repeatedly that the Japanese banking problem would be solved by threatening the banks with the removal of the blanket deposit guarantee. Such a claim is nothing short of madness, and shows how little these commentators know about rebuilding credibility in financial circles. Trust can be lost in one day, but rebuilding it can take years if not decades.

On the other hand, if stability of the economy and of asset prices is obtained, it will be just a few more years before Japan's corporate balance sheet problems are resolved. Even though these corporate balance sheet problems and the banks' NPL problems are near mirror images of each other, the fact that the banks are by their very nature highly leveraged means that it will take much longer for the banks to come clean than the companies.

Once the corporate balance sheet problems are resolved and the economy comes out of balance sheet recession, there is a chance that the banks will start to improve as the corporate demand for funds returns. When that time comes, the government should also shift its policy emphasis from supporting the economy through fiscal stimulus to making sure that the banks' capacity to supply credit does not become a constraint on economic growth. But that time is not now. For now, priority should be given to helping the corporate sector repair their balance sheets so that they can start looking forward and, hopefully, start borrowing money again.

In a nutshell, a systemic risk in finance is a situation where there is a large number of sellers of assets but hardly any buyers. It is similar to the situation of a person who has a great deal of assets to sell relative to the size of the market. If the volume of assets that can be sold in a time period without causing a drastic decline in prices is only 10% of his total holdings, he has to think twice before selling more than 10% at a time. If he ignores this rule and tries to sell 20% of his assets at one stroke, the asset prices will plummet. This means the value of the remaining 80% of his assets will also decline sharply.

This example reflects exactly the situation in which the Japanese banks and financial authorities now find themselves. If the disposal and liquidation of NPLs are pressed ahead in the present market where there are hardly any buyers, asset prices could decline further, sharply depressing the value of ¥150 trillion in problem loans which the banks still hold. If such a situation is allowed to develop, the amount of NPLs newly created could be far greater than the amount of NPLs originally disposed of.

In a balance sheet recession, a premature attempt to reduce the government's budget deficit or the banks' NPLs could result in the opposite of what was intended. In 1997, the then prime minister Hashimoto's decision to reduce the budget deficit resulted in a sharp *increase* in the deficit. The same holds true for the disposal of NPLs. If implemented at the wrong time, NPLs can multiply to several times the original amount.

Although some people have pointed out that NPLs are continuing to increase, this is because of the poor economic conditions, as I have mentioned earlier. If business conditions are poor because of the NPLs, interest rates in Japan should be surging. The fact that interest rates are falling shows that the new NPLs are rising because of the poor economic conditions. The causality in this direction means that a policy that could further worsen the economic conditions and depress asset prices is almost guaranteed to increase NPLs. Indeed, both the deflation and NPL problem of Japanese banks have the same root cause: the corporate behavioral shift to balance sheet restoration which weakened the aggregate demand. In such a situation, measures to improve the macroeconomy are the best measures both to fight deflation and to reduce the NPLs. With limited fiscal resources available, what the above means is that Japan should fix its economy first before fixing its banking system.

ENDNOTES

1 Interest rates in Taiwan are also the lowest since the founding of the Republic of China in 1911.
2 *Nihon Keizai Shimbun*, April 18, 2001.
3 Heizo Takenaka, "Scenario for Japan's Economic Revitalization (*Nihon Keizai no Saisei Shinario ni Tsuite*)," *CEFP*, June 21, 2001.
4 Bank of Japan, "Japan's Nonperforming Loan Problem," October 11, 2002, p. 7.
5 Japanese Bankers Association.
6 *Nihon Keizai Shimbun*, October 7, 2002.
7 *Financial Times*, November 21, 2002.
8 Richard C. Koo, "Postpone the Removal of the Blanket Guarantee (*Pay-off no Jissi Miokuri wo*)," *Nihon Keizai Shimbun*, June 18, 1999.
9 Sei Nakai, *Squint-Eyed Bank Supervision (Yabuniramino kinyu gyosei)* (Zaikei Shohosha, January 2002), pp. 5–7.
10 Moody's Investors Services, "Pay-off Extension: No Impact on Japanese Bank Ratings," January 24, 2001.

9

REAL CHALLENGES FACING ASIAN ECONOMIES

THE NATURE OF THE ASIAN CURRENCY CRISIS

Although Japan is the only country that has been suffering from a balance sheet recession since the early 1990s, it gained a number of colleagues after the Asian currency crisis of 1997. Indeed, all the countries in Asia that were affected by the currency crisis have encountered balance sheet problems because of the asset-price bubble that preceded the crisis. Unfortunately, the majority of English-language reporting on Asia has been written from a purely American or European financial perspective. As a result, some of the key factors that contributed to the crisis have not received the attention from the press that they deserve. This is because, just as in Japan, many reporters of the Western press could not speak the local language and had to rely on Western financial institutions operating in the country for information and analysis of the economy. Since the incentive of those financial institutions is to further their businesses or recover the losses incurred, many of the articles ended up reflecting these financial institution's "talking the books," especially in regard to their own roles in the crisis.

The countries of Asia slipped into a currency crisis and chaos after the Thai baht plunged in value in July 1997. This led to serious economic deterioration and a credit crunch throughout the region. In some countries, such as Indonesia, economic activity shrank so much that the situation could justifiably be called a depression.

Various explanations have been put forward for this Asian crisis — that the concentration of dictatorial power in the hands of a few administrators had led to distortions, or that Asian values were doomed to failure. American and British commentators were particularly vociferous in their belief that banking and legal reforms are needed to make Asian economies more transparent and accountable along Anglo-Saxon lines, and that organizations such as the IMF should move in to ensure structural reforms in these countries.

However, as someone who actually witnessed the Asian meltdown at the time, I would like to assert that the main reason for the Asian currency crisis was not structural problems within the Asian economy, but rather issues with the yen–dollar exchange rate and international capital flows. Although various structural problems contributed to the crisis in no small way, they alone could not have created a fiasco of such magnitude. This is because these structural problems were present in the region for years, if not decades, before the crisis.

For many years prior to the crisis, investors and media representatives throughout the world were focusing on what was then known as the Asian miracle. Asia was basking in the glory of its description as the growth center of the 21st century.

The key driving force behind the brilliance of Asia at that time was, without doubt, the strong yen, which started with the Plaza Accord in 1985. Under the terms of this accord, the G5 nations decided to coordinate their exchange rate policies in order to curb the strength of the dollar so as to avoid the protectionist pressures growing everywhere in the U.S.

At that time, the yen traded at ¥240 to the dollar, and the Deutschmark at DM2.8 to the dollar. American industry could not remain internationally competitive at such rates, and this was leading to growing protectionism within the U.S. Indeed, at the time of the Plaza Accord, commentators in the U.S. were saying that industries that should have taken 30 years to disappear were folding in only three, which shows just how badly American industry was hollowing out.

Concerned that the protectionism in the U.S. spawned by this hollowing-out process would deal a fatal blow to the world trade system, authorities in the G5 started to work to lower the value of the U.S. dollar and raise the value of the yen and of the European currencies. In the decade following the start of this policy, the yen continued to rise, albeit with some slight fluctuations. By April 1995, or 10 years later, it had risen to an all-time high of US\$1 = ¥79.75.

A change from US\$1 = ¥240 to US\$1 = ¥80 means that the dollar lost two-thirds of its value, while the yen trebled in value. Confronted with this exchange rate appreciation, many Japanese companies that had grown by producing things in Japan and selling them to the rest of the world found that they could no longer sustain their domestic production activities. As a result, Japanese manufacturers were forced to move offshore. For many Japanese companies, this was their first experience of shifting production bases overseas. However, they had no other choice, and many moved their plants to Asia.

THE COUNTRIES THAT BENEFITED FROM THE STRONG YEN

Four countries benefited most from the rise in the value of the yen. The first was South Korea. Because South Korea has been competing with Japan in many of the same product areas, such as steel and shipbuilding, any loss of Japanese competitiveness as a result of a rise in the value of the yen will lead to a rise in orders at South Korean companies. The rise in the value of the yen therefore brought major benefits to South Korea.

The other three countries were Thailand, Malaysia, and Indonesia. These countries benefited from inward direct investment by Japanese companies, which opened the majority of their plants there. The U.S., which signed the Plaza Accord, had expected Japanese companies to move there, but with certain visible exceptions such as the autos, the majority of Japanese companies moved into Thailand, Malaysia, and Indonesia.

As a result of these moves by Japanese companies, these three countries suddenly found themselves living in a dream world. Japanese companies brought in state-of-the-art facilities and machinery. They purchased land, leveled it to build plants, and hired and trained staff. Then they made things, and exported them through a marketing network that spanned the whole world. In other words, these three countries enjoyed the best of all worlds, with production, incomes, jobs, and exports all growing at the same time.

I remember visiting Southeast Asia on business in 1990 and being asked by a locally based executive of a Japanese household electronics company which country was the second-biggest producer of VCRs in the world. Of course, Japan was number one, and I honestly believed that either South Korea or Taiwan was number two. This was because South Korea boasted powerful household electronics manufacturers such as Samsung, while Taiwan was also a major producer of household electronics.

However, the correct answer was Malaysia. I was surprised, and asked the executive why. He replied that the lack of any domestic component producer in Malaysia was the main reason why many Japanese companies had set up shop there.

Many countries that receive inward investment from overseas manufacturers require that the foreign companies moving in must source a certain proportion of their production to local suppliers. These local-content requirements sometimes discourage foreign manufacturers from investing in the country, because they cannot be sure of the quality or price competitiveness of the local component manufacturers.

There were no such worries in Malaysia, however, because the country had virtually no local component producers at that time. Moreover, Prime Minister Mohammad Mahathir welcomed the influx of Japanese manufacturers. As a result, the Japanese companies that moved into Malaysia were able to source parts from wherever they wanted (including Japan), which enabled them to keep product quality standards as high as in Japan. By 1990, only five years after the Plaza Accord, Malaysia was already the second-biggest producer of VCRs in the world.

The Japanese investment in Thailand and Indonesia expanded rapidly as well, which increased jobs, production, incomes, and exports in these countries. This is how the Asian miracle started.

Japanese companies thus constituted the initial driving force behind the upturn in economic activity within Southeast Asia. From the Asian standpoint, the hollowing out of industry which had attracted such concern in post-Plaza Japan translated into industrialization for them. As the economy took a turn for the better, people's incomes increased. As they found themselves with more money to spare, they spent more. As spending picked up, local companies benefited. This virtuous cycle of economic expansion lasted until 1995. In other words, it lasted for as long as the yen continued to rise against the dollar, from US$1 = ¥240 in 1985 to US$1 = ¥80 in 1995. The dream world lasted for a decade, but things changed from April 1995 onwards.

EUROPEANS REPLACING JAPANESE AS CAPITAL PROVIDERS

From April 1995 onwards, the yen moved in the opposite direction to the previous decade and started to weaken against the dollar. When this happened, many Japanese companies that had moved into Asia began losing their raison d'être for producing there, or for purchasing products from Asia. Once the yen fell in value, Japanese companies could remain internationally competitive even if they produced in Japan.

The tide then turned as Japanese companies started asking themselves why they had to move into Asia when it was more important to preserve jobs in Japan. As a result, the facilities and capital that had been transferred to Asia became increasingly irrelevant.

Exhibit 9.1 shows the sheer scale of the currency movements. This graph starts in April 1995, when the yen hit its peak against the dollar. The yen then slid rapidly from that point. However, the majority of Asian currencies did not move, because at that time they were all pegged to the dollar. This peg meant that when the dollar became the strongest currency in the world, these Asian currencies also became the strongest currencies in the world. As a result, Asian countries lost international competitiveness, which caused their trade balance to deteriorate. The relatively high domestic inflation rates of these countries during this period also eroded their competitiveness. The deterioration of their trade balance in 1996 can be seen in Exhibit 9.2.

By late 1996, some Japanese retailers were already saying that there was no point in purchasing anything from Thailand because everything was so expensive. Because the yen had weakened so much, there was virtually no profit to be made in some product lines that were coming from Thailand. Under normal circumstances, a country experiencing deterioration in its trade deficit should expect its currency to fall in value. However, something else happened at this time — namely, Asian fever on the part of global investors.

Exhibit 9.1   Asian currencies are now trading below the yen

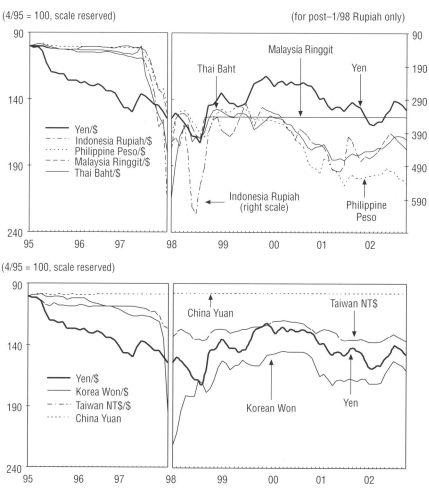

*Except Chinese yuan and NT$.
Source: Nomura Research Institute (NRI).

Exhibit 9.2 Trade balances of ASEAN countries and South Korea

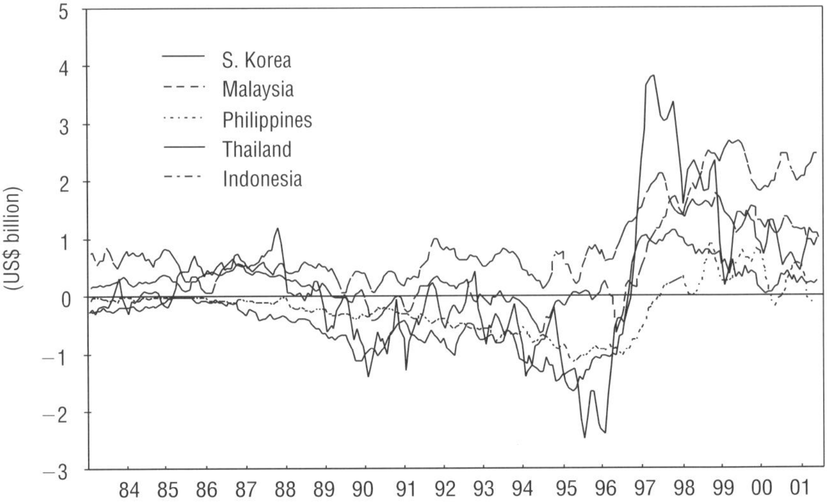

Sources: CEIC database, Nomura Research Institute (NRI).

Global funds flooded into Asia, fueled by the belief that investments in Asia would definitely pay off. At the time, even the World Bank was saying that Asia would be the growth center of the 21st century. The peoples of Asia had high savings rates and high education levels. They were diligent and entrepreneurial. Investors thought that they could not possibly lose money investing in these countries.

American and Japanese investors thought that way too, but European investors were the most enthusiastic of all. The U.S. and Japan had always kept up economic, diplomatic, and security links with Asia over the preceding decades, with the result that many U.S. and Japanese companies had invested in Asia even prior to the signing of the Plaza Accord in 1985.

By contrast, European countries had ruled Asian countries as colonies, in some cases until the end of the 1960s. Since their presence as (sometimes brutal) colonial rulers was not appreciated by the Asians, European companies and investors kept a low profile in Asia, feeling it would be best to stay away from the economic affairs of countries that they had once conquered and ruled.

However, 20 or 30 years later, their former colonies in Asia started to blossom, and Japanese, American, and Taiwanese companies were apparently making serious money in Asia. Investors and corporate executives throughout Europe started to ask themselves why Japanese and American companies should walk away with all the goodies from Asia, when the entire region had been theirs not too long before.

INTERNATIONAL CONFERENCE TO BRING EUROPE AND ASIA TOGETHER

In 1996 an international conference took place in Venice, Italy. Hosted by the European Commission, it brought together 500 European and Asian politicians, diplomats, academics, and business leaders. Its aim was to look at ways of reinitiating links between Europe and Asia. There were 250 delegates from Europe, and the same number from Asia.

Of course, some countries were not well represented at this conference — namely Japan, the U.S., and Taiwan. The latter was excluded because the delegation from China would not have attended otherwise, but in the case of Japan and the U.S. it was cold-shouldering. Indeed, the main aim of the conference was to work out how Europe could return to Asia, which was now making so much money for Japanese and U.S. companies. However, for some reason, I was invited to this conference. This struck me as somewhat odd, given that I was a U.S. citizen with a Taiwanese (and Chinese) background, born in Japan, and working for a major Japanese company.

Nevertheless, I was there to hear the EU Commission come straight out with the comment that the best of Europe's former colonies were now enriching the Americans and Japanese, and that Europe had to get back into Asia. Even more surprisingly, I heard not only private-sector individuals, but also bureaucrats, calling for greater European investment in Asia. I kept a relatively low profile over the three days of the conference, as I was naturally regarded as having links with Japan and the U.S., but at the final plenary session of 500 people I could not contain myself and decided to make a few comments of my own.

I told the assembled delegates that it would be great for Europe to move into Asia; indeed, it would be wonderful if Japanese, Americans, Taiwanese, and Europeans came and applied themselves to making good products, as this would help to achieve social progress in Asia. Everybody was aware that Japanese and American companies were succeeding in Asia, but this was not an overnight thing. Many of these companies had been in Asia for 10, 20, 30 years, or in some cases even longer. It had been a trial-and-error process, with some major setbacks and major losses over the years, and it was only now that everything was starting to come together. I therefore urged my European audience to study the Asian economies thoroughly before investing in the region.

I then went on to stress the remaining political risks in Asia, such as the rift between China and Taiwan and the division of the Korean peninsula. I said that foreign investors could panic if insufficient preparations had been made to cope with these political and economic risks. I added that although overseas investors would suffer major losses if they panicked, even greater damage would be inflicted on the Asian economies. I therefore urged my audience to do their homework on Asia before moving in, so as to avoid panic reactions when things do not go as planned.

My only intention had been to state the obvious. But far from finding agreement in the hall, I found myself denounced as a front man for the Japanese or as a CIA spy. Some people stood up and told the audience to ignore what I was saying, and there was some booing. The atmosphere was so bad that I said I understood what the deal was, wished the participants luck, and sat down again. It brought home to me just how wildly enthusiastic the European private and public sectors were about investing in Asia.

As a result of such enthusiasm, huge sums flowed into Asia, from Europe as well as from Japan and the U.S. Even though Asian countries' international competitiveness and trade balances were deteriorating, the inflow of capital from abroad was more than enough to offset the increasing trade deficit, thus keeping the Asian currencies strong.

ASIA BOOMS WITH CAPITAL INFLOW

What did this foreign enthusiasm look like from an Asian perspective? Up until then, Asian countries had been treated like second-class citizens whenever they attended international conferences. The U.S. and European media paid them little attention, and it was a good day if they were ever featured in the news coverage.

Come the mid-1990s, though, and blue-chip U.S. and European investment banks were rushing up to Asian countries with offers of investment funds at rates so advantageous that they would have been inconceivable only a few years earlier.

Just think about it for a moment. Imagine that you were an Indonesian businessman. Only 30 years previously, Indonesia was one of the poorest countries on earth. Until a few years ago, not a single top-notch global bank would have touched you with a barge pole. The only way to borrow money from abroad would have been at exorbitant rates of interest. Then suddenly, in the 1990s, swarms of people from global investment banks turn up asking if you would like to borrow money at low rates of interest. Others turn up asking for an equity share in your investment projects. With such generous offers, it is hardly surprising that the Indonesian business community became ecstatic, believing that they had finally received recognition from their counterparts in the West, and that 30 years of toil had not been in vain.

With their newly gained recognition and respectability, they of course borrowed the money offered and invested in various projects, such as taller buildings and bigger dams. As a result, Asia at that time witnessed a whole range of so-called mega-projects. The inflow of funds from blue-chip

Western investment banks was like manna from heaven for the Asian business community.

Ten years earlier, Japan too was so swept away by exuberance that it ended up producing a major asset-price bubble. (Recall Ezra Vogel's book, *Japan as Number One.*[1]) Indeed, one of the key reasons for the land-price bubble in Japan in the late 1980s was that so many Western investment banks came into Japan at that time and opened offices in Tokyo; they often were willing to pay *any* amount to secure the most modern and prestigious locations. The willingness of the Western investment banks to pay such high prices for office space in Tokyo shocked the usually cautious Japanese, and led them to think that something bigger and better must be happening to the Japanese economy.

As such, it comes as no surprise that people in Indonesia too got carried away and invested in all sorts of projects. Thus, massive inflows of funds from overseas created an asset-price bubble in the Asian economies. Indeed, capital inflows from overseas in the period from 1995 to 1996 were so great that the Thai central bank had a difficult time keeping the baht from breaking free of its dollar peg and trading *higher*. Such was the intensity of the foreign-investor-driven Asian investment boom.

THE UNFOLDING OF THE ASIAN CURRENCY CRISIS

These conditions in Asia lasted until 1997, causing a region-wide bubble in asset prices as more and more mega-projects were unveiled. However, the trade deficits of the Asian countries were getting worse and worse, as shown in Exhibit 9.2. By the beginning of 1997 the situation had deteriorated to the point where some observers began to fear that Asia would collapse if things carried on as they were. Nomura's Singapore office, for example, issued warnings to global investors to reduce their Asian exposure starting in early 1997.

But at that time so many people were still spellbound by the talk of the Asian miracle that they failed to take the warnings seriously. Indeed, I remember at the time trying to explain to Western investors about the problems in Asia, only to be told on several occasions that I was being pessimistic because I worked for Nomura, a Japanese company that was suffering in the weak Japanese economy. This is how caught-up everyone was in the Asian boom.

However, by summer 1997, even the overseas investors that had flocked to Asia were starting to ask themselves whether things could really go on like this. People had become increasingly concerned about whether it was still OK to invest in countries with such a deterioration in their trade accounts, and somebody decided to sell up. Once the selling started, however, panic followed quickly.

Up until then, investors had been brimming with confidence that they were on to a definite winner with Asia, believing that nothing could go wrong. They were so confident, many of them did not consider hedging their Asian risks. This is in contrast to normal practice, where global investors spread their investments over several countries in order to prevent all assets from turning bad in the event of problems in one country. Through diversification, they try to avoid putting all their eggs in one basket.

Diversified investment does not just mean investing in different places at random. The assets are carefully chosen so that their risk characteristics tend to offset each other. For example, a foreign investor looking to invest in Japan might also want to invest in Mexico. This is because Japan is not an oil producer. Thus, it is vulnerable to rises in the price of oil. If oil prices spike, Japanese asset prices might fall. By contrast, because Mexico is an oil producer, a spike in oil prices will probably cause Mexican asset prices to rise. Invest in both countries, and it should be possible to avoid incurring major losses even in the event of an oil shock. Investors construct shock-absorbent portfolios by skillfully combining investments with different risk characteristics. Risk hedging is at the core of diversified international investment.

However, the more one hedges, the more profitability declines. Taking the example in the previous paragraph, 50:50 investment in Japan and Mexico would mean that if Japanese equities were rising, the investor would only stand to make half as much as if he had invested all of his money in Japan. From the standpoint of absolute returns, it goes without saying that putting everything in Japanese equities would have produced better results.

At the time, many of the people investing in Asia had no risk hedging at all, because they all thought they could not go wrong investing in Asia. In other words, many of them were totally exposed when the Asian currency crisis started.

Moreover, many foreign investors who invested in Asia in the mid-1990s knew very little about those economies and had made no attempt to learn. For example, they did not bother to check whether there was any difference between the quality or coverage of Indonesian banking statistics compared with those from the U.S. Federal Reserve. They did not check the difference in bankruptcy laws between the U.S. and Thailand either. In other words, they had not done their homework on Asia. They had simply jumped in because they believed that they should not miss the bus.

As a result, as soon as these investors realized that something was not right, the only thing they could do was to get out. Everybody therefore rushed for the exit. With everyone trying to sell Asian currencies for dollars at the same time, the former plunged overnight. This is how the Asian currency crisis started.

Given that it was the strong yen which had created the Asian miracle, it was tantamount to suicide for the Asian economies to allow their currencies to have become uncompetitive relative to the yen. In other words, when the yen started to fall in 1995, the Asian currencies should have fallen with it. However, hardly any government officials and economists in Asia thought so at the time. This is because 10 years of yen appreciation had rendered a strong yen axiomatic. By 1995, it was entirely taken for granted. The same is probably true for anything, if it lasts for 10 years.

Moreover, people in Asia thought it was self-evident that Japanese companies would come to them, because they were diligent, had high levels of education, and high savings rates. Even though the most important reason for the Japanese investment in Asia was the strong yen, by 1995, most people had forgotten about this factor because it had been with them for so long. Furthermore, when the Japanese stopped coming due to the weakening of the yen, Europeans came as major capital providers. As a result, hardly anyone was concerned about the yen exchange rate during the 1995–97 period, even though that was the most important determinant of Asia's international competitiveness.

Put differently, the fall in the Asian currencies to where the yen was in July 1997, shown in Exhibit 9.1, probably represented a healthy adjustment that was two years overdue. However, once the selling started, the whole market was engulfed in a panic, and the Asian currencies fell way beyond what might be called a healthy adjustment. Instead of stopping at where the yen was in Exhibit 9.1, the Asian currencies fell nearly twice as far as they should have. Overseas investors panicked in the way that I had anticipated when I spoke at the conference in Venice.

SAD STATE OF AFFAIRS AT BLUE-CHIP INVESTMENT BANKS

When this happened, the Western media suddenly started talking about the need for structural reforms in Asia. Western investment banks as well as policymakers in Washington, including the IMF, started to come up with all sorts of arguments that laid the blame on structural problems in the Asian economies — the fact that Thai banks had been borrowing indiscriminately in foreign currencies, that bankruptcy laws were not good enough, that there were problems with the Malaysian legal system and with Indonesian accounting, and that there was not enough transparency and accountability all around.

There is no question that all of the above are areas in which reforms are urgently needed. However, to argue that they were the causes of the Asian currency crisis is absolute nonsense. This is because the above structural problems had been around for decades and had not appeared overnight. In other words, Western investment bankers could have investigated those deficiencies long in advance, had they chosen to do so. If they wanted to find out how corporate bankruptcy law worked in Thailand, all they had to do was to look at the law books in Thailand. It was all out in the open. Had they wanted to, Western investors could have checked everything, including the quality and coverage of banking statistics or corporate accounting in Asia, long before the crisis.

More importantly, the fact that these investment bankers were full of structural arguments against Asia proves that *they did not do their homework* as lenders before investing money in Asia. If they had known in advance about Thailand's bankruptcy laws, they should have reflected this risk in their loan pricing to Thai entities. And if this problem were fully reflected in the loan pricing, there was no reason for those bankers to be making noises about the Thai bankruptcy laws after the crisis had erupted.

Investing is equivalent to moneylending. If the borrower has hidden something from the lender and runs into problems, the borrower must be held responsible. If Thailand and Indonesia had been deliberately fiddling their trade statistics, they should have been punished severely for their criminal activities.

But if the lender lent money without first having checked out the borrower, the lender should also be held responsible for any money that is lost. After all, it is the responsibility of the lender to check out certain things in advance. What sort of political and social problems are there in the country concerned? What are the legal and accounting systems like? How transparent and accountable is corporate governance, and what do the government's statistics mean? These checks should be the lender's first step toward making investment decisions. It is only then that the investor should decide either that it is worth investing at the current price despite the risks attached, or that the figures cannot be trusted, in which case the investment should be called off.

However, many of the global investors that moved into Asia between 1995 and 1997 knew absolutely nothing about Asia. Had they done their homework and thought a little more about Thai bankruptcy laws, for example, they might not have worked themselves up into such a boom first and panic later. Moreover, it was preposterous for the blue-chip investment bankers who had been such cheerleaders for investment in Asia suddenly to turn into social reformers the minute they started losing money. What happened in Asia represented a complete lack of due diligence on the part of lenders.

WHY INVEST IN DEVELOPING COUNTRIES?

Financial problems are always partly the responsibility of the borrower and partly the responsibility of the lender. During the Asian currency crisis, though, the Western media, together with private-sector economists and the IMF, pointed the finger of blame almost exclusively at the borrowers. However, some blame should also have been laid at the feet of the global investment banks, which lent huge sums to Asian businesses without carrying out all the necessary checks in advance.

Moreover, one needs to consider why investors from advanced countries invest in developing countries. Why, for example, do American investors invest in Malaysia, rather than in the U.S.?

In countries like the U.S. with extremely well-developed markets, investors are unlikely to gain unusual returns vis-à-vis their competitors unless they are exceptionally skilled or extremely lucky. This is because there are no major differences between investors in terms of the volume and quality of information supplied to them. The fact that the majority of investors invest on the basis of broadly identical information makes it unlikely that one group will gain significantly higher returns than other groups operating in the same market. At most, any difference in returns will only be in the order of a few percent.

However, in developing countries, many things are not yet fully functional and there are many structural challenges. In those countries with less than perfect markets, good connections with those in power will probably enable one to purchase assets cheaply. Indeed, until the crisis hit in 1997, many blue-chip investment banks were boasting to their clients back home just how close they were to the people who held the reins of power in Asia. The Western media may be critical of Indonesia's former president Suharto now, but during the Asian investment boom, many foreign investment banks were boasting that they enjoyed the closest of links with him.

These investment banks felt that with the help of those in power, they would be able to gain higher returns in those countries compared with what was available in the developed world. After all, it is the possibility of higher-than-average returns that stimulates people to invest in developing countries in the first place. In other words, it is the very presence of structural challenges that constitutes one of the attractions of investment.

From the standpoint of investors, the bottom line is whether the price is cheap enough to offset the structural and other risks involved in investing in a developing world. If the risk-adjusted price is right, investors will come. In this sense, the Asian currency crisis cannot possibly have been caused by structural problems in the Asian economy. Rather, it was caused by the overvaluation of their currencies relative to the yen, and by the huge inflow and subsequent outflow of funds from investors who had not made sufficient study of the Asian economy before investing their money.

ASIA RECOVERED IN SPITE OF WARNINGS FROM "WASHINGTON CONSENSUS"

It is understandable why Western investment banks urged structural reforms on Asia. They wanted to deflect attention from their own inadequacies and ignorance. However, what was even more shocking was the behavior of some academics and critics in the U.S., in that many of them actually talked as though they welcomed the Asian currency crisis.

The U.S. is founded on Anglo-Saxon rationalism and liberal market principles. For some people who believe in those ideas, the success of Asian countries, including Japan, which have not necessarily conformed to their models of liberal market principles, has constituted the antithesis of their version of rationalism. For them, the downfall of Japan after the bubble burst in 1990 and the downfall of Asia after 1997 proved that their Anglo-Saxon rationalism was correct all along. The fact that the U.S. economy and stock market were very strong in the late 1990s only reinforced that feeling.

In what is known as the "Washington Consensus," they argued after the crisis that the Asian economies would not recover unless policymakers there implemented bold structural reforms along Anglo-Saxon lines. They warned the Asian governments in a very heavy-handed manner that they faced a choice between structural reform and prolonged stagnation.

In spite of such a dire forecast coming out of Washington, the Asian economies subsequently recovered much faster than the U.S. government or the IMF had expected. The reason for this quick recovery was very simple. The Asian economies recovered because the overvaluation of their currencies, the real cause of the crisis, was completely resolved when the crisis brought all the currencies down. As a result, the Asian countries once again became highly competitive on the international stage.

The Asian currencies fell sharply immediately after the crisis, but regained some of their lost ground after the panic subsided. However, as Exhibit 9.1 shows, they are mainly trading below the dollar–yen exchange rate and not higher than the yen. Having got through the crisis, the Asian central banks have now learned that their currencies should not trade higher than the yen.

In 1999, I had the opportunity to talk to central bankers from Thailand and South Korea. When I explained to them the relationship between the yen–dollar rate and the Asian economies, they replied that they too had realized the need to treat the relationship with the yen most carefully. They now recognized, they said, how important the yen rate was in maintaining their international competitiveness, and were now working to ensure that their currencies stayed below the yen.

Indeed, with the exchange rates fully corrected, the Asian countries have once again become highly attractive production locations for Japanese companies. As a result, Japanese companies have been boosting capacity utilization rates at Asian plants, deepening their alliances with Asian companies, and making new products such as DVDs in Asia. This is why Asia started to recover from the crisis much faster than the U.S. Treasury and the IMF had expected.

The Asian countries still face a number of structural problems. There are problems in the banking system. There are also problems in the accounting system. However, with the exchange rates as they are at the moment, the Asian countries are enjoying strong international competitiveness. The engine that propelled the Asian miracle following the Plaza Accord in 1985 has returned.

DOMESTIC BALANCE SHEET RECESSION AND THE CHINESE CHALLENGE

The Asian economies were all caught in asset-price bubbles that subsequently collapsed. The major decline in domestic asset prices has led to large NPL problems at Asian banks. Just like in Japan, many companies and individuals who bought assets during the bubble days are stuck with excess liabilities. As a result, there are probably several million damaged balance sheets in Asia. Those entities that have been affected are in the process of repairing their balance sheets by reining in their spending and investment activity and using any cash flow to repay loans.

In other words, even though Asia's international competitiveness is back, their domestic economies are very much in balance sheet recession. As a result, interest rates have come down sharply in many parts of Asia. Some interest rates are already at their historical lows. These symptoms of balance sheet recession all suggest that the recovery in domestic demand will take some time.

However, even though domestic demand is weak, the exchange rates have ensured a certain level of international competitiveness and generated substantial external demand. What economists call the "initial condition" of Asia is very much along the lines of South Korea, as mentioned in Chapter 4. As such, the Asian countries should continue to recover, thanks to external demand, for the foreseeable future.

However, it is unlikely that the Asian economies will continue to grow at the pace they managed between 1999 and 2000. The recovery following the crisis was fueled by a kind of regeneration demand. It was a recovery from the chaos of the currency crisis in 1997. It is hardly surprising that a recovery from the abyss will be rapid, but new growth is likely to be more challenging.

Moreover, China is now Asia's main economic rival. With virtually limitless markets and the ability to supply cheap, high-quality labor, China has attracted the attention not just of Japanese companies, but also of companies throughout the world. In a sense, Asian countries were lucky in that when the Japanese were looking to move their plants overseas in the late 1980s, China was on no one's radar screen. As a result, the Asian countries got most of the factories leaving Japan.

Today, however, the first destination any manufacturer thinks about when relocating a plant is China. In too many cases, China is the *only* country on their radar screens. The fact that China is very close culturally to the two largest investors in the region, Japan and Taiwan, should also be a cause for concern in Asia.

In order to overcome the Chinese challenge, Asian countries will have to offer things that are not available in China. For example, China does not have a properly functioning court and legal system, but the Asian countries could have one if they just made a little more effort in this regard. There are also some questions as to the ease of moving money out of China, whereas the Asian countries have fairly open systems when it comes to money flows. Making improvements in these areas would be the key for Asia to improve its competitiveness relative to China.

Put differently, a country with structural problems would, all other things being equal, need a weaker currency than a country without structural problems to attract investment from overseas. This means the country with structural problems will have to work longer and harder to earn a dollar as compared to the country without structural problems.

It makes sense for all countries, therefore, to engage in reforms for their own sake in order to assuage investor concerns while maximizing the return on their labor. For example, raising accounting standards to international levels would probably enable overseas investors to invest in that country with greater peace of mind. That, in turn, may help increase the prices of assets at home, which would be of great help for an economy still mired in balance sheet recession.

Confounded by the fact that the Asian economies have recovered so much faster than their prognostications, the "Washington Consensus" now argues that the recovery will prove to be short-lived, or that it will all end in tears as the Asian governments become complacent and take their finger off the throttle of structural reform. However, their economic prognosis failed to materialize because their basic analysis was wrong. Furthermore, any slowdown in Asia today has its causes in the slowdown in the U.S.

economy, as well as in the emergence of the Chinese challenge, the two factors which the "Washington Consensus" never predicted in the past.

As part of Asia, Japan needs to make the facts better known in the West. Japan should speak out in forums such as the G7 so that the same mistakes of administering the wrong medicine are not repeated. The Asian countries should, of course, continue with their structural reform efforts, but structural reform is not the biggest issue for the Asian economies — the exchange rate is.

ARE THE MARKETS ALWAYS RIGHT?

In order to prevent tragedies such as the Asian currency crisis before they happen, it seems much more useful to discuss how to cope when uninformed investors turn up in droves, rather than just debating structural reform issues in Asia.

Within the economics profession, there is a belief that markets are always right. In some sense, this is true. It is true in the sense that those who disagree with the market's conclusions can always take positions against it. Since the market is the cumulative expression of all these different views, in some sense, it is what everybody has acquiesced to. However, for the market to produce optimum resource allocation in the medium to long term, an additional assumption is needed. That assumption is that investors have done their homework properly and are fully aware of what they are getting into. Unfortunately, though, that is not always the case in the real world.

When I was assigned to the foreign exchange desk of the Federal Reserve Bank of New York, my boss told me that although I may have been told in my graduate school economics classes that markets are always right, that is not necessarily true on the ground. In her opinion, only around 15% of investors at any one time really thought about what they were doing; the remaining 85% were just sheep. The defining characteristic of sheep is that they are flock animals. In other words, if a market moves in a given direction, people will be dragged along with it.

This is not to suggest that 85% of investors are stupid. Indeed, in most cases it is not the fault of the investors themselves. This is because many of those investors have their performances judged against a benchmark index. If that index happens to contain an asset that is rapidly increasing in value, and if one's own portfolio did not contain a sufficient portion of that asset relative to the benchmark, the fund manager is placed under tremendous pressure to increase the holding of that asset so that his portfolio will track the performance of the benchmark better.

Even if there is no formal benchmark to beat, the fund manager may get a call from the final investor checking to see whether the fund manager has those assets that are going up in value and are in the news every day. If the fund manager does not have the assets in his portfolio, such a call will put tremendous pressure on him to acquire the assets in question, and to do so quickly. In such a situation, the fund manager typically does not have much time to study the risk characteristics of the assets. This kind of arrangement is sure to produce a lot of (sometimes unwilling) sheep.

Of course, a truly independent-minded fund manager will be able to withstand such pressures. But most ordinary souls will find it difficult to stay away from such a "popular trend," especially when the media is full of praises for the trend.

At times, these 85% of investors get carried away. And it is at times like these that bubbles or panics happen. When large numbers of less than fully informed investors all pile on to the bus, others jump on for fear of missing it; by the same token, when people start to get *off* the bus, lots of others follow suit. For example, during the late 1990s' IT bubble in the U.S., it is probably fair to say that the vast majority of investors who flocked to the NASDAQ market had very little idea of what they were really getting into. It is this type of investor that causes problems.

Given these dangers of uninformed investors flooding the place and then panicking, some restrictions on capital flows might be justified, especially for a small, developing country. This is because when these global investors pile into a small, developing country and create a bubble and its aftermath, the balance sheet recession, it is the poor local residents of that country who have to live with most of its consequences.

As such, the policymakers of these countries should be looking at ways of reducing the risk that ignorant investors will come in and wreak devastation in their economies. In other words, some kind of rules should be put in place so that investors would have to do their homework before they enter these countries.

FORCING INTERNATIONAL INVESTORS TO DO THEIR HOMEWORK

Chile once had such restrictions on capital flows, based on its bitter experience of something similar to the Asian currency crisis 15 years earlier, the Latin American debt crisis of 1982. At that time, as mentioned in Chapter 6, there was a major boom among global banks to lend money to South American countries, thereby generating a boom in these countries.

However, the Mexican debt crisis, which erupted in August 1982, made the banks realize that their risk assessment of Latin America was wrong. And as a result, they all tried to get out of Latin America at the same time, just as foreign financial institutions all tried to get out of Asia at the same time in 1997. Although the then chairman of the Federal Reserve, Paul Volcker, moved in right away and kept the international banks from leaving Latin

America, the crisis also led to a decade-long (balance sheet) recession in virtually all of Latin America.

From this devastating experience, Chile learned an extremely valuable lesson. A former top official of the Chilean central bank told me that "even if top Western banks come offering money at extremely favorable terms, it is very dangerous to accept them all." Chile learned that, because not all lenders do their homework, taking money from such lenders is extremely risky for the borrower. Based on this bitter experience, Chile imposed restrictions on capital flows.

In Chile's case, foreign investors were free to invest in the country, but they had to pay high levels of tax if they attempted to withdraw their funds after a short period of time. The way the system worked was that tax rates would be high if investors attempted to withdraw their funds early — for example, within three months — but it would become progressively lower and eventually would disappear altogether.

This way, outside investors know that they would lose a lot of their money to tax authorities if they attempted to pull out quickly. They therefore would not invest unless they were sure that they could make a profit in the medium term. In order to determine whether they could make a profit in the medium term, they would first have to do their homework properly, considering such issues as what economic conditions were like in Chile, what the accounting system was like, whether the legal system worked, how much they could rely upon lawyers and courts in the event of difficulties, and what local trade union activity was like.

Having done their homework, they would then decide whether they wished to invest in Chile. Because the investors that moved into Chile had done their homework and were able to look at the situation rationally, they were less likely to panic when confronted with problems. Thus, Chile did not turn away overseas investors. It merely said that the country wanted only those investors that had done their homework properly.

This is a very smart way of dealing with uninformed investors, and should be regarded as a useful benchmark in any discussion on the subject. Indeed, in September 1998, Malaysia borrowed the idea from Chile and implemented similar restrictions until stability was regained in the markets.

These restrictions on capital flows have attracted the wrath of free-market adherents within American economic circles. Indeed, views in favor of restrictions are not accepted readily in today's economics profession where it is a given that any restriction on the freedom of international capital movements is a bad thing. Their objections would be correct providing that investors had done their homework properly. However, the real world is not like that, and the human cost of repairing the damage after a bubble has burst is too large for most developing countries to ignore.

It should be noted that putting up this kind of capital controls actually requires tremendous courage on the part of the host country government, especially when its neighboring countries seem to be doing so well with unrestricted foreign capital inflow. Just before the Asian currency crisis, for example, the Taiwanese central bank was under tremendous pressure to deregulate capital flows, as its Southeast Asian neighbors were enjoying wonderful economic growth with foreign money. In the end, however, it turned out that Southeast Asian growth had a large element of bubble, while the Taiwanese growth was real.

Since no one feels bad when he is offered money at very attractive terms by the world's top investment bankers, tremendous courage is needed to say "No, thank you." However, when temptation wins over reason, disaster will not be very far off.

Meanwhile, some people argue that there should be a differentiation between short-term and long-term capital flows. In their opinion, the latter are OK, but the former should be regulated. However, this is much easier said than done.

Many foreign investors who moved into Asia in the mid-1990s did so because they thought that Asia would be the growth center of the 21st century. Initially, therefore, they thought that they would be there for the long term; indeed, until the 21st century. However, when the currency crisis erupted in 1997 they took fright and bolted for the exit, with the result that their investments ultimately turned out to be of a short-term duration. What this means is that it is difficult to establish restrictions that differentiated between the long term and the short term from the beginning.

This being so, it is much smarter to do what Chile did and design restrictions so that investors that withdraw their funds after a short period of time are penalized heavily through taxation, while those that remain for a longer time face progressively lower taxes. If the investors know that this kind of system is in place, they are much more likely to do their homework and make a proper study of a country's economy before making their investment decisions.

ECONOMIC SCIENCE HAS NOT DEALT WITH LIBERALIZATION OF CAPITAL FLOWS

Many critics think it so self-evident that the free flow of capital is a good thing for a country's economy that they do not feel any need to justify it. However, as the Nobel laureate Joseph Stiglitz in his *Globalization and Its Discontents* has pointed out, economic science has not yet sufficiently proved under what circumstances the liberalization of capital flows is good for a country's economy.[2]

Although the economics profession has been talking about the "open economy" for a long time, up until recently this concept in economics only referred to the free movement of goods and services across national borders. The concept never referred to the free movement of capital across national borders. Indeed, in most theoretical treatments of the open economy, it is implicitly assumed that the free movement of capital does not exist.

Since the beginning of the 20th century, the economics profession has carried out detailed research into the welfare, efficiency, taxation, and terms of trade implications of the free movement of goods across national borders. However, until recently, there has been hardly any empirical or theoretical analysis of what happens when the capital market in an economy is opened up. This is simply because, until recently, hardly any capital markets were completely open, even in advanced countries.

The U.S. started to liberalize international capital flows in the 1980s. Up until then, there were various regulations, including eurodollar reserve requirements, that regulated international banking flows: Regulation Q, which governed domestic interest rates, and the "Bank of America letter," which discouraged foreign currency deposits at domestic banks. In other words, it was not easy for the ordinary American to move financial capital in and out of the dollar and the U.S.

Similarly, Japan basically forbade free flows of capital until December 1980, when the foreign exchange law was revised. This was followed by further gradual deregulation; since 1997, capital flows into and out of Japan have been completely deregulated. Restrictions also remained in the U.K. until the end of the 1970s.

What this means is that as late as the first half of the 1980s, people who studied economics did not study, and had no experience of, economies in which capital flows had been deregulated. Although these are the people who are now making policy decisions as part of governments, the economics that they learned in school cannot tell them anything about the current situation in which cross-border capital flows are no longer restricted.

Former Singaporean prime minister Lee Kuan Yew made this point very well. When confronted with Western critics who argued for the need for structural reforms in Asia immediately following the currency crisis, he shot back by saying that none of his critics had ever told him that capital flows should *not* be liberalized unless these structural issues were all sorted out in advance. He was right.

Indeed, none of the so-called Western experts now lecturing Asia in such a high-handed fashion saw any need for these measures until the crisis actually happened. They failed to notice the need, because the liberalization of capital flows did not feature in the economics courses they had studied.

As a result, they had no idea of what might happen if capital flows were actually liberalized, especially in a small, developing country.

Furthermore, even though the IMF and the Clinton-era Treasury Department often said that capital markets needed to be opened and deregulated in Asia, there is very little empirical evidence to prove that such measures actually yielded better results. In other words, there is insufficient evidence to prove that the countries that had deregulated and opened up their capital markets enjoyed significantly higher economic growth than countries that had not.

On the contrary, both Taiwan and China, which still maintain numerous restrictions on the flow of capital, did not suffer any major disruption due to the Asian currency crisis, and maintained steady economic growth thereafter. In particular, the fact that the Taiwanese economy did not experience a major bubble and continued to develop in a stable fashion constitutes an important counter-argument to the belief that capital markets should be deregulated at all costs.

Similarly, when Malaysia imposed some capital controls in September 1998, Washington was furious and, together with the Western press, argued that Malaysia would lose out on everything. For example, the September 21, 1998, issue of *Business Week* stated:

> Mahathir's bet is likely to be a loser. ... because Malaysia has effectively burned its bridges with foreign portfolio managers, its beleaguered companies will be deprived of an important source of capital to rebuild. By closing off parts of Malaysia's economy, Mahathir may find that he has crossed Malaysia off the world investment map. ... Mahathir has discredited free markets. And the world is watching to see if his economics of defiance works.[3]

Pretty strong reactions, indeed. But, in fact, no disaster followed, and the Malaysian economy continues to do well. Even though *Business Week* predicted Malaysian GDP growth to fall 2–3% in 1999 and blamed this squarely on Prime Minister Mahathir who is said to be "wounding his nation with every step,"[4] the country actually recorded 6.1% growth for 1999 and 8.3% growth for 2000. Malaysia achieved the highest growth in the region, in part because the country only restricted some capital flows; it did not restrict the free flow of goods and services. And it is the latter that is proven to be important for the efficient allocation of resources.

This *Business Week* episode shows how thoroughly the Western media is influenced by the Western financial institutions operating in the region. Those financial institutions have a reason to worry about capital controls, since those controls mean fewer money-making opportunities for them. That is why they made such a fuss. For 99% of the Malaysian economy, however, the key issue is whether or not they can continue to get the parts from abroad to assemble and export VCRs. To them, whether or not investors in New York or London can play the Malaysian stock market is largely irrelevant.

This is not to argue that capital flows should not be deregulated. The point is that the arguments in favor should be based on theoretical and empirical analysis, not on blind faith. As Lee Kuan Yew's remarks have made clear, at the moment, there is insufficient analysis of the conditions under which the deregulation of the flow of capital will prove beneficial to the economy. In too many cases, arguments in favor of capital market opening are nothing more than a mindless extension of the market opening arguments that worked so well for the cross-border trade in goods and services. Without solid understanding of what free capital flows can do to an economy, however, the mistakes of Latin America prior to 1982, and of Asia prior to 1997, are likely to be repeated, with costly consequences for the countries involved.

JAPAN HAS BEEN SAVED BY INTERNATIONAL CAPITAL FLOWS

However, there are two countries that have derived huge benefits from the liberalization of capital flows: Japan and the United States. Japan has been in serious economic difficulty since the 1990s as a result of the collapse in asset prices and the subsequent balance sheet recession. However, it has been lucky in that, over the past 10 years, foreign investors, mainly Americans and Europeans, have continuously propped up the Japanese equity market. Exhibit 9.3 shows the supply–demand conditions in the Japanese equity market over the past decade. It reveals that domestic individuals and corporations have been net sellers — in other words, they have sold more than they have bought — for almost the entire period. Moreover, domestic institutional investors, life insurers, and trust banks have also been net sellers virtually every month. By contrast, foreign investors such as American pension funds and hedge funds have been net purchasers. (Although the entry for banks shows a large net buying, it is mostly government's PKO, or price-keeping operations.)

Where would Japanese equities be now but for the inflow of funds from overseas investors? As indicated in Exhibit 1.1 in Chapter 1, markets that foreign investors did not invest in, such as the commercial real estate market and the market for golf club memberships, fell to nearly one-tenth of their peak values. In comparison, the share market, which attracted large foreign buying, fell only 70% from its peak value. This suggests that if it were not for the foreign capital inflow, the Japanese share market could have fallen much further than where it is now. In other words, in the 1990s the biggest beneficiary of the liberalization of international capital flows was Japan.

Exhibit 9.3 Japanese stock market has been led by foreign investors

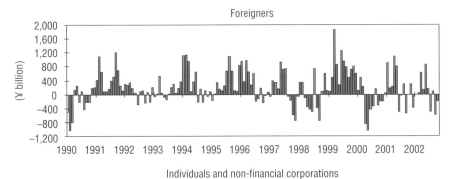

Foreigners

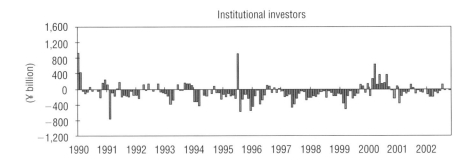

Individuals and non-financial corporations

Institutional investors

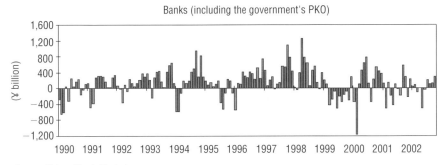

Banks (including the government's PKO)

Source: Tokyo Stock Market.

In the 1980s, however, the situation was just the reverse. At that time, it was the U.S. that was suffering from a severe shortage of domestic savings as exemplified by the mushrooming trade deficit, while the government was running a huge budget deficit. As a result, there was a constant fear that interest rates would go sky-high, as the financial market continuously worried about the twin deficits.

In this predicament, it was the Japanese institutional investors' healthy appetite for U.S. treasury bonds that saved the U.S. By buying a large portion of U.S. treasuries as they were issued, Japanese investors simultaneously kept the dollar up and U.S. interest rates low, thus supporting President Reagan's supply-side revolution in no small way. Had it not been for the presence of Japanese investors, U.S. economic adjustments could have collapsed by the mid-1980s with sky-rocketing interest rates and a collapsing dollar. Although U.S. money was plentiful in its stock market, it was the Japanese money in the most critical U.S. bond market that kept the U.S. economy going during those now distant days of the 1980s.

It has to be more than a pure coincidence that when the U.S. most needed money in its bond market, the Japanese were there to help, and that when the Japanese most needed money in its stock market, the U.S. investors were there to help. These two countries are really allies in more ways than one. A friend in need is a friend in deed!

THE LESSONS OF THE ASIAN CURRENCY CRISIS

Unfortunately for Asia, foreign investors blinded by the talk of an Asian miracle flocked into the market without doing their homework and ended up contributing significantly to both the bubble and the subsequent panic. As a result, Asians were forced into considerable tribulations as, one after the other, their economies fell into serious balance sheet recession. By keeping their currencies competitive, however, the Asian countries are making good use of foreign demand to keep the economy going and help domestic entities repair their balance sheets.

In terms of information flow, however, the attempt by foreign financial institutions to pin all the blame for the Asian currency crisis on structural problems in Asia has been 99.9% successful. The fact that even now Western forums on the Asian currency crisis carry titles along the lines of "Is Asia Making Progress with Structural Reforms?" and not "Are Investors Doing Their Homework?" shows how successful they have been. Of course, Western opinion is not completely monolithic. People such as the former World Bank chief economist Joseph Stiglitz have gone so far as to say that some of the responsibility lies with the Wall Street lenders as well as the borrowers. However, he was dismissed from his post after crossing swords with the U.S. Treasury Department, which was all out to produce structural reforms in Asia.

The only option for Asia, which is under the thumb of the West in terms of who controls the information flow, is to take steps to protect itself from a further reoccurrence of the desperate events of 1997. That means, in addition to maintaining competitive exchange rates and implementing structural reforms needed for their own sake, the Asian governments *have to be courageous enough to refuse overseas money*, no matter how attractive the terms are, unless they can be sure that the overseas investors offering the money have made a proper study of their country's economic conditions.

ENDNOTES

1 Ezra Vogel, *Japan As Number One: Lessons for America* (Harvard University Press, 1979).

2 Joseph E. Stiglitz, *Globalization and Its Discontents* (W. W. Norton & Co., 2002), p. 64.

3 "Renegade Economy," *Business Week* (Asian edition), September 21, 1998, pp. 20–22.

4 "Report Card on Asia," *Business Week* (Asian edition), November 23, 1998, pp. 16–21.

10

JAPAN'S LESSONS FOR THE U.S. ECONOMY

U.S. CORPORATE SECTOR ALREADY IN BALANCE SHEET REPAIR MODE

What does Japan's experience of the last 10 years mean for the post-IT-bubble or post-Enron United States? There are certainly many similarities as well as differences.

There is no question that the U.S. economy is already suffering from many of the symptoms of a balance sheet recession. After the collapse of the IT bubble, a lot of wealth was lost, leaving a hole in the balance sheets of both corporations and households. The collapse of Enron and subsequent discoveries that many U.S. companies may actually have more debt than they show on their financial statements has prompted everyone to look at the liability side of balance sheets with far more care than in the past. The subsequent disclosures that many other companies have been reporting inflated profit numbers have also added to the more careful scrutiny of both balance sheets and profit and loss statements.

These revelations and the subsequent national uproar are now forcing corporate executives in the U.S. to produce strong balance sheets as quickly as possible. As a result, the demand for funds from the U.S. corporate sector has collapsed altogether, in spite of the fact that the Federal Reserve has lowered interest rates 12 times to a level not seen since the 1950s. In fact, as seen in Exhibit 1.4 in Chapter 1, corporate demand for funds in the U.S. has continued to fall in spite of the lower interest rates, a very clear sign that U.S. companies are concerned about their financial health.

The last time the corporate demand for funds fell so drastically was in 1991. Indeed, it was at that time that the term "balance sheet recession" was first coined by the Federal Reserve Bank of New York to describe the recession of that time when so many corporations, banks, and households were talking about the debt overhang. At that time, the chairman of the Federal Reserve, Alan Greenspan, was somewhat slow in realizing what was happening, and was still of the opinion, right up until December 1991, that there were no signs of a generalized decline in economic activity.

By December, however, Greenspan realized that the situation was very different from a typical recession, and he started to use the term "50 mph head wind" to describe the difficulties faced by the U.S. economy. He also lowered the discount rate by a full 100 basis points, a highly uncharacteristic move by the central banker known for his gradualist approach. At the same time, a fat spread was provided to the commercial banks to resolve their capital problems.

The recession in 1991, although very severe, was still largely confined to the banking sector. As mentioned earlier, the commercial banks were suffering from the collapse of both the leveraged buyout market and the mini-bubble in the commercial real estate market. As a result, many major U.S. money center banks, including Citibank, came mighty close to collapsing during this period.

At the same time, bank supervisors were becoming extremely stringent as they were trying to recover the credibility lost during the Savings and Loan fiasco, which had unfolded only two years earlier in 1989. Thus, there was a nationwide credit crunch in the U.S. where bankers were withdrawing loans left and right to meet the capital adequacy ratios imposed by the regulators. The credit crunch got so bad that, at one point, President George Bush, Sr. had to beg the bank examiners to be a little more reasonable.

Because of the difficulties faced by the U.S. banks, many foreign banks, including those from Japan, had a field day extending loans to U.S. corporations. Indeed, many U.S. corporate executives traveled to the headquarters of Japanese banks in Tokyo and asked for lines of credit to offset the financing they were losing at home from U.S.-based banks.

The point here is that the decline in the corporate procurement of funds in Exhibit 1.4 for 1991 probably included a large involuntary component in that even if corporations wanted to borrow more, no supply was forthcoming from the banks. This can also be inferred from Exhibit 8.1, which shows that when there was a massive credit crunch in the U.S. between 1991 and 1993, those companies that had access to the capital market moved their funding activities there.

In other words, the epicenter of the 1991 balance sheet recession was the banks. In contrast, the epicenter of the 2002 balance sheet recession is the corporations. In that sense, it is much more like the Japanese balance sheet recession of the last 10 years. It is similarly harder to tackle than the 1991 recession because there are so many more entities involved. Furthermore, with so many companies involved at the same time, it is easy to fall into the fallacy of composition problems, as has happened in Japan during the last 10 years.

In 1991, however, only the banks needed to be fixed. As can be seen in Exhibit 8.1, once the banks were fixed via the policy of fat spread, the credit crunch ended in the fourth quarter of 1993. Once the banking problems — the bottleneck of the economy — were removed, the rest of the economy recovered quickly as well.

REAL ESTATE PRICES WERE STILL RISING WHEN THE MONETARY EASING BEGAN

So, how does the U.S. today compare with the Japanese experience of the last 10 years? First, in terms of the magnitude of wealth lost as a result of the collapse in asset values, the U.S. situation so far is only a fraction of what has happened to Japan over the last 10 years. For example, the combined loss of market capitalization in the NYEX, NASDAQ, and AMEX from their peak levels is around US$7 trillion (as of January 22, 2003). That is about 70% of U.S. GDP for the year 2001. In comparison, the Japanese loss of wealth was 2.7 times the yearly GDP of 1989, and 2.3 times the GDP of 2001. This means the damage in Japan is three to four times that experienced in the U.S. up to now.

The key difference here is the value of real estate. Nearly 70% of the loss of wealth in Japan was due to the collapse in land values. In the U.S., however, even though the price of commercial real estate in some hard-hit areas such as Silicon Valley in California has fallen badly, housing prices rose in most parts of the country until recently. The fact that the real estate market in the U.S. is still holding is limiting the negative wealth effect coming from the bursting of the IT bubble in the stock market.

This difference — the collapse of the real estate market in Japan but not in the U.S. — is due almost entirely to the different schedules of monetary easing undertaken in the two countries. In Japan, the Bank of Japan was still raising interest rates after the stock-market bubble burst in early 1990. In fact, two more monetary tightenings followed after the stock market crashed. It was more than a year after the stock-market crash that the BOJ began easing its monetary policy.

The reason for this action by the BOJ is that, at that time, the whole nation was very upset about the rapidly rising land prices. Indeed, it was the time when the Imperial Palace in the center of Tokyo was said to be worth as much as the entire state of California. The social and political uproar over this land-price craze forced the BOJ to keep raising interest rates until the bursting of the land-price bubble was confirmed. Thus, the short-term money market rate was raised to well above 8% in 1991, before monetary policy was reversed. At that time, the Japanese CPI inflation rate was still less than 3% per annum, so the real rates were well in excess of 5%.

Therefore, the land-price bubble had already burst when monetary policy began to be eased in July 1991. In other words, when the BOJ began lowering rates, both the share market and the real estate markets were collapsing. Once the bubble bursts, however, lowering of interest rates becomes ineffective in turning the tide of asset prices because people in those markets are already convinced that they were chasing the wrong asset prices. Once this realization spreads, the momentum toward the downward adjustment of asset prices becomes almost unstoppable. This phenomenon was also observed in the U.S. during 2001 when, in spite of 11 cuts in interest rates by the Federal Reserve, share prices, particularly in the NASDAQ market, continued to fall. Thus, Japan was stuck with both land and share prices collapsing at the same time, resulting in huge damage to the balance sheets of corporations and banks.

In the U.S., the Fed chairman, Alan Greenspan, followed developments in Japan very carefully, as he was determined not to make the same mistake the BOJ had made. The fact that Greenspan was slow in understanding what was happening in the U.S. in the 1991 recession, which cost his long-time friend, George Bush, Sr., his re-election bid, probably made the chairman particularly alert to the possibility that the U.S. might face the same balance sheet problems again.

After analyzing the Japanese and other bubbles carefully, the Federal Reserve apparently came to the conclusion that it was not wise to push interest rates higher in order to crush the bubble. They concluded that if the bubble would burst under its own weight anyway, there was no reason for the central bank to get involved. Their view was that the central bank should concentrate on traditional or conventional macroeconomic indicators and not be swayed unnecessarily by asset-price bubbles in certain parts of the economy. In other words, the Fed was determined to tighten monetary policy only if the aggregate economic performance warranted such tightening, not because asset prices were rising in some regions or sectors of the economy.

Although this mindset kept the Federal Reserve out of the share-price bubble when the bubble was still expanding, when it burst, the Fed's action in the opposite direction was extremely swift. Indeed, starting with the cut in interest rates in January 2001, Greenspan dropped short-term rates all the way from 6.5% to 1.75% in less than a year. This speed of rate cuts was an all-time record for the Fed, and was done in less than half the average time it took the Fed to cut interest rates in the past.

More importantly, Greenspan started to cut interest rates as soon as share prices started heading south. But at that time, the U.S. economy was still doing very well, with a booming housing market. In other words, Greenspan cut interest rates when housing prices were still on an upward trend. Since nothing responds more to a cut in interest rates than the housing market, the lower interest rates pushed housing prices even higher, thus creating an important offset to the wealth lost in the share markets. When Greenspan spoke before Congress in July 2002, saying that the negative wealth effect from the collapse of the share market was largely offset by the positive wealth effect coming from the housing market, he was referring to this development. It was a brilliant strategy.

Greenspan probably reasoned that if the bursting of a bubble in one asset class cannot be avoided, why not offset it by raising prices of some other assets? The Federal Reserve's strategy today seems to be to keep the housing market as strong as possible until other elements in the economy get their act together and start moving forward. For example, if the housing boom keeps the economy going for another year or two, that will give the battered corporate sector badly needed time to repair its balance sheets. Once the corporate sector regains its health, the economy's dependence on the housing market can be eased.

In a sense, Greenspan was also lucky. This is because, at present, there is no uproar in the U.S. about the high cost of housing, which was the problem that haunted the Bank of Japan in 1990. Thus, the BOJ had to continue tightening monetary policy until the real estate market started heading south. But by then, *all* asset prices were collapsing, and there were no asset categories left that could respond positively to monetary policy easing and offset the negative wealth effect stemming from other asset categories. In the U.S., the fact that the real estate market was not the target of monetary tightening saved a key portion of the monetary transmission mechanism which was lost to the BOJ in the 1990s, as mentioned in Chapter 3.

Although the strategy of offsetting one asset price decline with another asset price increase is a brilliant one, it is not without problems. First of all, housing prices are rising when the rest of the economy is at a near standstill. Since the only reason housing prices are rising is the low interest rate, there is a danger that another bubble is in the making. After all, it is difficult to imagine a world where housing prices are going up when income and employment are going down. MIT professor Charles Kindleberger, for example, has been warning that the housing bubble might not last.[1] There are already reports that in some areas housing prices have peaked. If this bubble crashes before other elements needed for economic growth are in place, the U.S. economy will find itself in a most difficult situation.

REBUILDING CORPORATE CONFIDENCE IS NOT EASY

In this regard, how the corporate sector in the U.S. might recover from the current accounting fiasco needs to be examined carefully. The problem of overstated profits and understated liabilities is not an easy one to resolve.

Even though producing accurate numbers is a simple matter, replicating past ROE and ROA performances is not. This is because the past numbers were overstated in the accounting sense, and were obtained during a booming economy. Now that accounting tricks are no longer overlooked, and the economy itself is much weaker than before, regaining the same ROE as in the past is going to be a real challenge for the management.

Since past share prices were attained on the basis of high ROEs, stock prices must necessarily adjust downward to reflect the true reality. Furthermore, in those cases where good profits were partly a result of higher-than-reported leveraging, the de-leveraging that is under way will necessarily lower the return on capital. To gain the same return on capital as in the past, but with a lower leveraging, is not an easy task. This means that, for share prices to regain their upward momentum, cleaning up the accounting mess alone will be far from sufficient.

Moreover, if the reaction of President George W. Bush to the U.S.'s corporate accounting problems is any guide, corporations might have to reinvent themselves in order to regain the social acceptance they have lost since the Enron affair became public. For example, in his July 9, 2002 speech, the president said, "The pay package sends a clear signal whether a business leader is committed to teamwork or personal enrichment. It tells you whether his principal goal is the creation of wealth for shareholders, or the accumulation of wealth for himself. I challenge every CEO in America to describe in the company's annual report — prominently and in plain English — details of his or her compensation package, including salary and bonus and benefits."

Suddenly, it is not so cool to have a huge pay package, even in the United States. Remember, that wasn't Lenin or Mao speaking, but the president of the United States in mid-2002. For those U.S. corporate executives who have worked hard to get bigger and better pay packages, hearing such a statement from their president must have been a bewildering experience. At the minimum, it must have reduced their incentive to work hard for a bigger pay package. Many are probably unsure about what is the right thing to do in this new environment.

All of this will tend to make U.S. companies more cautious. They will wait to see what is acceptable and what is not in the new social and political, if not accounting, environment. Unless the new game plan is stated clearly for everyone to understand, it will be difficult to expect companies and executives to forge ahead at full speed.

Indeed, if we were to take the president's statement — "Responsible leaders do not collect huge bonus packages *when the value of their company dramatically declines* ..." — and replace the italicized portion with "when hundreds of employees are losing jobs," we would be talking about the once highly regarded, but now largely ignored, Japanese management principles! For many U.S. business leaders, this must be a very confusing period indeed.

FALLACY OF COMPOSITION PROBLEMS MORE SEVERE IN THE U.S.

Moving from the accounting and management issues to macro issues, it has been argued in Chapter 2 that the balance sheet recession is really caused by the fallacy of composition — that everyone is trying to do the right thing by repairing their balance sheets, but with everyone doing it at the same time, the economy is collapsing into a vicious cycle. This fallacy of composition problem could become particularly acute in the U.S. compared to Japan, because U.S. companies typically do not keep much of their financial and other resources within the corporation. Because they do not have much of a "cushion" within the company to absorb shocks, they typically take actions to cut costs much more rapidly than the Japanese.

For example, U.S. companies typically distribute large bonuses when times are good, but start laying off workers and cut costs as soon as times turn bad. Japanese companies, on the other hand, wait until times are *really* good or *really* bad before taking such action. This is because many Japanese companies that were set up at the end of World War II had as a basic premise that employees cannot be laid off easily. In fact, I remember how shocked I was when I moved from the Federal Reserve Bank of New York to Nomura in Tokyo and discovered that, in Japan, labor is considered a fixed cost. In all my years as an economist in the U.S., labor cost was always considered a variable cost.

But how do Japanese companies manage with such a huge fixed cost when there are large fluctuations in demand stemming from business cycles? There is only one solution: during the good times, they do not distribute all the profits, so that during the bad times they have reserves available to carry them over. (Some downward flexibility in wages is also available to the management in the form of adjustment of bonuses.)

Since Japanese companies followed this principle in a rapidly growing economy for nearly five decades following the end of the war, they ended up accumulating huge reserves by the end of the 1980s. Thus, when the balance sheet recession hit those companies in the 1990s, they were in a very cash-rich position.

Not realizing that this recession was very different from previous recessions, they relied on their reserves to weather the storm for the first few years. Indeed, in the early years of this recession, many corporate employees fully expected their employers to cover for them, because during the good times in the late 1980s they were never paid their marginal product. The employers also fully expected to keep their employees as much as possible.

As a result, the Japanese bankruptcy rate and unemployment rate grew only very slowly in spite of the massive loss of wealth and the massive contraction in corporate activities, as seen in Chapter 1. In effect, the corporate reserves, together with the fiscal stimulus from the government, acted as a cushion in keeping the fallacy of composition problems from multiplying quickly.

Of course, many corporate executives now regret their earlier decisions. Had they known that this was no ordinary business cycle-induced recession and that it would go on for so long, they might have taken a very different course of action, especially in terms of relying on past reserves. There is no question that the rich reserves made both employees and employers in Japan more complacent about the balance sheet recession than they might otherwise have been.

In the U.S., however, where companies typically do not have such reserves, cost-cutting and layoffs start very quickly in a downturn. Even though that is good in an ordinary recession, when there is a massive fallacy of composition problem in the economy, too fast a corporate reaction can easily push the entire economy into a vicious cycle.

In Japan, as seen in Exhibit 3.1 in Chapter 3, it took more than three years after the share price collapsed before the demand for funds from the corporate sector disappeared. In the U.S., as seen in Exhibit 1.4, the same thing is happening in less than two years. In the U.S. today, the number of bankruptcies is already at a record high, whereas in Japan, it is still less than the record reached in 1984.[2] In this sense, the United States' need for fiscal stimulus to fill the demand gap created by the rapid shrinkage in corporate activities might surpass that of Japan.

U.S. HOUSEHOLD SECTOR RAISING SAVINGS RATE

The other difference between the U.S. and Japan that could make the fallacy of composition problems worse for the U.S. is the behavior of consumers. As noted in Chapter 1, during the last 12 years, Japanese consumers really did not change their behavior. During the boom days of 1990, when Japan was on top of the world, the Japanese household sector was saving 7–8% of GDP; in 1999, when it was at the bottom of the world, the household sector was still saving 7–8% of GDP. Most recent numbers show a slight decline in savings, largely because of the weakness in income and employment.

This stability of household saving behavior is truly remarkable in view of the fact that the Japanese were so confident in 1990, and so depressed in 1999. After all, the end of the 1980s was characterized by almost global worship of so-called Japanese management, so that any book with a title that included the term was almost guaranteed to make it on to the *New York*

Times bestseller list. Indeed, it was a period when the whole world thought that Japan had got everything right, and the U.S. had got everything wrong. The statistics on productivity growth, income distribution, trade and budget surpluses, educational level, employment rate, crime rate, and credit ratings of financial institutions all showed Japan to be way ahead of the U.S. and other countries.

Given how far Japan is today from that "Japan as number one" state of only 10 years ago, it is remarkable that household savings stayed stable for so long. It is perhaps an indication that the supreme confidence displayed by Japan's business leaders in the late 1980s and early 1990s was really confined to business*men* only, and that Japanese housewives, who make the savings decisions, were nowhere near as confident as their men-folk.

The significance of this savings behavior is that the household sector in Japan is not responsible for the weakness of the economy during the last 10 years. As mentioned earlier, it was the change in *corporate* behavior that weakened the economy, not the behavior of the household sector. The household sector remained cautious throughout this period.

In contrast, the U.S. household sector played a huge role in keeping the economy going during the late 1990s by reducing their savings rate dramatically. As shown in Exhibit 10.1, the U.S. household savings rate was above 5% up until 1995. But from that point, and in conjunction with the stock-market boom, the savings rate fell dramatically to almost zero by 2001. This dramatic fall in the savings rate played a major role in keeping the U.S. domestic demand strong.

Exhibit 10.1 U.S. savings rate going up as U.S. share prices come down

Sources: U.S. Department of Commerce; Dow Jones.

There is a reason for this drop in the savings rate, of course. This period was characterized by a dramatic fall in the unemployment rate, as well as by dramatic increases in asset values and income. The increase in share prices and, to a lesser degree, housing prices made it unnecessary for many to save so much. With nearly 80 million Americans holding stocks in some form, the dramatic increase in the value of shares during the period from 1995 to 2000 added trillions of dollars to their wealth. The market capitalization of the three markets, for example, increased by US$13.5 trillion during this period. This is equivalent to decades of accumulated savings, and as a result, people felt safe enough to spend.

My uncle in San Francisco, for example, was over 75 when the stock-market boom doubled his retirement portfolio. Realizing that he was not going to live twice as long just because his retirement fund had doubled, he started spending money by inviting his friends and relatives for dinner every night. This was a man who had left war-torn China in 1949 with just one suitcase and a few dollars of American money in his pocket. He had always lived simply, despite becoming a successful chief engineer at a major U.S. engineering firm. The stock-market bubble completely transformed him. Similar stories were repeated all over the U.S.

What this means is that if asset prices start heading south, the wealth effect will work in the opposite direction, which may result in a sudden contraction in consumer spending all around the country. The fact that US$7 trillion in market capitalization has been lost in the share market is not a good sign in that regard, and the recent savings rate figure in Exhibit 10.1 suggests that the savings rate is now creeping upward. Although some of the wealth lost has been offset by the rise in house prices, as mentioned earlier, any further increase in the savings rate could make the situation dramatically worse. In contrast, less than 20% of Japanese households were involved in the stock market when it began collapsing in 1990.

The point is that the Japanese balance sheet problems have been largely confined to its corporate sector, whereas the U.S. balance sheet problems potentially involve both the household sector and the corporate sector. In other words, the fallacy of composition problem could become that much more serious in the U.S. with both sectors affected by the fall in asset prices at the same time.

Of course, U.S. banks are in much better shape than the Japanese banks, thanks largely to the stability of real estate prices in the U.S. compared with Japan. However, the Japanese banking problem has not been the constraint on economic growth, as mentioned earlier. On the other hand, given the precariousness of the U.S. economy at the moment, especially in regard to housing prices, even a slight increase in the household savings rate could cause a very large contraction in demand. With U.S. corporations trying to find ways to reinvent themselves, a cautious note from consumers might be all that is required to push the U.S. into a vicious cycle.

TRADE DEFICIT COULD LIMIT POLICY OPTIONS

Another possible weakness of the U.S. situation compared with the Japanese one is the presence of a huge trade deficit in the United States. Although the U.S. has been running huge trade deficits for decades, when the economy is doing well, the deficits themselves seldom cause a problem, both at home and abroad.

In fact, the vibrant economy, together with the generally higher rates of return available in the U.S. market, has brought lots of foreign money into the United States. As long as the inflow of foreign capital is large enough to finance the U.S. current account deficit, the demand for and supply of dollars in the foreign exchange market will be balanced and there is really no reason to worry. In other words, as long as the dollars the Toyotas and Hondas are selling in the foreign exchange market in order to pay their workers at home in yen are bought by Japanese life insurance companies and pension managers looking for higher returns in the U.S., there is no reason for the dollar to fall.

Once the economy weakens, however, those in the U.S. who are losing jobs begin to complain about the foreign penetration of their markets. Import-competing manufacturers also begin to complain that foreigners are dumping in the U.S. market. Once these issues become important in Washington, however, the foreign exchange market participants suddenly start paying attention to the trade imbalance, which is the root cause of the problem. There, they cannot help but notice the United States' huge trade deficit and Japan's large trade surplus, as shown in Exhibit 10.2.

Foreign exchange participants start paying attention to these trade issues because one of the most straightforward policy responses to a trade imbalance is exchange rate adjustments. In other words, people begin to contemplate the possibility that the U.S. government might be forced into a weak dollar policy in order to keep the workers and import-competing industries happy. Even if the administration did not openly argue for a weak dollar, it may still acquiesce to the falling currency.

Since investors, both foreign and domestic, have the right not to buy dollars or even to sell dollars, there could be a sudden fall in the demand for dollars from those investors who become concerned about the trade imbalance. Some of them may decide that even though the return on the dollar assets is higher, they will wait until the dollar has bottomed before resuming purchases of dollar assets. When that happens, the demand for both the dollar and U.S. assets, such as U.S. treasury bonds, could dry up quickly.

Exhibit 10.2   U.S. trade deficit is still huge

Sources: U.S. Department of Commerce; U.S. Department of Treasury; Ministry of Finance, Japan.

On the other hand, the Toyotas and Hondas have no choice but to sell the dollars they earned in the U.S. in the foreign exchange market in order to pay their workers at home in yen. Thus, when foreign investors become cautious, there will be only sellers and no buyers of dollars in the foreign exchange market.

Once the dollar begins falling, however, foreign investors become even more cautious about investing in the U.S. because of the foreign exchange losses incurred. Some may be forced to dump their holdings in order to cut their losses, resulting in both a weaker dollar and weaker asset prices in the U.S. But a situation of weaker asset prices in the U.S. today would be nothing short of a nightmare, because it would make the present balance sheet recession worse. Furthermore, if foreigners dumped their huge holdings of U.S. treasury bonds, U.S. interest rates could skyrocket, as weaker bond prices mean higher interest rates. Higher interest rates will play havoc with the housing market, which is the only bright spot left in the U.S. economy today.

This simultaneous weakness of both the dollar and the bond market is difficult to stop, because the typical policy remedy of raising interest rates to defend the dollar by making dollar assets more attractive runs the risk of weakening the bond and stock markets even further. The departure of foreign investors would therefore make the balance sheet recession worse, because their departure would accelerate the already serious fall in asset prices.

These are not just academic possibilities either. As mentioned in Chapter 4, over the last 20 years, there have been a number of occasions of this kind that have almost resulted in a financial meltdown. As Exhibit 4.1 indicated, in March 1987 there was a simultaneous fall of both the dollar and long bond prices in the U.S. which was perfectly correlated with the fall of the dollar vis-à-vis the yen. The fact that it happened only four weeks after the G7's ill-fated Louvre Accord, which tried to establish the bottom for the dollar, made the situation that much worse. At that time, the long bond yield in the U.S. went up 150 basis points in just six weeks.

This March 1987 crisis was finally contained using some of the nastiest tools available to the monetary authorities.[3] But the damage was done, and the credibility of the monetary authorities lost during this incident had a part to play in bringing about the infamous Black Monday in October 1987.

Since foreign investors hold nearly 40% of all U.S. government bonds, the U.S. policymakers must pay close attention to the dollar exchange rate in order to ensure that nothing like 1987 happens again. After all, if foreigners dumped even a small portion of their bondholdings, it will have a major impact on the U.S. interest rate structure. And if the long bond yield goes up by 150 basis points now, the U.S. housing market will be finished in no time.

With U.S. interest rates already so low, the attractiveness of U.S. assets to foreigners is shrinking. The U.S. trade deficit, on the other hand, is still huge. Furthermore, the fact that some corporate accounts turned out to be fraudulent means that the so-called high rates of return on capital in the U.S. may also come under suspicion, especially from those foreign investors who are also worried about the risk of a falling dollar.

Put differently, the U.S. today has (1) a weak economy, (2) a huge trade deficit, and (3) corporate accounts that are suspect. This means it has macro, international, and micro problems all at once. If the U.S. had problems in (2) and (3), but not in (1), it probably would have weathered those problems without much difficulty. For example, as long as the U.S. economy is strong, nobody really cares about the trade deficit, and micro problems will remain just that — micro problems of a limited number of corporations.

If the U.S. had problems in (1) and (2), but not in (3), the situation would be tougher, but there might still be bargain-hunters to keep the bottom from falling out of the stock market. If the U.S. had problems in (1) and (3), but not in (2), the dollar would be fundamentally strong and the departure of foreign investors would not be an issue. Indeed, if the U.S. were running a current account surplus, it would have no reason to depend on foreign capital inflows to keep the economy moving. Unfortunately, the U.S. today has all three problems, which is a handful for any policymaking authority.

Japan today basically has problem (1), and may possibly have problem (3). But as far as (3) is concerned, since the Japanese have never bragged about the supreme accuracy or completeness of their corporate accounts, nothing much has changed from the past. If anything, they have been in the process of resolving problem (3), albeit slowly and from a low base. Furthermore, only 5% of Japanese government bonds are held by foreigners, and Japan's trade surplus is still one of the largest in the world.

All of this suggests that even though the balance sheet damage which the U.S. has sustained so far is much smaller than that of Japan, the fact that it has a huge trade deficit in a weak economy does put constraints on policymakers that Japanese policymakers never had to worry about.

BETTER POLITICAL LEADERSHIP IN THE U.S.?

The biggest advantage the U.S. has over Japan today is probably in the area of political leadership. The Koizumi government is ignoring all the signs of a balance sheet recession coming from the market and insisting that structural reform along supply-side ideas is the key to economic recovery. In fact, the similarity of the mindsets of the current Cabinet and President Herbert Hoover's administration is unmistakable. Even though there are people such as Taro Aso and Shizuka Kamei, the present and former heads of the Policy Planning Committee of the LDP, and Yasuhiro Nakasone, the former prime minister, who understand the danger of balance sheet recessions, they are not at the steering wheel.

In the U.S., on the other hand, there is Alan Greenspan, who is determined not to repeat the mistakes the Japanese have made during the last 10 years, or his own slow reaction to the balance sheet recession of 1991. The administration of George W. Bush is also determined not to repeat the mistakes of his father's administration, which placed too much emphasis on diplomatic matters and was late in responding to the balance sheet recession.

When a top White House aide on economic policy told me in April 2002, "If we hadn't put in place the tax cuts and other fiscal stimulus measures [in 2001], the U.S. economy would have been in the same condition as the Japanese economy is in today," he clearly showed his understanding of the dangers of a balance sheet recession. In view of the fact that this is a Republican administration, which traditionally does not like fiscal stimulus, it was a remarkable statement.

Indeed, there was an interesting twist to the current policy thrust of political parties in the U.S. The Democrats, who traditionally prefer big government and more fiscal spending, were advocating a balanced budget in 2001, just like Herbert Hoover in the early 1930s. (Hoover was a Republican.) The Democrats were trying to capitalize on the budget surplus which the Clinton administration managed to achieve in its later years. The Republicans, on the other hand, were worried about the economy and were willing to try anything to avoid making the same mistake the previous Bush administration had made in not paying sufficient attention to the economy.

In this sense, the fact that there was a change of administration in Washington just as the bubble was bursting was an extremely fortunate development for the U.S. economy. If the Democrats were still in power, they would be most reluctant to mobilize fiscal policy, which would nullify their most cherished achievement of the previous eight years of Clinton's administration. In other words, they should be most opposed to anything that would push the federal budget back into deficit again. Although the Democrats returned to their traditional position of favoring more government spending just before the mid-term election in late 2002, they were thoroughly defeated by the Republicans in both houses of Congress.

A TAX CUT ALONE IS NOT SUFFICIENT IN A BALANCE SHEET RECESSION

The Republicans are not without their liabilities, either. The new economic team in Washington which took over after the mid-term election may take a while before they realize that the U.S. is in a balance sheet recession. Furthermore, the Republican Party, in pursuit of smaller government, always prefers tax cuts to spending increases. For the efficient allocation of resources, allowing the private sector to spend money as it sees fit is infinitely preferable to the government spending money. Indeed, when most companies are forward-looking and maximizing profits, the smaller and less intrusive the government, the better it is for the economy.

The problem is that a balance sheet recession is no ordinary recession. In this recession, which is brought about by the fallacy of composition, the economy is weakening because most companies are looking backward as they try to repair their balance sheets. But because the companies are minimizing debt instead of maximizing profits, demand is lost all around the economy. If no one came in to fill the shortfall in demand created by everyone paying down debt, the whole economy could fall into a vicious cycle, as mentioned earlier.

Since individual companies are all doing the right thing at the micro level, the government cannot tell them not to repair their balance sheets. In such a situation, the government itself must fill the demand gap so as to keep the economy from falling into a vicious cycle. Furthermore, it has to fill the gap proactively if it does not want to fall behind the curve.

In order to fill such a gap with a tax cut, however, one must prepare a tax cut perhaps several times larger than the deflationary gap to ensure that after all the leakages, it is still sufficient to fill the gap. This issue of leakage is particularly important, because so much of the tax cut in a balance sheet recession could be redirected to pay down debt or replenish the savings pool which has been depleted by the fall in asset prices. Since the amount of leakage is very difficult to estimate in advance, the government will have to put in a tax cut that is many times larger than the estimated demand gap just to ensure that the deflationary gap will be filled completely.

What this means is that, for a given size of budget deficit, the tax cut will not be very efficient in filling the demand gap, especially when the economy is in a balance sheet recession. In this kind of recession, public works spending is far more efficient in the sense that (1) there is no uncertainty regarding the leakage, and (2) for a given amount of fiscal deficit, it generates maximum demand.

If the Republicans, because of their traditional aversion to public spending, remained committed to the idea of a tax cut only, they could fall behind the curve, so to speak, in dealing with this kind of recession. Even though there is nothing wrong with tax cuts themselves, when push comes to shove, the government should be ready to implement direct spending measures to supplement tax cuts to ensure that the economy does not fall into a vicious cycle.

The White House aide that I spoke to in April 2002 seemed fully aware of these challenges, but the new team might not be well disposed to this kind of thinking at first. This means that precious time will be lost before effective countermeasures are put on the table. If the Republicans still refuse to contemplate an increase in government spending at that time, however, the only option left will be a weak dollar, with all its attendant risks for U.S. interest rates and asset prices, as mentioned earlier.

RECOGNIZING THE LIMITS OF MONETARY POLICY

Another area in which the U.S. leadership seems to be ahead of the Japanese is in recognizing the limits of monetary policy. Because the Koizumi government is fully committed to the mistaken notion that fiscal stimulus has been largely ineffective, it has tied its own hands by saying that the issuance of Japanese government bonds in a year will be limited to ¥30 trillion. Since the amount of savings the household sector is generating but the corporate sector is not borrowing is more than ¥30 trillion, both the economy and asset prices have been heading south.

In response, Economics Minister Takenaka has been pushing the Bank of Japan hard to ease further. He has even threatened to take away the BOJ's independence if the central bank does not go along with the government's wishes. But, as mentioned in Chapter 3, there is a solid reason why monetary policy does not work in a balance sheet recession, and the government's refusal to understand or acknowledge these reasons does not bode well for the economy or the stock market.

In the U.S., the limits of monetary policy have been recognized relatively early in the process. For example, Chairman Greenspan changed his stance in late 2000 to approve the tax cut that he was not favorably disposed to earlier. He probably felt that the fall in demand at that time was so severe that monetary policy easing alone might not be enough to stop the economy from contracting. Following the September 11, 2001 attacks, he even went on record as asking for a fiscal stimulus of 1–1.5% of GDP. This is probably the first time in recent memory, if not the first time in history, that the top central banker in the U.S. has asked for a fiscal stimulus.

These actions show that Greenspan obviously understands the limits of monetary policy, and is ensuring that the public does not depend excessively on it. Although there are some in the administration, as well as in the Federal Reserve, who still believe in the almighty powers of monetary policy, Greenspan is not likely to be one of them.

Putting it all together, there are some areas where the present-day U.S. is better positioned than Japan, especially in the area of the real estate market, but there are other areas, such as the trade deficit and the low savings rate of the household sector, which might constrain U.S. policymakers in a way the Japanese never had to worry about.

Although awareness of the dangers of a balance sheet recession seems higher among policymakers in the U.S. than in Japan, whether the Americans can make use of the lessons they have learned from the Japanese experience remains to be seen. For example, if the consensus-building needed to implement fiscal stimulus within the administration and with the law-makers in Congress is delayed, the net result for the U.S. could still look very similar to the Japanese one today. Similarly, if excessive demands are placed on the Federal Reserve and the central bank cannot deliver, precious time will be wasted debating the same issues that the Bank of Japan has been debating during the last 10 years.

It is hoped that those who understand the dangers of a balance sheet recession will join hands across the Pacific and help each other so that no more time is wasted repeating the arguments of the 1930s.

EUROPE IS MOST VULNERABLE TO A BALANCE SHEET RECESSION

A short note on Europe. The European share markets also experienced a massive IT bubble and its collapse. The price declines in some of the European markets are almost as bad as in Japan, with the German DAX index falling 68% and the French CAC index falling 62% from their respective peaks. All of this naturally has huge balance sheet implications for the involved entities.

If the number of affected companies and individuals is large, and if they are all moving to repair their balance sheets at the same time, Europe could also become engulfed in a balance sheet recession. The fact that the European economies have been losing their forward momentum recently may suggest that the balance sheet recession is already here.

The problem, however, is that Euro-zone countries are restricted from using fiscal stimulus by the Maastricht Treaty. This treaty specifies that Euro-zone countries cannot run a budget deficit greater than 3% of GDP. This limit is very low, relative to where the countries are already. More importantly, as discussed in the section on Prime Minister Koizumi's ill-advised pledge to limit Japanese government bond issuance to ¥30 trillion, this kind of restriction keeps the government from applying a proactive fiscal policy, which is very much needed in a balance sheet recession.

Since fiscal stimulus is the most effective — if not the *only* — remedy for a balance sheet recession, as soon as the symptoms of balance sheet recession are observed in Europe, the EC Commission is strongly advised to take action to free the Euro-zone economies from the restrictions of the Maastricht Treaty. Failure to do so may result in Europe falling into a vicious cycle with an ever-larger deflationary gap. Indeed, of the three regions — Japan, the U.S., and Europe — Europe is by far the most vulnerable when it comes to balance sheet recession because of the restrictions placed on it by the Maastricht Treaty.

KEYNES AND THE IMF ALL OVER AGAIN

If the Europeans fail to agree on relaxing the Maastricht Treaty, the only option available to them will be to weaken the Euro and rely on foreign demand to keep the European economies going.

The same holds true for the U.S. If and when the new economic team in Washington realizes that the U.S. is in a balance sheet recession and that the tax cuts are not sufficient to deal with it, the only options left will be to increase government spending or weaken the dollar. If, at that time, the Republicans are still opposed to increasing government spending for ideological reasons, the only option left will be to weaken the dollar.

In Japan, too, with Prime Minister Koizumi refusing to contemplate increasing government spending, the temptation to weaken the yen is getting stronger within the Cabinet. This is in spite of the fact that Japan is already running one of the largest trade surpluses in the world.

However, it would not only be impossible for the U.S., Japan, and Europe all to weaken their currencies at the same time, but would also represent an exact repetition of the mistake made in the 1930s. Then, competitive devaluation was followed by massive hikes in tariffs, with the result that global trade volumes slumped to a fraction of what they had been before and the world economy plunged into depression. For one country on its own to rely on external demand may be OK, but for all countries to do so at the same time represents a global fallacy of composition.

Keynes created the International Monetary Fund in 1945 because he was concerned that, whereas individual governments could deal with balance sheet recessions caused by domestic fallacies of composition by increasing fiscal spending, the lack of a world government meant that countries could not deal with international fallacies of composition brought about by all countries trying to rely on external demand by weakening their currencies at the same time. The IMF was created to deal with these contingencies because of the bitter lessons of the 1930s.

However, the IMF has never been called upon to perform this role. I would imagine that hardly any of the current IMF workforce knows what its original purpose was. Indeed, what the IMF has done or been made to do subsequently has deviated substantially from its original mandate.

The distinct possibility that all the major economies will be relying on external demand from around 2003 raises the likelihood that the global economy will revert to the 1930s unless the IMF functions properly. When ideological aversion toward public spending among Republicans in the U.S. is combined with the bureaucratic limitations of Maastricht and the characteristic stubbornness of both Prime Minster Koizumi and the Japanese Ministry of Finance, the possibility that a global fallacy of composition will actually materialize cannot be ruled out.

When it appears that the world is heading in that direction, the IMF must tell each country that weakening the exchange rate is not a remedy when the whole world is engulfed in balance sheet recession. The IMF must tell its members that each country must contain the fallacy of composition within its borders through fiscal stimulus so as to avoid a 1930s-like global meltdown.

Of course, there are major differences between 2003 and the 1930s — the deposit insurance system, to name but one example. However, even the stabilizing effect provided by this system could be swept away by misguided policy choices. For example, the Koizumi Cabinet contains people such as Heizo Takenaka who are so ignorant of the lessons of the 1930s that they attempt to remove the blanket guarantees on deposit accounts in the midst of a severe balance sheet recession.

FED OPPOSITION CAN TURN THE DEBATE AROUND

Although the above is very depressing, a somewhat more positive scenario can also be drawn. Minutes of the Federal Open Market Committee (FOMC) meetings, the policymaking body of the Federal Reserve, from late 2002[4] reveal that some participants are beginning to worry that the U.S. might slip into deflation if things continue the way they are. Indeed, some U.S. price indexes[5] have already slipped into negative territory. Share prices and unemployment are also weak. This is in spite of the fact that the Fed has lowered interest rates 12 times to almost zero.

As such, before long, the Fed might start saying that monetary policy alone will not be enough, and that fiscal policy will also be needed. In particular, if somebody like Greenspan said this, it would definitely trigger a major policy as well as academic debate in the U.S. If that were to happen, public opinion in both the U.S. and Japan on fiscal policy would likely change. There could also be a major shift in attitudes toward the Maastricht Treaty conditions in Europe. Such a shift may constitute the first step toward global economic recovery.

On the other hand, until the Fed speaks out, monetarists in the U.S. are likely to repeat the mantra they have adopted for Japan for several years now — that just one more piece of monetary loosening will do the trick. Some prominent economists in the U.S. are already urging the Fed to set an inflation target.

U.S. policymakers are likely to start focusing on the true cause of the problem — namely, balance sheets — only after they realize that monetarist solutions do not work in the U.S. either and that tax cuts are not sufficient to turn the economy around. In order to shorten the time to get there, it is hoped that those who understand the dangers of a balance sheet recession will join hands across the continents and help each other, so that the dreadful mistakes of the 1930s will not be repeated.

ENDNOTES

1 Charles P. Kindleberger, "Housing Bubble Might Not Last (*'Jutaku Bubble' Houkai he Susumu*)," *Nihon Keizai Shimbun*, August 10, 2002.

2 Teikoku Databank, "Bankruptcy Reports." http://www.tdb.co.jp. U.S. Bankruptcy Courts, "Judicial Business of the United States Courts," Appendix: Detailed Statistical Tables, Table F-2 Business and Nonbusiness Cases Commenced, by Chapter of the Bankruptcy Code. http://www.uscourts.gov/judbus2001/appendices/f02sep01.pdf.

3 Richard C. Koo, "International Capital Flows and an Open Economy: The Japanese Experience," in Takagi Shinji (ed.), *Japanese Capital Markets* (Oxford: Blackwell Publishers, 1993), pp. 78–129.

4 Board of Governors of the Federal Reserve System, "Minutes of the Federal Open Market Committee," November 6, 2002.
http://www.federalreserve.gov/fomc/minutes/20021106.htm.

5 U.S. Department of Labor, "Producer Price Index," November 2002.

11

REAL CHALLENGES FACING JAPAN

"DEBT REJECTION SYNDROME"

This final chapter will discuss the real structural issues facing the Japanese economy. The non-performing loan disposal and fiscal deficit issues are both repairing the damage of the bubble, so to speak. These issues will be solved if proper planning to match the needs of the balance sheet recession is put in place. But resolution of these issues does not change the structure of the Japanese economy or the way in which it operates. In this sense, they are not the issues for the future, but rather are backward-looking issues akin to repairing war damage.

The real issue in Japan, then, is neither fiscal rehabilitation nor the disposal of NPLs. The real issue facing post-balance sheet recession Japan is likely to be the corporate "debt rejection syndrome" in the short term, and convincing the Japanese household sector that savings are not always a virtue in the long term. There is also the infamous "land problem" to resolve.

Businesses have been working very hard to clean up their balance sheets by paying down debts. So far, approximately 20–30% of businesses have already solved their balance sheet problems. In fact, among the listed companies, slightly under 1,000, or slightly less than 30% of the total, have borrowed in order to invest. However, even these firms are showing extreme symptoms of debt rejection. They are very reluctant to borrow, although their balance sheets are clean and interest rates are low. Even when they borrow, the loans they take out are very small.

In fact, Japanese business executives today in all sectors are saying, "We are through with borrowing." When investing in plant and equipment, they do not raise funds from outside but try to invest within the limits of their cash flows. In the world of historically low interest rates, this is nothing but a debt rejection syndrome.

From the perspective of individual businessmen, no-debt management is the soundest of all management practices. After all, companies with no debt are much less likely to go bankrupt than are those with debt. The fact that Toyota, one of the most highly regarded companies in Japan, has virtually no debt is prompting other companies to follow suit by reducing their dependence on debt financing. The need to lower their leveraging to match the environment of slow growth is also discouraging companies from borrowing.

The problem is that the Japanese household sector is still saving enormous amounts each year. This means that the economy does not function properly unless someone borrows and spends all these savings. In other words, if all companies in Japan operated like Toyota, the Japanese economy would have been dead long ago.

In a country where the household savings rate is very low, as is the case in the United States, it makes good macroeconomic sense for businesses to limit their investments to below the levels of their cash flows. However, in Japan, where the household sector is still hell-bent on saving, if businesses limit their investment to within their cash flows, private-sector savings and investment will remain forever in disequilibrium. This means that there will always be a deflationary gap and that the government will have to close it with budget deficits almost indefinitely. This would be the worst-case scenario for Japan, in which private-sector fund demand will never recover fully, making it necessary for the government to keep operating in the red.

U.S. EXPERIENCE WITH THE SYNDROME

A similar phenomenon occurred in the United States following the Great Depression of the 1930s. Those people who had experienced great hardship in repaying their debts in the 1930s vowed never to borrow money again. Known as "depression mentality," many Americans aged in their seventies and eighties today who experienced the Great Depression in their youth still refuse to borrow money even now. The trauma of paying down debt under duress has completely transformed their attitude toward debt.

As a result, even though there were massive fiscal stimuli in the form of President Roosevelt's New Deal Policy, World War II, and the Korean War, U.S. interest rates remained remarkably low for a very long time. Exhibit 11.1 shows the movement of interest rates in the United States during this period. The stock-market crash of 1929 plunged the country into the Great Depression. From that time on, it took a full 30 years, or until 1959, for U.S. interest rates to return to the average level for the 1920s which were still only 4.1% both at the short and the long end.

Exhibit 11.1   U.S. interest rates took 30 years to return to their 1920s level

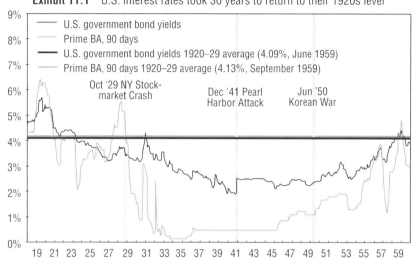

Source: Board of Governors of the Federal Reserve, *Banking and Monetary Statistics 1914–1970*.

With the government adopting such large fiscal stimuli and creating such huge budget deficits, it is remarkable that it took so long for interest rates to return to normal levels. Although it is unimaginable from the current household savings rate in the United States, the interest rates remained low probably because their experience of paying down debt was so difficult and painful for Americans in the 1930s that many were determined never to borrow money again. In other words, it took the U.S. economy 30 years to overcome the trauma.

If the Japanese today experience the same trauma the Americans experienced in the 1930s, the same debt rejection syndrome that Americans displayed in the 1940s and 1950s may become apparent in Japan as well. If that happens, Japanese businesses may not return to borrowings even after their balance sheets are fully restored. But if they refuse to borrow, the Japanese economy will still suffer from the deflationary gap caused by the household sector saving but the corporate sector not borrowing. Even if the situation is an improvement over the present case where corporations are not only *not* borrowing, but are actually paying down debt, the deflationary gap can still remain to haunt the economy.

TODAY'S JAPAN RELATIVE TO THE U.S. IN THE 1930s

If the U.S. experience of the 1940s and 1950s is any guide, the problem of debt rejection syndrome in Japan is likely to be very serious. After all, it took 30 years for U.S. interest rates to return to normal levels.

One consolation, however, is that thanks to an active fiscal policy from the beginning, the damage Japan has sustained so far is less than that in the United States in the 1930s. By 1933, the damage in the U.S. was such that the GNP had declined to half of what it was in 1929. By contrast, Japan has managed to maintain zero growth, or within the range of a few percentage points above or below this figure. Since the damage is smaller than that in the United States during the 1930s, there is a possibility that it will not take 30 years for interest rates to return to normal levels. Even though Japan has been in a balance sheet recession for over 10 years, since the wound has never opened all that wide, the recovery is not likely to take a very long time.

On the other hand, in several respects, Japan's situation is worse than it was in the United States. As Europe and Asia had been turned into battlefields during World War II, the United States emerged as the sole-surviving production center in the post-war period. Therefore, even when domestic demand was not very strong, abundant reconstruction demand overseas enabled the United States to sustain its economic growth. In other words, in the absence of the war and the subsequent export demand, it might have taken the U.S. even longer than 30 years to restore its interest rates to normal levels. By contrast, Japan today cannot rely on such an extraordinary demand either from the military or from abroad, which makes it possible to argue that the recovery might take longer than in the U.S.

THE REAL ROLE OF STRUCTURAL REFORM

Nevertheless, the wound is not so deep at the present moment and the economy has not plunged into a real depression. Furthermore, the pressure of global competition does not allow corporations to sit still for very long.

Unfortunately, there are many obstacles at home in the path of Japanese companies wishing to resume their investment activities. For example, Japan is still a high-cost country in which to do business, while its next-door neighbor, China, is an ultra-low-cost producer. As a result, many companies in Japan today are coming to the conclusion that investment within the country is not worthwhile, and that investing in China makes more sense.

This is where the need for real structural reform comes into play. In order to overcome severe corporate debt rejection syndrome, Japan must make itself into a nation several times more attractive for companies to invest in than is currently the case. If regulations are eased both to lower the cost of doing business and to increase the number of interesting business opportunities, business executives suffering from severe debt rejection syndrome may re-think their positions on debt. They may be tempted to borrow money if they feel there are some very exciting investment opportunities available. Besides, interest rates are so low. In order to overcome debt rejection syndrome, therefore, structural reform to open up investment opportunities in Japan is absolutely essential.

There are, however, a large number of barriers to overcome before new investment opportunities can be created, and it will take an enormous amount of political energy to surmount them. Furthermore, it takes a long time for structural reform to bear fruit. However, unless this problem is firmly dealt with, new investment prospects will not be created, and Japan will be stuck with the debt rejection syndrome even after corporate balance sheets are fully restored. Since it takes a long time for deregulation to result in greater economic activity, and Japan is behind many other countries in this respect, there is no time to waste. The government must move quickly so that companies will see new investment opportunities when they come out of their balance sheet repair mode.

This raises two questions: (1) In which fields should structural reform be carried out at the micro level? and (2) Will such efforts be sufficient to close the gap between household savings and corporate investment at the macro level? In other words, even if all desirable structural reforms are put in place, there is still a possibility that the gap between savings and investment will remain within the economy.

The micro-level question on where to direct structural reform efforts can have many answers, but the key criterion in all such efforts must be the creation of investment opportunities. Thus, those matters that do not add to investment opportunities may be put on the back burner, while those that will increase investment opportunities immediately should be given the highest priority. The government should also direct its fiscal spending toward those projects that will lower the cost of doing business for the private sector. This may include everything from better and less costly access to Tokyo's Narita Airport to reduced traffic congestion in the major cities.

INCREASE PERSONAL CONSUMPTION TO BRING BALANCE TO THE JAPANESE ECONOMY

By contrast, there are causes for long-term concern at the macro level. Without doubt, once the corporate balance sheets are clean, the situation will greatly improve from the present picture, in which companies are hell-bent on paying down debts. The annual ¥20 trillion net repayment of debt should come to an end. But the gap between the present levels of savings and investment is very wide. Even though it may be possible to narrow this gap considerably by implementing every possible measure to increase investment opportunities inside the country, there is still a danger that a fairly large gap remains at the end of the structural reform process.

If a gap remains after every possible structural reform aimed at increasing investment opportunities for the corporate sector is implemented, increasing personal consumption and reducing household savings is the only possibility left to close the remaining savings–investment gap. In other words, if the gap remains, the Japanese people must be persuaded and convinced that their traditional fondness for saving must be changed in order to free the Japanese economy from the fallacy of composition problems.

Although increasing personal consumption in Japan is highly desirable, especially in the absence of investment demand, it is also extremely difficult to achieve in practice. This is because how much people consume and how much they spend is closely related to their cultural background. Furthermore, as seen in Exhibit 1.2 in Chapter 1, Japanese households have not really changed their savings behavior during the last decade. If they had changed, it may be possible to locate the reason for the change and to use that knowledge to affect people's current savings behavior. But if they have not changed their savings behavior at all in decades, then one cannot be too optimistic about effecting a quick change in something that is rooted so deeply in people's character.

The same problem was faced in the U.S., but in the opposite direction. The savings rate of Americans has been very low for the past few decades. Since the early 1980s, the U.S. government has taken many measures to correct this low savings rate. One measure was a scheme called All Savers' Accounts, which paid tax-free interest. Although there was an annual ceiling for these accounts, they were introduced as a national effort to increase Americans' savings rate. The 401K scheme, which has recently been attracting attention in Japan, was also introduced as a part of this effort.

The outcome, however, was a total failure. In spite of such efforts, the savings rate in the United States continued to fall and reached almost zero in 2000. What we have learned from the All Savers' Accounts and 401K accounts is that when incentives are offered for certain types of savings, people who normally save anyway just shift their money from other types of accounts into the one with the incentives, and the overall savings rate remains the same.

SAVINGS ARE NO LONGER A VIRTUE

The U.S. experience in the 1980s and 1990s illustrates how difficult it is for the government to change people's savings behavior. The United States was unable to increase its amount of savings, however hard it tried. Japan must increase its consumption, but the problem is basically the same. Nothing will change unless people's philosophy on savings and consumption is fundamentally changed. Perhaps due to the influence of Confucius, savings rates are high everywhere in East Asia: in South Korea, Taiwan, China, and Japan. The citizens of these countries have been told for centuries that "savings are a virtue." Everyone tries their best to save in order to prepare for a rainy day and old age. This commitment to savings may already be part of the East Asian DNA.

However, savings are a virtue in a macro sense only when there is demand for investment within the economy. When there is a strong demand for investment, a high savings rate enables the economy to experience high growth. And that is exactly how Japan managed to grow so quickly right up until the end of the 1980s. By contrast, if people save when there is no demand for investment, the whole economy falls into a deflationary spiral toward depression while the saved funds stay idle at financial institutions. Japan has been in this situation since the early 1990s. In such a situation, savings are a vice rather than a virtue.

To understand that savings are a vice when there is no investment demand, one has only to go back to the example cited in Chapter 1. Let us suppose that a person with an income of ¥1,000 spends ¥900 and saves ¥100. In the past, that ¥100 in savings was lent by the bank to someone who spent that money. Against the initial ¥1,000 income, therefore, ¥900 of consumption plus ¥100 of investment for the total of ¥1,000 of expenditure materialized, and the economy moved forward.

When no one borrows that ¥100 even at 0% interest rates, however, the money remains in the bank unused. In this case, because only ¥900 was spent and ¥100 remains idle at the bank, the total income of the economy has dropped to ¥900. It is easy to imagine what will happen next if the person whose income is ¥900 spends only 90% of his income and saves the remaining 10%. Consumption declines to ¥810 and the ¥90 in savings become idle at the bank. As shown in Chapter 1, if this cycle is allowed to continue, the contraction will end only when everyone is too poor to save any money. And this is precisely the danger facing Japan and many other economies today.

At the moment, the government, through deficit spending, is barely managing to keep this vicious cycle from starting. The point is that, when there is no demand for investment, savings are a definite vice. In such a world, the economy will be in constant danger of falling into a vicious cycle the minute government's deficit spending is stopped.

EXHORTATION NEEDED TO BRING THE SAVINGS RATE DOWN

Since deficit spending cannot be used forever and structural reform efforts might not be able to close the investment–savings gap completely, a massive effort is needed to educate the public that savings are not a virtue at present, because companies are not borrowing money. In other words, a strong campaign is needed to exhort Japanese households to reduce their savings because there is no investment demand at present. (Of course, the same campaign can be used in reverse to increase savings again when investment opportunities present themselves.)

First, the government needs to explain why savings are a vice in present-day Japan. The government should explain to the people as follows:

> When companies are paying down debt even when interest rates are zero while the household sector continues to save as before, the economy will plunge into depression unless the government borrows and spends the money the household sector saved but the corporate sector did not borrow. The resultant budget deficits must be paid for with your future tax money. On the other hand, if you spent more and saved less now, there would be less need for a budget deficit and lower taxes in the future. The choices you have, therefore, are for you to spend the money yourselves now, or let the government spend it through deficit financing and pay for them in taxes later. This being the case, it would be better if you spend the money yourself now.

The government should try to exhort people into changing their savings behavior, using the above argument.

"Exhortation" means urging people to do something. For example, during World War II, every country waged a campaign to increase its weapons production. "Give ¥100 if you are rich. Give just ¥1 if you are poor. Let's give to build a fighter plane." What is needed now is to do exactly the opposite of this campaign. In other words, the government must exhort people to "spend ¥100 if you are rich, spend ¥1 if you are poor. Let's spend a little more than before so as to get the Japanese economy out of the balance sheet recession."

In view of the fact that the idea of "savings are a virtue" has been so deeply ingrained in the mind of the Japanese public for centuries, the government must clearly explain to the people that the priority of the country has changed. Without such a campaign, changes in tax codes and the other measures explained below are not likely to be sufficient to bring about the desired outcome.

Such exhortation is not part of ordinary economics. The major premise of economics is that everyone who participates in an economy is making rational judgments and that it is not proper for the government to exhort people into taking a different course of action. However, in ordinary economics, it is assumed that businesses are behaving to maximize their profits. In other words, ordinary economics does not take into account a situation in which companies are behaving to minimize debt. However, the fact that it is not assumed does not mean that it will not happen. It happened in the United States 70 years ago and has been happening in Japan for the past 10 years.

Moreover, the present balance sheet recession stems from the fact that everyone is behaving rationally. When there is this sort of fallacy of composition, it is essential that someone does something that is different from what is correct at the micro level. If no such corrective actions are taken, the whole population can fall off the cliff precisely because everyone is behaving rationally.

Some people may say that exhortation as a policy option is outrageous. However, we are already adopting a great many policies that are outrageous, the first among them being a 0% interest rate. This is an outrage to depositors. The budget deficit of ¥660 trillion is bigger than Japan's annual GDP. This is also outrageous. However, since we have come this far, exhortation may be the least outrageous among many policies that might have been considered out of the question.

INCENTIVES NEEDED TO CHANGE PEOPLE'S MENTALITY AND BEHAVIOR

Of course, exhortation alone will not be sufficient. It will have to be matched with a scheme in which those who have increased their spending can see its benefits clearly. Although there are a number of conceivable mechanisms, the best would be to give tax refunds to those who have spent more than a certain percentage of their income, provided the government can track the total spending of each individual. For example, one could build a scheme that gives people who have spent more than 80% of their income a tax refund (credit) equivalent to a proportion of their spending above 80%. Although it will take a lot of effort to make something like this work, if the total spending of each individual can be monitored, it would be the smartest and most straightforward approach.

If it is difficult to grasp the total consumption of each individual, there are many other ways. Up until the end of the 1980s, the United States allowed its taxpayers to deduct interest expense on their credit cards or car loans. Although these incentives have been pared down because of the very low and falling savings rate, such a tax exemption was widely allowed up to that time. Since Japan's problem today is the exact opposite of that in the United States during the 1980s, it might be worth considering employing such tax deductions. If the benefits are visible, then people's behavior might change.

Another possibility is to use tax exemptions. Japan's income tax laws allow certain personal exemptions whether the person spends the money or not. When the economy is weak, as it is today, it is likely that people are not spending as much as is assumed in the tax exemptions structure. By making the exemptions conditional on actual spending, however, people may be tempted to spend more, because they will be able to see the direct benefits of such actions. For example, if office workers were allowed to claim business suits as a necessary business expense for tax purposes, they would have the incentive to purchase more suits or to purchase better-quality ones, knowing that some part of the purchase price will come out of the government's pocket.

It should be noted that the change of behavior needed from consumers is not very large. For example, a 5% increase in spending would go a long way in filling the deflationary gap. This is because, since personal consumption accounts for 60% of GDP, even if it were increased by only a few percentage points, it would have the same effect as businesses increasing their capital investment many times over. It is unrealistic to expect businesses that are busy repairing their balance sheets to make significant investments, but it may be possible to make the household sector spend just a few percentage points more if the right incentives are offered. Although it is difficult to change people's behavior because of its cultural background, it is worthwhile giving it a try, especially if the alternative is to rely on budget deficits almost indefinitely.

CHANGE IN JAPANESE LIFESTYLE LONG OVERDUE

In discussing the expansion of consumption, one topic that cannot be avoided is the issue of lifestyle. This is because how people think about their consumption and savings depends very much on their lifestyle.

A couple of years ago, *Nikkei Ryutsu Shimbun* conducted an extensive survey of Japanese consumers in metropolitan areas, asking them what they really wanted to buy. Shockingly, more than half of the respondents answered "nothing."[1] However, if consumers cannot find anything they want to spend their money on, the economy cannot possible grow. The goal of reducing people's savings rate will be hopeless as well.

After this survey was published, Isao Shirai, my colleague at Nomura Securities, came up with an eye-opening interpretation of the survey results. He argued that the survey results were fully consistent with the Japanese lifestyle. In particular, he argued that with so little freedom to take holidays and so few holidays, most Japanese people are just too busy even to think about spending money. He suggested that if the lifestyle of the Japanese were changed to match those of other developed countries, so that people had more time to enjoy themselves, they would suddenly want to buy all sorts of things that they had never even thought about buying. Working in a Japanese company myself, I must say that he is absolutely right.

Japan is an advanced, industrialized nation, with per capita income equal to or greater than that of the U.S. The fact that it is an advanced industrialized nation means that almost everyone owns all of life's necessities. Those nations in which not all people own these necessities can be called the developing nations. In the former, no matter how much of the necessities are supplied, people do not feel the need to purchase them since they already own them. This means that the only way to increase consumption in these developed countries is by offering luxury goods or services.

However, the world of luxury goods and services is entirely different from that of necessities, because these things never sell unless consumers have the time to enjoy them. In Japan, people hardly have the time to enjoy such items.

Although the number of holidays in Japan has increased over the years, the vast majority of people are still not well disposed to buy country houses, as people in other advanced countries might do. This is because, even in summer, they are lucky to get 10 straight days off work, including two weekends. With such limited holidays, the utilization rate of country homes would be so low that no one wants to buy one.

However, if the law were to require everyone to take a vacation of at least 25 days, as it does in France, the situation would be dramatically different. People in Japan might suddenly find that they want to purchase a country house or a pleasure boat. Having a second home, however, doubles the need for everything from TVs to curtains. Indeed, such a change might cause an explosive increase in demand for all those items that are "necessary" in time-intensive hobbies, such as better fishing rods or mountain bikes. Furthermore, if Japanese workers were allowed to take longer vacations more freely, not only would they be able to do many different things, but they may want to do things that they have never previously thought of doing.

Since they already have the money, if they are allowed more leisure time in which to entertain themselves, consumption in those areas could increase sharply. Compared to other advanced countries, therefore, there is a huge potential for consumption growth in Japan by just altering the lifestyle of the average person. The advanced industrialized nations in Europe, such as France, have been able to make their economies function properly, in part because they offer their citizens both luxury goods and time in which to enjoy them.

Indeed, the Japanese should have changed their traditional lifestyle when the country became affluent. However, since it has always been said in Japan that savings and labor are virtues, while consumption and play are vices, it has been very difficult even to think of the need to change their lifestyle. Furthermore, because of their strong work ethic, the Japanese have prided themselves on working very hard, and not taking the holidays they are entitled to. This "production is good, but consumption is bad" mentality, together with the horrendous land usage problem described below, has resulted in an economy that is excessively strong on supply but extremely weak on demand.

For the last 30 years, Japan has tried to close the resultant shortfall in domestic demand by relying on exports. This was successful in the beginning, but it ran into an impasse when the resultant massive trade surplus pushed the yen exchange rate to extraordinary heights. This is where Japan is stuck today.

In order to break away from the present impasse, the Japanese government should give more holidays to the average person. And this must be done in a form that makes people want to spend more money. The stingy strategy of just creating long weekends by moving national holidays to Mondays or Fridays is not enough to overcome the present economic crisis. The government must fundamentally change people's lifestyles by making it possible for everyone to take two or three weeks off at a stretch at any time.

Narita Airport and Tokyo Railway Station are packed with people during the stepping-stone holidays in May, the Bon festival in August, and the New Year holidays, indicating that only when people have the time to enjoy themselves is there an enormous demand for consumption. The unfortunate thing is that, since these holidays are nationwide holidays and very short, people's behavior patterns become more uniform, which leads to congestion everywhere. For example, during these national holidays, it is not unusual to see 200-kilometer-long traffic jams and stories of people taking 12 hours to drive to a resort only 150 kilometers from Tokyo. Indeed, the congestion can get so bad that many people give up altogether on the idea of going anywhere and of spending money during those holidays.

"FALLACY OF COMPOSITION" IN THE VACATION PROBLEM

Some people will argue against such a proposal by saying that if vacations are significantly increased, Japanese business, especially small and medium-sized companies, would suffer further due to cost increases. This is true at the micro level, or from the perspective of individual businessmen. But it is not always so at the macro level, or from the perspective of the Japanese economy as a whole.

The fact that there is so much over-supply in the economy as a whole means that people go to work to "work," but in fact there is a great deal of meaningless "labor" that is producing nothing. Moreover, the harder the people work because of the recession, the greater is the supply and the smaller the demand, which just aggravates the situation. Here, again, is the fallacy of composition. At a time like this, stimulating the total demand by giving people more holidays could ultimately lead to better corporate earnings because the demand will be there to make people's work effort worthwhile.

A macro-level concept such as this would never be put forward by a corporate executive, because individual businessmen will only see the immediate cost increases such a proposal would entail. Therefore, the government, which is not part of the fallacy of composition, must take a bold step and implement holiday increases. It is perhaps for this reason that many advanced, industrialized nations require by law that people take long vacations. By creating a better-balanced domestic demand structure, these long vacations not only increase the overall health of the economy but also its growth potential by creating new business opportunities.

Since requiring Japanese to take longer holidays does not add to the budget deficit like the other forms of fiscal stimulus, this idea should be promoted vigorously. After all, Japan is already 20 to 30 years behind the United States and Europe in this regard. Like other advanced, industrialized nations, Japan has reached the stage at which it needs to normalize its economy by taking such a measure. It has to recognize that it is no longer a poor, developing economy.

If Japan's domestic demand begins to grow soundly in line with its income levels, it will not only contribute positively to the economy but also greatly ease such problems as trade friction and a strong yen, which have besieged the country for so long. This is because with a healthy domestic demand, Japanese companies will not have to depend so much on exports. In this sense, also, it is hoped that the government will take strong leadership in creating a lifestyle that befits an advanced, industrialized nation.

HIGH COST OF JAPANESE RESORTS

There is concern that even if more vacation time is provided, Japanese people will only increase their amount of overseas travel and not increase their spending at home. Every year, 13 million people take overseas vacations, while some tourist destinations in Japan are becoming more and more desolate.

The key reason for the Japanese taking overseas vacations is that Japanese resorts are extremely expensive relative to their quality. But the reason for this goes back to the fact that Japanese people cannot take vacations freely. Since people cannot take much time off, they use resort facilities only during weekends. As a result, the occupancy rates of Japanese resort hotels are high only during weekends, while there are hardly any guests during the week, no matter how big a discount is offered, resulting in extremely low occupancy rates. There is no way for facilities that operate only two days a week to offer reasonable prices.

The reason why prices are reasonable at overseas resorts is that, since people can take vacations more freely, these resorts operate seven days a week, which enables even luxury hotels to offer reasonable rates. Indeed, there is now a vicious cycle in that in Japan, because of the low occupancy rates, even poorly equipped facilities charge exorbitant fees, which drives people to overseas vacation spots, which in turn makes domestic vacation spots even more desolate or more expensive. If people can take a vacation at any time, it will benefit domestic resorts by raising the utilization rate for the whole week. That, in turn, will allow the resorts to offer more reasonable prices.

INEFFICIENT USE OF LAND

The next hurdle in increasing domestic demand in Japan involves the use of land. Indeed, if there is one area where Japan still does not qualify as an advanced industrialized economy, it is in the area of housing. Although it has always been said that Japan does not have enough land, this has never been the case. One only has to think about how many Hong Kongs or Manhattans could fit into the Kanto plain (in the middle of which sits Tokyo) to realize that the amount of land is not the key issue. In Hong Kong, six million people live rather comfortably in a tiny area. By contrast, Japanese people have to live in homes that are so tiny even people from Hong Kong are astounded. This is because, while Hong Kong uses its land very efficiently, the Japanese use it very badly.

It is true that Japan's land area is only one-twenty-sixth of America's. If that is the case, the Japanese should be using their land 26 times more efficiently than the Americans, but the land utilization rate in Tokyo is several times lower than that in New York City. This abnormal situation needs to be corrected as soon as possible.

Basically, three factors hinder effective land use. Of the three, the simplest reason is resignation. Many people have given up any hope of having spacious housing comparable to that available in the West, because the supply of land in Japan — level land, in particular — is limited. Most school children learn during their elementary school days (I was one of them) not to expect bigger housing. In fact, however, the population density in central Tokyo's 23 wards is much lower than in Manhattan or Paris. Thus, neither absolute population size nor the amount of land available explains why people live in cramped apartments ridiculed by foreigners as "rabbit hutches." It is too early to give up for this reason.

The next-often-cited reason is the occurrence of earthquakes. It is true that earthquakes in Japan, including the 1995 Great Hanshin Earthquake, have wrought great damage. It is also said that one-tenth of all earthquakes in the world take place in and around Japan. From the viewpoint of modern architectural technology, however, the problem of earthquakes is virtually a thing of the past. Actually, if one is seriously worried about earthquakes, it is more troublesome that traditional low-level houses are built so close together, along streets that are too narrow for fire engines to navigate with ease. People would be much better protected from earthquakes if land were used effectively, allowing the construction of wider roads and larger, modern buildings incorporating the latest in earthquake technology. Indeed, most of the people who perished in the Hanshin Earthquake were living in traditional houses built around narrow and crowded streets, instead of in modern buildings.

The principal reason why land cannot be used efficiently lies in the tax system and the nature of government building regulations. The property tax rate in Japan, when compared to that of the United States, is extremely low. The tax rate varies from state to state in the United States. But as an example, I sold my house in New Jersey, in a suburb of New York, where I had lived until 1984, for US$92,000. The property tax at the time was US$3,000 a year. This amounted to 3.2% of the market price.

Contrast this with the situation in Japan. I once lived in a house in Shirogane, Minato-ku, Tokyo. While I was there, a developer offered an equal-value trade for the real estate with a market price of ¥400 million. The property tax on this house at that time stood at ¥250,000 a year. This means the tax rate would be 0.065%. This is one-fiftieth of that on my New Jersey home. What effect does this difference have? In the United States, if the price of land goes up and the person owning the land cannot put it to good use, he will be unable to pay the tax. Thus, he will have no choice but to rent or sell the land to someone who can use it more effectively.

The tax on land in Japan, however, is almost nil. Even if land prices surge suddenly, there is almost no pressure to use the land more effectively and to gain a profit. This becomes apparent when one sees that many shops and houses in areas such as central Tokyo's Chiyoda-ward or Chuo-ward, where land prices have already reached astronomical levels, are no taller than two stories.

It is often said that in Japan, land is sold only at the time of inheritance. Many such sales involve fragmentation of ownership, as owners must parcel out their land and sell it in order to pay the inheritance tax. As a result, land ownership becomes even more segmented. As a result of these tax systems, Japanese developers must spend enormous sums of money and an unbelievable amount of time in order to assemble a plot that is large enough to sustain high-rise buildings. It is not uncommon for developers to take as long as 20 years to build the final building. Those who cannot wait or do not have the requisite resources often end up constructing what are called "pencil buildings," generally five- to 10-story structures on extremely small lots. This makes for a most inefficient use of land. The United States and many European countries prohibit the selling of land in such small pieces.

Construction regulations, such as restrictions on height limits or floor area ratios, also prevent the effective use of land that is already available in the form of large lots. Although cities everywhere in the world have some sort of height limit on buildings, the limit is set at extremely low levels in Japan. This, together with the so-called sunshine laws, makes effective use of land difficult even for owners of large plots. Unless there is major deregulation, if not abolition, of restrictions on floor area ratios, effective use of land will continue to remain out of reach.

There is almost unlimited demand for affordable and roomy housing in Japanese cities. However, if all regulations, including floor area ratios and the right to sunlight, are satisfied, housing with only very limited floor space will be affordable for consumers. For example, if only a three-story building can be built on a piece of expensive land, then regardless of the ingenuity put into its layout, the builder's only choice is between offering spacious, but very expensive, housing, or affordable, but cramped, housing. While wealthy consumers may pay high prices, the general public will find the offerings less than attractive. This keeps the Japanese domestic demand well below its potential.

On the other hand, if these regulations are relaxed or removed altogether so that it becomes possible to construct a building up to 30 stories high on a lot that was originally limited to three-story structures, the situation will change dramatically. First of all, the return on investment in real estate will increase several-fold. That will provide the floor to the fall in real estate prices that will be of great help in dealing with the balance sheet recession. Even if the eventual competition among developers halves the rent for each unit of floor space, there will still be plenty of investment projects that will pay for themselves. Only then will it become possible to supply the affordable and roomy housing that Japanese people have always wanted.

Drastic deregulation of land usage, especially those laws relating to the ratios of ground floor space to land area, total floor space to land area, the right to sunlight, and land and house leases, is essential if the land is to be used more efficiently. In recent years, the ratio of total floor space to land area has been raised somewhat, but piecemeal deregulation is the worst choice, since people would wait if they think that the restriction will be eased again in the future. If the restriction is to be eased, it should be done in one big step, such as allowing up to 30-story buildings in one step, rather than allowing up to three-story buildings this year and four-story buildings next year. Otherwise, it will be impossible to turn all the potential demand into actual demand.

The Public Housing Loan Corporation also has a strange regulation that prohibits loans if the house is too big by its standards. Such a regulation does not encourage consumption. The rule should be changed so that the bigger the house, the bigger the loan.

One of the pillars of structural reform by the Koizumi Cabinet is urban reconstruction (rehabilitation). It would be most useful if the government rigorously promoted the efficient use of land so as to turn the almost infinite potential demand that exists in this area into actual demand. The radical promotion of efficient land use is the best solution to the demand problem that Japan faces today.[2]

INVESTING IN GOOD HOUSING IS A FORM OF SAVINGS

The U.S. savings rate is said to be low, and statistics prove that it is. But the savings rate in the United States is somewhat different from that in Japan in that a significant proportion of Americans' consumption expenditure is for home improvements, such as repainting walls, remodeling the kitchen, or putting on a new roof.

In the statistics, most of these expenditures are treated as consumption. But investing money in homes will raise their value, so that home-owners can ultimately recover some of those expenditures when they sell their homes. In other words, it is savings as well as consumption for the home-owner. American home-owners know that they are saving money by taking care of their homes, and they plan to recover their investment when they sell them.

This type of "consumption," however, does not happen in Japan. This is because of the shoddy quality of Japanese homes. In the United States, wooden homes can be used for 100 or 200 years with careful repairs and maintenance. By contrast, many Japanese homes are unusable after 20 years or so and their asset value falls to zero. It is only in fortunate cases that the asset value is zero, for often the existence of an old house on a property reduces the value of the property. This is because the house has to be demolished before a new house can be built. Indeed, it is often said in Japan that a vacant lot has more value than the same plot with a house on it. This means that the buyer must have ready the money for home construction as well as land, which leads to a still higher savings rate.

The Japanese are wasting a great deal of money and effort in not building houses that last. Instead of adding wealth on top of wealth, they are pulling down houses to build again, only to pull them down again. As long as they continue to repeat this process, they will never be able to enjoy a rich life in the true meaning of the word.

Even though the post-war conditions in Japan, where everyone had to start from virtually nothing, did not allow many people to build good homes, now that they have the means, there should be a system to encourage the building of high-quality homes that will last for 100 or 200 years. Then, as the structure will not deteriorate easily, people will have the incentive to invest in their homes to increase their value. This increases the "consumption" while reducing the need for savings, since the house itself is the savings. Furthermore, since the owner is the one who uses the new kitchen or air conditioner, he can enjoy life that much more.

The government can lead the way by establishing standards for truly high-quality buildings. Then the builders will have the incentive to build "100-year condominiums" which will command higher prices. Wealth will then increase if people invest in these condominiums in order to maintain and increase their asset value.

In Japan, unless the efficient use of land is encouraged, its domestic demand will forever remain far below its potential. That will have adverse consequences for people both within and outside Japan. In order to unleash the almost unlimited demand that still remains unsatisfied in the country, a drastic deregulation of land use is urgently needed.

PLAN TO DOUBLE THE FLOOR SPACE OF HOMES AND VACATION TIME

In order to surmount the present difficulty, Japan, as an advanced, industrialized nation, should boldly announce, as its visions for the future, plans to double both the floor space of homes and vacation time. Since these plans represent a paradigm shift, the government must explain to the Japanese people why such changes are necessary. If the government explains clearly why savings, which had been a major virtue, have become a vice; why holidays, which had been such a vice, are a virtue now that Japan has become an advanced, industrialized nation; and why spacious homes, which people had thought to be beyond their reach, are actually a possibility if efficient land use is encouraged, the Japanese people will understand.

Indeed, during the so-called U.S.–Japan Structural Impediments Initiative (SII), which started in 1990, many of these issues, especially the efficient use of land, were widely discussed for the first time in Japan. Furthermore, unlike the other pressures from the U.S., this one was widely supported by the Japanese public. Unfortunately, just as the SII talks were gaining momentum in Japan, Saddam Hussein invaded Kuwait and the U.S. leadership had to redirect its energies to conducting the Gulf War. The subsequent change in U.S. administration, together with all the vested interest against change in Japan, ended up scuttling the goals of SII.

At that time, SII was viewed as a way to create a more balanced Japanese economy in order to address the trade imbalance problem between the U.S. and Japan. Today, however, the same efforts are needed to pull the Japanese economy out of the balance sheet recession and its aftermath, the corporate debt rejection syndrome. And in both cases, it is in Japan's own interest to improve the land use and lifestyles of its people so that they can truly enjoy the fruits of their labor. Indeed, all of these changes are long overdue.

"RESIDENTS' EGO" STIFLES THE JAPANESE ECONOMY

Before the Plaza Accord of September 1985, most Japanese executives never questioned the fact that, because they were born Japanese, their task was to manufacture goods in Japan to sell in the world market. They had thought that the costs they incurred in Japan were reasonable because they knew nothing else.

Once they stepped out of Japan as a result of the post-Plaza Accord strong yen, however, they discovered that their costs, which they had never questioned at home, were actually exceptionally high by international standards and that some of those costs, such as highway tolls, were close to zero in many countries. Of course, they only migrated to places where costs were low or nil. But, when they stepped out of Japan in search of such low-cost production sites, they discovered that there were actually many such places. In addition, there were plenty of young, eager workers who were willing to work very hard. Once they had seen such a world, the executives felt that it was difficult to justify investing in plant and equipment in Japan which required a great deal of cumbersome red tape.

In fact, even among those businesses that are not making any capital investment in Japan, there are many companies that are building new plants outside Japan. When asked why they do not build plants in Japan, they respond that they cannot operate in Japan's absurdly high-cost structure. Structural reform to rectify Japan's high-cost structure is therefore essential. It is by far the largest disincentive to domestic capital investment by Japanese businesses.

One of the reasons why the costs are so high is that community ego, or the so-called residents' ego, is tolerated in Japan to an unbelievable degree. This is most obvious in the example of Narita Airport, a gateway to Japan, where a few farmers are obstinately refusing to move and thus obstructing the construction of a runway as planned. This is the second, and even uglier, "land problem" that Japan must solve in order to use land efficiently. Even though the concept of eminent domain exists in Japan's law books, it is never put into practice for fear that the social uproar would be too great for political leaders to handle. It is said that one official who tried to enforce the eminent domain provision during the construction of Narita Airport was beaten so severely by angry protesters that all the bones in his hands and legs were broken to pieces. Indeed, his injuries were so bad that he lost the use of his hands and legs. No perpetrators of this crime were ever apprehended. This incident also made bureaucrats and politicians extremely cautious about enforcing eminent domain provisions.

Furthermore, a certain newspaper always takes the side of the residents, even when only one resident is making the noise. It agitates without regard to the fact that millions or tens of millions of people will be adversely affected and that it is against the interests of the population as a whole.

The reason that electric power is so expensive in Japan is because it entails enormous cost even just to erect a transmission tower. Even when a tower is to be erected in the middle of a paddy field where it will not obstruct anything, enormous amounts of time and compensation are required to obtain the consent of the land-owner. All of these costs are reflected in the high tariff for electric power. These stories are a dime a dozen in Japan. Because such actions by local residents have been tolerated (and in many cases amply rewarded), they have become endemic and are now blocking the smooth working of the economy all over the country.

POST-WAR BACKLASH GOING TOO FAR

The reason that community power has become so strong and pervasive probably has its origins in Japan's past. Before the end of World War II, the government, and especially the military, was so powerful that the people were totally unable to stand against it. They lost land and property to the state, and even their children were taken away from them to serve in the military. The reaction to this unfortunate past has appeared in its extreme form in post-war Japan.

Following the war, as the Japanese people strived to protect their rights as individuals, they somehow felt justified in suppressing the interests of the powerful elite in the center. In other words, the pendulum has swung to the other extreme compared with where it was during the war. This is why airport or road construction does not proceed unless unanimous consent is obtained. Even when only two or three people resist the project, the construction does not proceed as long as they stand against it. The pendulum has swung too far.

People often complain that public works projects are a waste of money, as they often end up building grand highways through barren mountain areas. However, if one tries to build really useful projects in Japan, it takes easily 10 to 20 years before the actual work can be launched because of the lengthy negotiations required with the local residents of affected areas. For example, everyone in Japan will welcome the efforts to expand the always-clogged Metropolitan Expressway from its current two lanes into four lanes in each direction. However, it will probably take a stupefying amount of time to negotiate with the title-holders before such work can begin.

On the other hand, the deflationary gap needs to be closed right now in order to keep the entire economy from plunging into a depression. This being the case, public works projects must be carried out in places where no one will raise objections and work can start immediately. That is why one finds grandiose roads constructed deep in the mountains.

It is often said that public works projects are carried out so that the bureaucracy and contractors can collude to skim taxpayers' money. This may be partly true, but the real reason why public works projects that people can be truly grateful for cannot be built lies in the fact that such projects typically involve too many lengthy negotiations with the title-holders of the land.

Unless this issue of expropriation for the public domain is solved, truly useful public works projects will continue to be impossible to complete and the money will move in an increasingly bizarre direction. Indeed, some parts of Japan may best be described as a dictatorship by residents, rather than a democracy. This is because any decision made democratically can be blocked, literally forever, by the opposition of a few affected residents. This situation is driving disgusted businesses to make investments elsewhere, which in turn is weakening the economy further. In addition to making the use of land more efficient and increasing workers' paid holidays, putting a scalpel to this problem is probably the most important structural reform Japan could put in place for the future.

ARE GENERAL CONTRACTORS THE ONLY PARTY TO BE BLAMED?

Regarding public works, a word or two about Japanese construction companies needs to be added. At present, they are being called the least efficient segment of the corporate sector. Critics claim that there are more than 600,000 companies in this sector, employing an enormous number of people, yet they are not building anything decent and their productivity is low. However, a closer examination is necessary to see whether the construction companies are really to blame, or whether the causes of the problem lie elsewhere.

A close examination is necessary, because in Japanese public works, construction companies are allowed little room to improve productivity. In most public works, the work schedule for each day is set by the government, which specifies which machines are to be used to do what. The general contractors have little room in which to try and reduce costs, and have to meet strict deadlines. On the other hand, if they complete the work ahead of schedule, their payments are reduced. If a planned three-month project is completed in two months, the contractors receive only two months' pay. Thus, there is absolutely no incentive to complete the work quickly.

By contrast, when the earthquake that occurred in Los Angeles on January 17, 1994 caused extensive damage to the city's freeways, the state authorities provided incentives for repair work to be carried out quickly. General contractors in California completed the job so quickly that they stunned even the state authorities. Thus, even in the U.S., whether or not there are incentives can make a big difference.

In Japan, a major car manufacturer decided to build a new plant and was asked to use the services of a local contractor whose business had been slow due to the decline in public works projects. The manufacturer decided to use this new contractor, who had specialized in public works projects, to build the foundations for the new plant. The job was scheduled to be completed by March 31 and the work started in December. For the first few weeks, the work proceeded very quickly and the job was almost done by the end of January. At that time, it seemed to require just a few more days of work before it would be completed. But from that time on, no one came to work at the site. When the company asked the contractor why work had ceased, he said, "This job is to be completed by March 31, right?" The manufacturer told him that it did not *have* to be March 31, and that the sooner the project was completed, the better. There followed a series of meetings to confirm that the contractor could in fact complete the work ahead of schedule without being penalized. When the contractor was reassured, he sent his workers back in and they finished the job in no time. This example shows that because contractors are penalized by being paid a lower fee whenever public works are completed ahead of schedule, it does not occur to them that the private sector actually *wants* jobs done as quickly as possible.

Furthermore, in Japan, a span of roadworks that would be tendered out to a single company in any other country may be divided into as many as 10 sub-projects, with 10 companies hired to do the work so that everybody shares in the jobs that are available. Although the cost would be much lower if the job was given to a single company, the Japanese system does not work that way.

Japanese contractors are doing good work all over the world, whether they are operating in the Middle East or on the Euro Tunnel. The reason that they are competitive abroad but have such low productivity at home lies in the domestic regulatory environment. The problem is not that these companies' productivity is low, but that the system forces low productivity upon them. If the system encouraged higher productivity by giving contractors bonuses for speedy work, rather than penalizing them by docking their pay, they would make every effort to raise their productivity. Needless to say, they should be severely penalized for shoddy work. However, if the private sector's principle of competition were introduced into the system wherever possible, the cost of public works would be much lower. There is no reason why the Japanese, who can produce such fine cars and appliances around the world, are unable to build decent roads and buildings at home.

People involved in the construction industry are working as hard as everyone else. If the system is the problem, the system should be criticized, not the companies themselves. Although there are many people both within and outside Japan who "bash" contractors and claim that structural problems would be solved only if contractors were forced to go out of business, they are barking up the wrong tree.

FULL EMPLOYMENT: MAJOR PREMISE FOR "GENERAL CONTRACTOR CRUSHING"

Some people have argued that if the Japanese economy is to develop and new industries are to grow, it is necessary to shrink the low-productivity sectors and transfer their human and financial resources to new fields.

Since Japan has a disproportionately large number of construction companies, with a workforce that actually grew during the last 10 years on the back of public spending, many critics argue that any reforms must start by shrinking this sector. They argue that without freeing resources from this sector, new and promising industries will not develop as quickly as they should in Japan.

Although this is a popular view, one should not forget that it is a view that is applicable only when the economy is enjoying full employment. In a full-employment environment, creating a new industry by definition requires taking resources away from existing industries. In such circumstances, those industries that are the least productive should be scaled down and replaced with imports so that their resources can be moved to the more promising industries.

However, Japan is now far from full employment and there are surpluses in people, money, and other resources everywhere. Indeed, the number of unemployed and the unemployment rate are both at record highs, while interest rates are at a record low. In other words, in terms of resource availability, there is absolutely no constraint on Japan starting new ventures today.

The real question the policymakers need to ask, therefore, is why new businesses are not springing up despite the abundant availability of resources. If excessive regulations are responsible for the present predicament, the government should ease or remove those regulations. If the problem is financing, the government should help nurture venture capitalists by reforming the tax system. If the problem is the education system, which has taught Japan's young people to fit in with society rather than have an entrepreneurial spirit that makes them stand out from the crowd, the overall educational system must be reformed.

The right order of doing things from the policy perspective, therefore, is to implement those reforms that are needed to encourage the birth of new industries, and to shake out low-productivity sectors only after the labor market has tightened. Poorly performing contractors should be allowed to go out of business when the economy reaches that stage.

Allowing construction companies to go out of business without new businesses springing up will only result in a dramatic contraction of the economy while increasing unemployment. It will also intensify the oligopoly among the surviving contractors. As the Nobel laureate Joseph Stiglitz has argued in his *Globalization and Its Discontents*, since the productivity of jobless workers is zero, the more unemployment there is, the greater will be the fiscal burden of the government and the lower will be the country's income.[3] Such is not the time to shut down companies in the name of structural reform.

Conversely, in the present situation where only a few new businesses are starting up while the economy-wide fallacy of composition problem has resulted in the worst unemployment since the end of World War II, keeping the existing businesses as much as possible so as to maintain jobs and income until new businesses emerge will better prevent the increase in budget deficits and maintain the productivity of the economy. This is precisely why the laissez-faire policy of President Hoover failed, but why the proactive fiscal policy of President Roosevelt succeeded, in getting the U.S. economy out of the Great Depression.

Of course, rotten businesses must be done away with. Those businesses judged to be hopeless by the involved parties in the private sector should be allowed to close down. However, this should be carried out through the initiative of the private-sector people on the front line, rather than through a top-down directive or guidance by the government. This is because the people on the front line are well aware of the extent of the negative chain reactions their decisions are likely to cause. In other words, they are not likely to produce too many nasty surprises for the economy as a whole.

LACK OF REFORM IS ALSO THE REASON FOR EXCHANGE RATE INSTABILITY

I have been involved with U.S.–Japanese relations, including economic, trade, and security issues, for the past 20 years. Over this period, no issues have been as troubling as trade friction and the instability of the yen–dollar exchange rate. Once the former issue makes it on to the political stage, it becomes so heated that it not only makes currency markets unstable, it also stirs up racial prejudices in both countries. Moreover, the exchange rate instability makes it difficult to provide a steady macroeconomic environment for economic recovery inside Japan.

After tackling the exchange rate problem for the last two decades, it is the opinion of the author that there is actually a structure in place in two countries that keeps the yen–dollar rate from stabilizing. The structure consists of the following components. First, Japan's comparative advantage over the U.S. in making and exporting manufactured goods remains intact. Second, the Japanese deregulation and market opening measures remain slow relative to the U.S., with the result that Japan will remain a less attractive destination than the US for both domestic and foreign investors. In other words, investment returns, including interest rates, will always be higher in the U.S. than in Japan. Exhibit 11.2 shows the consequences of these two assumptions.

Under these circumstances, Japanese investors, particularly institutional investors such as life insurance companies and investment trusts, will continue to find U.S. treasury bonds more attractive than Japanese government bonds. When they decide to purchase U.S. treasuries, the fact that Japanese people's savings are in yen means that they must first buy dollars and sell yen on the currency markets. They then use these dollars to purchase U.S. bonds or equities.

This dollar-purchasing, yen-selling activity leads to an increased supply of yen and an increased demand for dollars, which causes the dollar to rise and the yen to fall. When the dollar rises, U.S. treasuries become even more attractive, which draws in other domestic investors who, up until then, had been cautious about investing in them. That, in turn, exerts further upward pressure on the dollar and downward pressure on the yen.

When the dollar rises and the yen falls in this way, after a while Japanese exporters begin increasing their exports to the U.S. because they can make more money there than by selling the same product in Japan. At the same time, the rise in the value of the dollar causes imports to decline as they become less competitive in Japan.

At this time, both the investors that have invested in dollars and the manufacturers that have stepped up exports to America make large amounts of money out of the rise in the dollar and the fall in the yen. As a result, the former become even more aggressive about investing in the U.S. and the latter become even more aggressive in exporting to the U.S.

However, Japan has one of the biggest trade surpluses in the world, and additional growth in exports will only make the trade imbalance with the rest of the world bigger. At the same time, the countries sucking in Japanese

Exhibit 11.2   Structural instability of the yen–dollar exchange rate

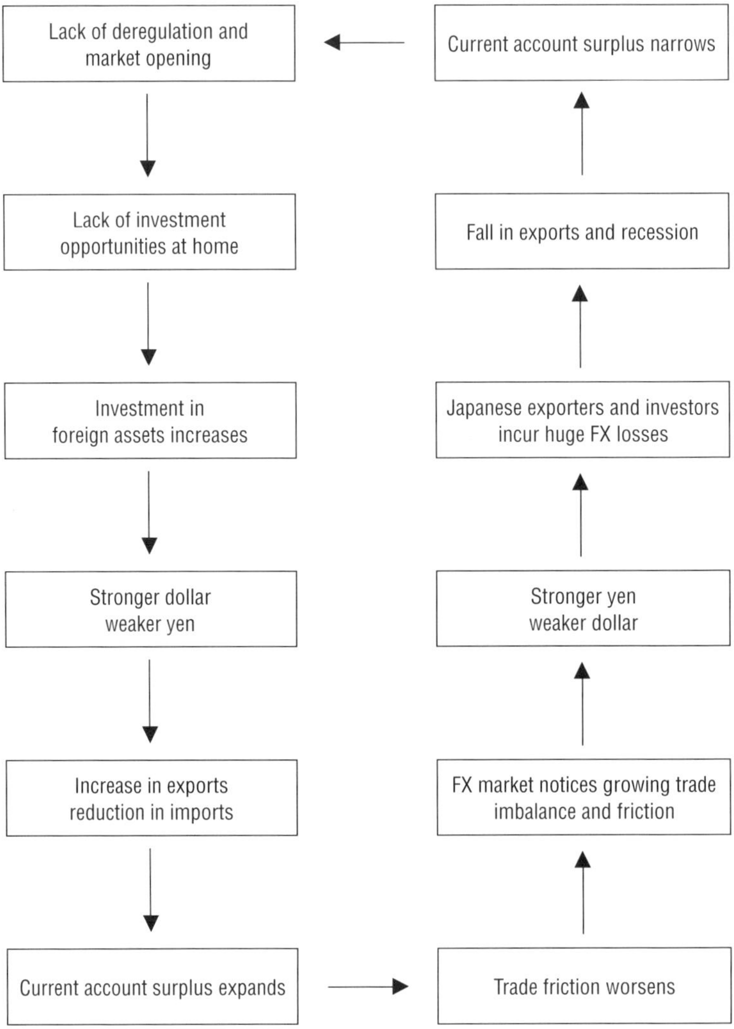

```
┌──────────────────────┐                    ┌──────────────────────────┐
│ Lack of deregulation  │  ◄───────────────  │ Current account surplus  │
│ and market opening    │                    │ narrows                  │
└──────────────────────┘                    └──────────────────────────┘
          │                                              ▲
          ▼                                              │
┌──────────────────────┐                    ┌──────────────────────────┐
│ Lack of investment    │                    │ Fall in exports and      │
│ opportunities at home │                    │ recession                │
└──────────────────────┘                    └──────────────────────────┘
          │                                              ▲
          ▼                                              │
┌──────────────────────┐                    ┌──────────────────────────┐
│ Investment in         │                    │ Japanese exporters and   │
│ foreign assets        │                    │ investors incur huge     │
│ increases             │                    │ FX losses                │
└──────────────────────┘                    └──────────────────────────┘
          │                                              ▲
          ▼                                              │
┌──────────────────────┐                    ┌──────────────────────────┐
│ Stronger dollar       │                    │ Stronger yen             │
│ weaker yen            │                    │ weaker dollar            │
└──────────────────────┘                    └──────────────────────────┘
          │                                              ▲
          ▼                                              │
┌──────────────────────┐                    ┌──────────────────────────┐
│ Increase in exports   │                    │ FX market notices        │
│ reduction in imports  │                    │ growing trade imbalance  │
│                       │                    │ and friction             │
└──────────────────────┘                    └──────────────────────────┘
          │                                              ▲
          ▼                                              │
┌──────────────────────┐                    ┌──────────────────────────┐
│ Current account       │  ───────────────►  │ Trade friction worsens   │
│ surplus expands       │                    │                          │
└──────────────────────┘                    └──────────────────────────┘
```

Source: Nomura Research Institute (NRI).

products, including the U.S., start to see their trade deficits increase, which constitutes a cause for concern.

It normally takes between six months and a year for a growing trade imbalance to be confirmed in trade statistics for both countries. It takes another quarter or two before import-competing industries and their workers in the U.S. and elsewhere begin screaming for help. And soon enough, the issue explodes in the form of trade friction in Washington. In other words, Congress and the United States Trade Representative start protesting about

Japanese products and initiate anti-dumping and other moves to help U.S. industry.

TRADE FRICTION PUSHES THE YEN HIGHER

The minute the trade imbalance becomes a political issue, those Japanese investors that have bought dollars start worrying about exchange rate risks. This is because correcting the exchange rate is the most effective and straightforward way of correcting a trade imbalance. Indeed, whenever trade friction intensifies, government officials and politicians are bound to call for a weaker dollar, although those officials who are directly responsible for the exchange rate policy are typically more careful.

When such voices are heard in Washington, Japanese investors start to behave differently, as indicated in Chapter 4. As they are free to purchase or not purchase dollars, they typically remove themselves from the foreign exchange market by either hedging their exposures or selling their dollars. Some may also take profits on the dollars they have at the moment with the idea of buying them back at some later time, when the dollar has become cheaper. This means that the demand for dollars disappears almost overnight.

On the other hand, dollar selling is bound to continue because Japanese companies exporting to the U.S., such as Toyota or Nissan, need yen in order to pay their bills in Japan. They do not have any option not to sell dollars. The fact that Japan has a surplus and the U.S. a deficit means that the amount of dollars Japanese exporters to the U.S. must sell is greater than the amount of yen U.S. exporters to Japan must sell in order to pay their bills in the U.S. Thus, trade flows alone would have pushed the dollar down long ago.

In order to keep the dollar from falling, therefore, this gap has to be filled by Japanese investors who have the yen to sell to the Toyotas and Nissans. However, when those Japanese investors that had been plugging this gap stop buying dollars, the market becomes awash with dollars. This causes the dollar to fall and the yen to rise.

When the yen rises, those investors who bought treasuries when the dollar was strong all incur currency losses. Many will be forced to sell their dollars, either to cut their losses or to hedge their remaining dollar exposure. When this happens, the dollar selling will come not just from the exporters to the U.S., but also from the investors who had previously bought dollars as well. With no one buying dollars, the forex market turns into a dollar bear market, and the yen rises rapidly.

Moreover, the fact that it takes a long time for the actual trade flows, and even longer for trade statistics, to respond to exchange rate movements means that trade statistics announced in both countries continue to show larger imbalances even when the yen is appreciating rapidly. Such a development makes investors even more cautious, because it suggests that an even greater appreciation of the yen might be necessary to correct the widening trade imbalances. This causes the yen to rise still further. In other words, the major time lags that exist between events in the real economy, such as expanding trade imbalances, and events in the financial markets, such as changes in exchange rates, mean that yen appreciation and dollar depreciation will tend to overshoot.

However, once yen appreciation reaches extreme levels, people will start thinking that Japanese exports are bound to fall and imports are bound to rise. By then, however, the Japanese investors have been hit so hard by the yen's appreciation that they need some time to lick their wounds.

Six months to a year after the yen has started rising, trade statistics began to confirm that Japanese exports are indeed falling and imports are indeed rising. This means that the trade balances are moving back toward equilibrium. Moreover, by this time the Japanese economy is probably in a serious recession due to the extreme strength of the yen and falling exports. With few investment opportunities at home (in the event that not much progress has been made with deregulation) and domestic interest rates remaining very low, Japanese investors once again turn their attention to opportunities in the U.S. market, including U.S. treasuries.

The cycle then starts up again, with the dollar rising and the yen falling. Because it takes some time for the trade balance to respond to changes in the exchange rate, however, it is entirely possible that during the first few months of the renewed interest in U.S. treasuries by Japanese investors, the trade balance will be moving toward equilibrium while the yen is falling and the dollar is rising. This makes Japanese investors even more relaxed about investing in treasuries, and turns even more of them into yen sellers and dollar purchasers. That, in turn, pushes the dollar even higher and the yen even lower. This time, therefore, the overshoot is in the direction of a strong dollar and a weak yen.

CREATING ATTRACTIVE INVESTMENT OPPORTUNITIES WILL STOP THE INSTABILITY

It should be added that even though the word "overshooting" is used here, these "overshooting" currency movements have a real and important impact on the economy. For example, countless Japanese companies faced real difficulties when the yen strengthened to US$1 = ¥80 in 1995. Moreover, it was only then that the government realized the need for market openings and other structural reforms. If the yen's appreciation had stopped at US$1 = ¥100, there is a chance that adjustments on the part of companies and the government would have been delayed, thereby creating the conditions in which the yen would have to rise to US$1 = ¥80 at some future date.

The same thing can also be said for Japan's trading partners. If the yen had remained at US$1 = ¥145, the trade deficit for the U.S. would have become so huge that it would have been forced to take drastic action (such as the Plaza Accord of September 1985), which could have resulted in an even sharper fall of the dollar than otherwise.

The history of the yen–dollar rate over the past 20 years has been the history of this cycle. The yen–dollar rate will never be stable for as long as these economic structures are in place. When the yen falls in value, the widening trade imbalance causes its next rise, and when it rises in value, the rush to purchase U.S. treasuries causes its next fall. If one is not careful, one will end up wasting most of one's life just following this cycle.

The best way to break this cycle and bring stability to both the exchange rate and the domestic economy is to deregulate Japan and thereby make it a more attractive place for Japanese investors to invest in. Opening the market would also make it more difficult for the trade imbalance to grow.

These changes, together with the reforms in lifestyle and land use mentioned earlier, would make the Japanese economy less dependent on foreign demand and exchange rates. Such reforms would create a true center of gravity for the Japanese economy and reduce its dependence on the U.S. economy. Moreover, it would go a long way to improving the living standards of the Japanese people.

Indeed, it is ridiculous that Japanese people, who live in such cramped housing and work so hard, are lending money to Americans, who live in much greater comfort. Many Japanese fund managers have been asking themselves why they should be investing in U.S. treasuries with all the attendant worries over the exchange rate, when there is so much room for improvement and investment within Japan, especially in the area of housing. They have been forced to invest abroad, however, because absurd regulations and tax codes make investment in needed domestic projects unprofitable. The answers to their prayers, therefore, lie in the deregulation of land use and lifestyle changes, both of which are long overdue.

DIFFERENT TREATMENTS REQUIRED FOR "PNEUMONIA" AND "DIABETES"

Putting all this in perspective, what Japan needs to do now is to assist, through an aggressive fiscal policy, those 70–80% of businesses that wish to repair their balance sheets so that they have the revenue to pay down their debts. At the same time, it has to implement forward-looking structural reforms in order to create exciting investment opportunities so that businesses that have repaired their balance sheets will not succumb to the debt rejection syndrome.

The former may be more properly called "repairing war damage" and is essential, but this alone cannot open future prospects or end the debt rejection syndrome. On the other hand, if only the latter policy (that is, structural reform) is implemented, it will only help 20% of companies while failing to solve the problems of the remaining 80%. But if 80% of the economy started sinking, the remaining 20% would also likely become defensive and cautious, so that the whole economy could collapse into a full-blown depression. It is for this reason that the government must carry out the two-pronged approach of repairing the war damage at a realistic pace, while applying full force to true structural reform, which is essential for improving the future prospects of the Japanese economy.

The fact that 80% of companies are trying to repair their balance sheets does not mean that 80% of the Japanese economy is bad. Quite the contrary, it means that these companies are getting leaner and meaner every day. The fact that they are still at it may mean that many of these companies have not yet reached the high standard of financial health they have set for themselves.

In other words, the fact that the economy is so weak does not mean the companies are all equally weak. The economy is weak because companies are trying to become leaner and meaner *all at the same time*. As long as the economy itself does not fall into a vicious cycle, Japanese companies, at the end of the day, are likely to come out stronger and meaner than ever before.

The reason that we have both macroeconomics and microeconomics is that the sum of micro behavior does not explain the behavior of the economy as a whole. The balance sheet recession stemming from the fallacy of composition is the prime example. When companies are all maximizing profits, strong companies mean a strong economy. When companies are all minimizing debt, strong companies mean a weak economy. Those who are competing with Japanese companies should keep this in mind so as not to write off Japanese competition prematurely.

On the other hand, those who are thinking of investing in Japan might find that now is a once-in-a-lifetime opportunity, as the fallacy of composition problem has depressed asset prices in the country to unusually low levels. Of course, such a person must have faith that the current almost exclusive policy emphasis on structural reform will be corrected to include realistic macroeconomic policies. Furthermore, they should be confident that realistic macroeconomic policies will be maintained until the fallacy of composition problem is completely eradicated.

Put differently, the Japanese economy today is like a sick patient who has both pneumonia and diabetes. Repairing balance sheets is like treating pneumonia, while overcoming debt rejection syndrome and making the economy an attractive destination for investments is like treating diabetes.

The two illnesses can happen at the same time. Furthermore, different treatment is required for each. In order to treat pneumonia, for example, the patient needs to be given plenty of nutritious food; whereas too much food is not good for a patient with diabetes. However, any doctor faced with both will treat the potentially fatal pneumonia first and then go after the diabetes. This is because treating pneumonia is an urgent matter where there is absolutely no time to waste. The necessary medications will have to be administered without delay and in sufficient doses to overcome the disease. On the other hand, treating diabetes requires a long and carefully monitored program to improve the patient's own bodily functions. It thus must be given a lower priority than the treatment for pneumonia.

In the same way that treating the pneumonia may worsen the patient's diabetes, the fiscal stimulus needed for the treatment of a balance sheet recession may add to the sense of complacency and delay necessary reforms in some quarters. However, this does not mean that the patient can go without the treatment. In such situations, it is critically important that the priority and sequencing are properly established so that as soon as the most urgent problem is fully resolved, attention can be redirected to treatments necessary in other areas for the complete recovery of the patient.

Unfortunately, the Koizumi government has been operating on the assumption that Japan only has diabetes, and has completely ignored the more serious complaint of pneumonia. As a result, both the economy and asset prices have been weakening. Earlier administrations, on the other hand, treated the pneumonia, often quite effectively, but they frequently forgot about the diabetes.

In terms of numbers, the Koizumi government is trying to help the 20–30% of companies with clean balance sheets, while previous administrations were trying to help the 70–80% of companies that were trying to repair their balance sheets. The truth of the matter, however, is that *both need help*.

Putting it all together, the government must both maintain economic stability through realistic fiscal policies while pushing for structural reform so that companies that have finished repairing their balance sheets will find ample investment opportunities at home. The household sector must also be persuaded and mobilized to reduce the deflationary gap. To do so, the government should lead the way in creating a lifestyle that matches the level of Japan's economic development. Promoting efficient use of land will also go a long way in alleviating the "excess savings" problem.

In doing so, the policymakers must make a clear distinction between repairs of war damage caused by the bubble, such as the fiscal deficit problem and the problems of non-performing loans, and structural reforms that are really needed for the future, such as better use of land and changing people's lifestyle. The latter should be identified as the true structural reform that calls for top priority and needs to be implemented with full force. The former tasks should be implemented to match the health of the economy at the time. If this distinction is made clearly and acted upon appropriately, Japan should be able to get out of its present impasse and grasp with both hands a new future that is not merely an extension of the past.

ENDNOTES

1 *Nikkei Ryutsu Shimbun*, August 29, 1995.
2 Some of these ideas were also presented in Richard Koo, "The Land Factor: An Economic Disaster," in Frank Gibney, *Unlocking the Bureaucrat's Kingdom* (Washington, D.C.: Brooking Institute Press, 1998), pp. 171–77.
3 Joseph E. Stiglitz, *Globalization and Its Discontents* (W. W. Norton & Co., 2002), p. 57.

Appendix 1: Summary of Balance Sheet Recession

This appendix summarizes the features of balance sheet recession. The key entries here in bracketed numbers are also shown in the flow chart (Exhibit A1.1) that is included at the end of the appendix.

THE ORIGIN OF BALANCE SHEET RECESSION

- A balance sheet recession typically emerges after the bursting of a nationwide asset price bubble that leaves a large number of private-sector balance sheets in need of serious repair (1).
- In order to repair their balance sheets, the affected companies are forced to move away from their usual profit maximization to debt minimization (2).
- Although debt repayment is a right and responsible action to take at the individual corporate level, when everyone moves in that direction at the same time, aggregate demand shrinks and worsens both the economy and asset prices (3). This, in turn, forces the companies to pay down debt even faster, resulting in a vicious cycle (4).
- This is a fallacy of composition problem in that individual companies are doing the right and responsible thing and therefore are unable to change their behavior. But collectively, they are making the situation worse for everyone.
- Large numbers of companies trying to pay down their debt at the same time are particularly troublesome for economies with a high savings rate because, in the absence of corporate borrowers, those saved but not invested funds from the household sector end up becoming the deflationary gap for the economy (5).
- The leakage to the income stream created by this deflationary gap, if left unattended, will continue to push the economy toward a contractionary

equilibrium until the private sector is too impoverished to save any money. That point is usually called depression.

- Since the economy will not enter self-sustaining growth until the majority of its companies are free of balance sheet problems, the government's policies must be geared to helping these companies finish their balance sheet repairs as quickly as possible.

FISCAL POLICY

- As the government cannot tell companies *not* to repair their balance sheets, the government itself must do the opposite of the companies and generate demand in order to offset the deflationary impact stemming from the fallacy of composition in the private sector (6).
- Fiscal policy can fill the deflationary gap in the balance sheet recession, because the government can borrow and spend the money the household sector saved but which the corporate sector did not borrow.
- The household and financial sectors are both happy to lend money to the government, because it is the only borrower left in the economy (7).
- Indeed, the only reason Japan managed to stay afloat in spite of the massive loss of wealth (equivalent to nearly three years of GDP) is that fiscal stimulus was applied from the very beginning so as to keep the vicious cycle from starting (8).
- Since no self-sustaining growth is possible for an economy without the majority of its companies having satisfactory balance sheets, the success of the fiscal stimulus in a balance sheet recession should be judged on its contribution to reducing private-sector debt overhang.
- Viewed in this light, the fiscal stimulus in Japan not only kept the Japanese GDP from collapsing, but it also allowed companies to pay down over ¥120 trillion in debt by maintaining their income, a truly remarkable achievement (9).
- The Japanese corporate debt overhang, therefore, is greatly reduced compared to 10 years ago. However, because of an even greater fall in asset prices, it will take a few more years of debt reduction before companies are satisfied with their balance sheets.

MONETARY POLICY

- When so many companies move away from profit maximization to debt minimization, the demand for funds disappears and the economy ceases to respond to monetary easing from that point onward, regardless of the level of interest rates (10).
- The subsequent weakness of the economy, however, prompts the central

bank to ease monetary policy aggressively, believing that at some point the economy would respond to lower interest rates and increased liquidity (11).

- However, nothing happens to the economy, because there are so few people left in the economy who can respond to monetary easing. With no response from the economy, the central bank panics and lowers rates even further until there is no more room to lower interest rates (12).
- The panic reaction from the central bank creates the world of a "liquidity trap," where very low interest rates coincide with a very weak economy. The fact of the matter, however, is that the economy lost its sensitivity to monetary easing because companies switched from profit maximization to debt minimization, not because interest rates have fallen to very low levels (13).
- In this environment, both the inflation target and quantitative easing will have no impact because, without the inflation actually being in place, the announcement of these policies alone will not change the behavior of those who are doing the right thing by paying down debt.
- Indeed, one almost has to assume criminal behavior on the part of borrowers and lenders of funds for those policies to work. This is because these people must be persuaded to forget their balance sheet problems and abandon their debt repayment effort, and bet on inflation materializing in the future when the reality is still deflation.
- It is not likely that too many people will take such irresponsible action. But without these people changing their behavior, inflation will never materialize.
- For the same reason that monetary policy failed to work in the 1930s, the last great balance sheet recession, there is no reason for monetary policy to work in today's balance sheet recession.
- Excessive purchases of government bonds by the central bank will weaken the banks by flattening the yield curve and depriving them of a key source of revenue.

PROACTIVE FISCAL POLICY NEEDED

- Even though Japanese fiscal stimulus has been helping companies repair their balance sheets while keeping the economy going, it was never applied in a proactive manner. Indeed, each time the fiscal policy was applied, it was always "behind the curve" in the sense that it was mobilized only after the economy showed significant weakness.
- In a balance sheet recession, such a reactionary fiscal policy is extremely inefficient. This is because it is applied after the wound has opened up, resulting in bigger medical bills and a less vibrant economy.

- In this kind of environment, a proactive fiscal policy is far more desirable in both keeping the economy going and in minimizing the medical bill, that is, the deficit.
- The last thing that policymakers should do in a balance sheet recession is prematurely withdraw the fiscal stimulus. As amply observed in 1997 in Japan and 1937 in the U.S., such a withdrawal can result in an instant collapse of the economy while enlarging the deficit by decimating the tax receipts.
- Once asset prices have fallen to a reasonable level, a proactive fiscal policy applied consistently can put the economy in a virtuous cycle and significantly shorten the time needed to repair private-sector balance sheets.
- Although Japan actually entered such virtuous cycles on two previous occasions, in 1996 and 2000, both were torpedoed by the Japanese Ministry of Finance, which is hell-bent on reducing the budget deficit regardless of economic conditions.

FISCAL AND MONETARY POLICY MIX

- This kind of recession caused by a large number of entities minimizing debt all at the same time has never been taken seriously in the economics and business literature. The inclusion of this possibility fills the key gap in Keynesian theories while clarifying the limitations of monetarism.
- Moreover, an active fiscal policy is needed to keep the money supply from shrinking in a balance sheet recession. This is because, in the absence of private-sector borrowers, the size of the money supply depends on the size of public-sector borrowings (14).
- Even though the central bank can inject any amount of liquidity into the banking system, in the absence of private-sector borrowers, the amount of liquidity that can come out of the banking system and enter the real economy depends on the size of the public-sector borrowings.
- In this sense, there is no independent monetary policy during a balance sheet recession. The effectiveness of monetary policy depends very much on the size of the fiscal stimulus.
- Once private-sector balance sheets are repaired and the companies return to the profit-maximizing mode, the government must reverse its course and start reducing the budget deficit in order to avoid crowding out the private-sector demand for funds.
- The signal for this change will come from higher interest rates in the market, supported by a strong demand for funds from the private sector.
- When the companies are back to profit-maximizing mode, however, the "invisible hand" will work to enlarge the economy. In this case, the

smaller and less intrusive the government, the better it is for the economy. Monetary policy should also be sufficient to fine-tune the economy in this normal condition.

- When the companies are in debt-minimizing mode, however, the "invisible hand" will work to shrink the economy. In this case, the more proactive the government is in filling the deflationary gap through fiscal stimulus, the better it is for the economy. Monetary policy, however, is largely irrelevant in this situation, because no one is interested in borrowing money.

- In such a world, deficit spending can actually increase the economy's long-term growth rates by keeping the "invisible hand" from pushing the economy into depression.

NON-PERFORMING LOAN PROBLEMS IN BALANCE SHEET RECESSION

- Even though a balance sheet recession typically comes with huge non-performing loan problems within the banking sector (15), the causality is from the poor economy and lower asset prices to NPL problems, not the other way around.

- This is obvious from the historically low interest rates observed in most balance sheet recessions. These low rates are the result of so many lending institutions competing for the few remaining borrowers.

- This means that banks' ability to lend is no constraint on economic growth in this type of recession. The bottleneck is in the demand for funds, not the supply of funds.

- With so few private-sector investors with strong balance sheets left in a nationwide balance sheet recession, government's attempt to dispose of banks' NPLs too quickly will depress asset prices to unimaginable levels.

- Such a fall in asset prices will worsen the NPL problems at banks while moving the goal of clean balance sheets further away from the corporations, thus causing havoc in the economy.

- Since the demand for funds is so weak, there is no reason to give highest policy priorities to the resolution of NPL problems with the banks.

- Unless there is a credit crunch, the available fiscal resources should be used to shore up the economy, which is the best defense against further increases in NPLs.

- The NPLs should be disposed of in an orderly and predictable manner. The pace of disposal should be determined collectively by the banking authorities and the private-sector banks to ensure that the resulting deflationary impact on the economy is minimized.

Exhibit A1.1 The anatomy of balance sheet recession and its cure

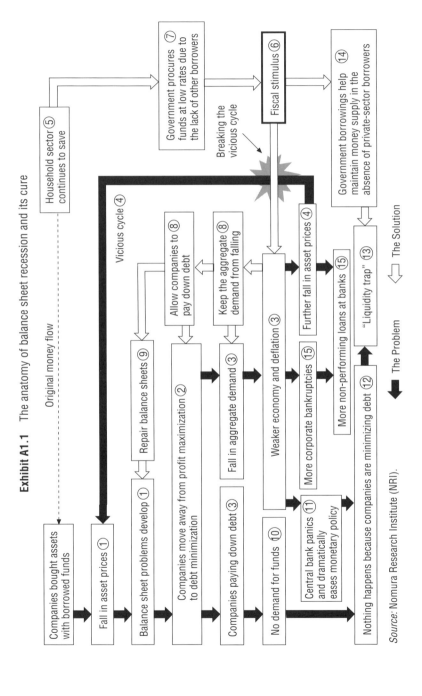

Source: Nomura Research Institute (NRI).

APPENDIX 2: REVISITING MONEY SUPPLY, HIGH-POWERED MONEY AND MONEY MULTIPLIER

Many commentators on Japan have been telling the Japanese monetary authorities that because money multiplier is falling in the country, the central bank must increase high-powered money so that the money supply can be maintained. They have argued that in order to do so, the Bank of Japan should increase its purchases of government bonds. Even though such demand contains serious misunderstanding as indicated in Chapter 3, for those who are not familiar with economic jargon, the above argument may make little sense one way or the other. Basically, they are saying that since the money supply is growing unusually slowly relative to the growth of liquidity supplied by the Bank of Japan, the central bank should increase liquidity faster to offset the slow growth of money supply.

Here, the term money multiplier indicates how much deposit money will be created from a unit of high-powered money supplied by the central bank. High-powered money is the liquidity that central bank supplies to the banking system and is the source of all deposit money. It consists of reserves provided by the central bank to private banks plus notes and coins in circulation. For the sake of simplicity, notes and coins are not considered in the following discussion because they are supplied entirely passively by the central bank and as such are not part of the policy debate. In other words, the issue is whether the central bank should supply more reserves to the banking system or not.

In a usual textbook world, high-powered money, money multiplier, and money supply are linked to each other in the following way. Suppose that a central bank supplies $10 of high-powered money to the banking system by buying $10 worth of government bonds from the banks. In modern fractional banking system, banks are required to keep a certain fraction of any deposit they obtained as reserves before lending the rest to their borrowers. If the reserve requirement in this example is 10%, the bank that received the $10 from the central bank will be able to lend $9. The $9 lent will eventually come back to the banking system when the initial borrower spends the money and its recipient deposits the proceeds with a bank. The bank that receives the $9 in deposit will then be able to lend 90% of it or $8.1. The process continues until the entire $10 of high-powered money supplied by the central bank is "reserved" by the banking system, that there are no excess reserves anywhere in the system.

In this process, a total of $100 of deposit money is created. This deposit money of $100 is called the money supply. Since the original high-powered money of $10 ended up producing the total money supply of $100 the $10 supplied by the central bank is called the high-powered money, and the money multiplier in this case is 10 or the inverse of the reserve requirement. This is how the money creation process is described in any economic textbook.

In Japan however, where so few companies are willing to borrow money today, the banks are not able to lend as much as they want. As a result, the money multiplier in Japan is much less than the usual inverse of the reserve requirement. With Japanese companies paying down debt to the tune of \20 trillion a year, it can be argued that the (private-sector) money multiplier is steadily shrinking.

In order to arrest the possible contraction in money supply, economists and commentators trained in monetarist thinking have been arguing that the central bank should supply ever-greater amounts of high-powered money in order to offset the fall in the money multiplier. They argue that by maintaining healthy growth in money supply through the rapid increase in high-powered money, the economy will eventually respond and prosper.

Although the above is a well-accepted argument among many economists, it actually contains serious problems. In particular, the above argument assumes that the deposit money and the high-powered money are good if not perfect substitutes. In the real world, however, nothing is further from the truth.

The key difference between the two is that, in spite of its name, high-powered money is not money that can be spent, whereas deposit money is money that can be spent by the owner of that deposit. The high-powered money cannot be spent in the usual sense because this money is for *lending*, not for spending by the bank. Just as banks are not supposed to spend the money depositors placed with them to pay their employees or update their computer system, the high powered money the banks get from the central bank is to be managed, not spent.

Furthermore, the bank does not feel any richer by having this high-powered money either because, as explained in Chapter 3, the bank merely exchanged one asset type with another asset of equal value. In other words, with the exception of notes and coins in circulation, an increase in high-powered money is *not recognized* by anybody in the economy as an increase in the money that they can spend.

The deposit money, on the other hand, is the money the owner of that deposit can actually spend. If he wants to buy a car with that money, he is free to do so. The increase in deposit money, therefore, is an increase in money that people can actually spend.

For the deposit money to increase, however, someone has to borrow the high-powered money provided by the central bank so that the above mentioned money creation process can began. In the absence of borrowers, the deposit money cannot increase and any high-powered money not lent will simply sit in the banking system waiting for the next borrower to show up. Indeed, if it there is no borrowers, any high-powered money that is not lent is worth nothing to the banking system or to the economy.

The implication of the above is that telling the Bank of Japan to increase high-powered money simply because deposit money is stagnating or falling is of no use. If the deposit money is stagnating or contracting because of the lack of borrowers, adding more high-powered money will do absolutely no good.

Of course, if the deposit money is stagnating or falling because of bank failures or other supply related factors, the central bank should provide all the high-powered money necessary to stabilize the situation. For example, if banks are short of reserves, the central bank might have to act as a lender of last resort. However, that is not the situation in Japan at all. Most banks in Japan today are flooded with excess reserves that they do not know what to do with.

As indicated earlier, what Japan lacks most is borrowers, there are over abundance of lenders. That is why the interest rates are so low. Commentators who have not thought it through have argued that if the Bank of Japan keeps on adding reserves, the economy and price level will eventually respond. In the real world, however, nothing happened, and for good reason. As indicated earlier, in the absence of borrowers, high-powered money is worth nothing. And adding more of things that are worth nothing does not change anything. That is what has been happening with monetary easing in Japan during the last ten years, and that is what happened in the U.S. during the similar recession in the 1930s.

Of course if the government increased its borrowing by selling government bonds to the banks, the high-powered money sitting in the banking system would have found the borrower and will be able to leave the banking system and enter the real economy. With the government replacing the missing private sector borrowers, the money multiplier process mentioned at the beginning will start working as well. That means both the economy and the money supply will began expanding with increased government borrowings (this means both the IS and LM curves will move to the right as indicated in Chapter 5.) When there is a severe shortage of private sector borrowers relative to the savings available in the economy, therefore, the government must become the borrower of last resort in order to get the economy and money supply moving again.

INDEX